DOC

The Life of Roy Halladay

Todd Zolecki

TRIUMPH
BOOKS

Library of Congress Cataloguing in Publication data available upon request.

This book is available in quantity at special discounts for your group or organization. For further information, contact:

    Triumph Books LLC
    814 North Franklin Street
    Chicago, Illinois 60610
    (312) 337-0747
    www.triumphbooks.com

Printed in U.S.A.
U.S. Edition ISBN: 978-1-62937-750-6
Canadian Edition ISBN: 978-1-62937-798-8
Design by Patricia Frey

For Ryan, Henri, and Margot

Contents

Chapter 1. Doctober 1

Chapter 2. The Basement. 15

Chapter 3. Bus 23

Chapter 4. Arvada West. 31

Chapter 5. Doc and Carp. 41

Chapter 6. 10.64 55

Chapter 7. Mel. 67

Chapter 8. A New Roy. 83

Chapter 9. Harvey 97

Chapter 10. Cy Young 111

Chapter 11. The Arsenal 125

Chapter 12. The Machine 137

Chapter 13. Time to Move On. 153

Chapter 14. Philly 171

Chapter 15. Four More Days 185

Chapter 16. Perfection 201

Chapter 17. It's Only Going to Get Funner 213

Chapter 18. The Rotation 229

Chapter 19. He's Human 247

Chapter 20. How You Fit In 267

Chapter 21. Second Callings 279

Chapter 22. I Love You Too 291

Chapter 23. The Legacy 307

Acknowledgments .323

Sources 327

Index 337

| 1 |

Doctober

Roy Halladay's eyes never left the TV.

It was October 6, 2010, a little more than an hour before Game 1 of the National League Division Series against the Cincinnati Reds, and Halladay pedaled a stationary bike alone in a room inside the Philadelphia Phillies' clubhouse at Citizens Bank Park. Halladay's routine dictated everything on game days, which meant he rode a bike a little more than an hour before every start. It did not matter if it was a midsummer game against the worst team in baseball or the first postseason game of his storied career. The routine never changed.

Phillies center fielder Shane Victorino walked past Halladay on his way to see the team's chiropractor. He looked at the Phillies ace, but Halladay's eyes never moved.

"Any human being, when somebody walks by them, that close to them, they will give some kind of look," Victorino said. "It's like I wasn't even in the room."

Halladay was more machine than human on the days he pitched. Everybody knew this. Nobody said hello to him. Nobody approached him. Nobody punctured his cocoon of preparation.

Victorino looked at the TV. He knew the man on the screen commanding Halladay's attention. Texas Rangers ace Cliff Lee was carving up the Tampa Bay Rays in Game 1 of the American League Division Series at Tropicana Field. Lee became an instant Philadelphia folk hero in 2009 when he joined the Phillies in July, then went 4–0 with a 1.56 ERA in five postseason starts, including an unforgettable complete game against the New York Yankees in Game 1 of the World Series at Yankee Stadium. Phillies fans loved Lee, but the team traded him to the Seattle Mariners a couple months later, at the same time it announced it acquired Halladay from the Toronto Blue Jays.

Halladay waited a lifetime for his postseason moment. He trained to be a pitcher since childhood. He was a first-round draft pick in 1995. He came within one out of a no-hitter in his second big league start in 1998. But after historic struggles put his career in jeopardy in 2001, he re-engineered his pitching mechanics and rewired his brain in a top-down physical and mental rebuild. Halladay remade himself into arguably the greatest pitcher of his generation, establishing an unparalleled work ethic and legendary mental approach. But after failing to sniff the postseason for more than a decade in Toronto, the man nicknamed "Doc," after the legendary gunslinger Doc Holliday, orchestrated a trade to Philadelphia. And now, a little more than an hour before he threw his first postseason pitch in front of a sellout crowd, he watched the Phillies' 2009 postseason hero strike out 10 batters and allow one run in seven innings in a victory over Tampa Bay.

"I think Roy was looking at Cliff going, 'Really?'" Victorino said.

A feeling overcame Victorino.

"Doc's going to go out and do something special," he thought.

Halladay went to see Phillies strength and conditioning coordinator Dong Lien. It was about 4:00 PM, which meant Halladay was right on schedule for the 5:08 PM first pitch. Lien stretched Halladay's legs about an hour before every game. The two were close, but Lien never talked to his friend on game days. He respected his process too much. Not that a conversation was possible anyway. Halladay wore earphones before he pitched. Sometimes he listened to nothing, wearing them to discourage interruptions. Sometimes he listened to Harvey Dorfman's career-saving *The Mental ABC's of Pitching,* which he had on his iPhone only because he paid somebody to read and record the book in studio. But Halladay mostly listened to music. He liked Enya. Her song "Only Time" regularly played when Lien stretched him. It might surprise people to know that, but Halladay, who stood 6-foot-6 and intimidated opponents, umpires, managers, and even teammates with a stare, did not pitch on emotion. He pitched in complete control of his thoughts and feelings.

Halladay learned a long time ago that negative thoughts lead to negative results, so he trained his mind to behave differently. He stopped thinking about the big picture and what might happen if he threw a bad pitch. He stopped worrying about what people might think if he failed. Dorfman taught him to focus on the task at hand, which meant the next pitch and only the next pitch. Doc struggled toward the end of the regular season, posting a 4.32 ERA in six starts before he tossed a shutout to clinch the Phillies' fourth consecutive National League East title. Halladay's conversations with Dorfman before the division-clinching game recentered him for the postseason.

"I had so many nights when I sat up thinking what it would be like, how I would do, how would I handle it," Halladay said. "I really went back to the basics. I thought about all of the things that have created this success for me; the thoughts of one pitch at a time, not worry about what will happen or what did happen, just concentrating on the moment. And had I not had Harvey, I wouldn't have done that. I would've been thinking, 'Crap, playoffs are coming up. I have one start left. If I don't pitch well here then no one is going to have confidence in me. I won't have confidence in me.' And that's just not the way I approached it. But I would've never done that without Harvey."

"So many guys talk about getting there and wait a long time to get there and then, when they do, they soil themselves," Dorfman said.

HALLADAY HAD NINE DAYS to prepare for Game 1, which he considered bad news for the Reds because they would not outwork him.

"There's no way," he said. "I'm going to know every single thing about every hitter. So going into that game I was as confident as I'd ever been. Even though I had all these feelings underneath, I knew as soon as I stepped on the mound they would go away."

Halladay met Phillies catcher Carlos Ruiz and pitching coach Rich Dubee in the Phillies' dugout at 4:30 PM. Halladay always met them in the dugout at half past the hour, whether the game started at 1:00, 5:00, 7:00, or 8:00. They walked to the outfield together. Halladay continued up the bullpen steps alone. He put his glove and jacket down, returned to the field and jogged to warm up his body. He returned to the bullpen to use the bathroom. Doc always peed after he ran.

"*Every time*," Dubee said. "I don't know how many starts he made with us, but every time he had to go up and pee because he was so hydrated. Nothing was left to chance."

Halladay grabbed his glove and returned to the field. He stretched his arm and shoulder against the fence. He long tossed with Ruiz from 100 to 110 feet.

Halladay, Ruiz, and Dubee went to the bullpen to warm up. Doc threw 20 pitches from the windup and 20 pitches from the stretch. He threw sinkers to both sides of the plate, cutters to both sides of the plate, changeups to both sides of the plate, and curveballs. He finished from the windup with one sinker to his arm side (the right side of the plate) and one sinker to his glove side (the left side of the plate). The routine never changed. If he missed cutters to his glove side, he moved on. He knew that warmup pitches did not predict his performance in the game.

"I think a lot of that had to do with Harvey," Dubee said. "Harvey was a great teacher. He was very thorough and disciplined about having routines, about being so locked in that you had a routine and nothing got in your way. It was physically, it was preparation, it was mentally the focus before each pitch."

Halladay's four greatest concerns in the Reds' lineup were: Brandon Phillips, Joey Votto, Jay Bruce, and Scott Rolen. Halladay studied hitters so thoroughly that he felt he knew what they were thinking. He never could figure out Phillips, though. Phillips baffled him. Votto was one of the smartest hitters in baseball; he thought along with the pitcher. Halladay considered Bruce a tough out because he changed his approach from time to time. Halladay knew Rolen because they played together in Toronto. Rolen was smart, like Votto, and he liked to get in the pitcher's head.

"Don't be scared that we're here," Rolen texted Halladay before the game.

"I'm ready," Halladay replied. "I'm waiting."

"That was a way to let him know, 'You're not getting the upper-hand, you're not getting that control,'" Halladay said. "'I'm not going to let you have that.'"

HALLADAY THREW 10 PITCHES in the first inning. Phillips hit a first-pitch sinker to Phillies shortstop Jimmy Rollins, who threw him out at first base. Orlando Cabrera flew out to Victorino on a cutter. Votto hit a cutter on one hop to second baseman Chase Utley to end the inning. Halladay's pitches moved more than normal.

"Everything was electric," Dubee said. "It was moving, darting, commanded. Going back and forth between different speeds and different looks, they just did not have good swings against him at all."

Phillies left fielder Raúl Ibañez watched the Reds flail at pitches from the outfield. He saw similar hacks from the Florida Marlins in Miami on May 29, when Halladay became the 20th pitcher in baseball history to throw a perfect game.

"He's going to do it again," Ibañez thought to himself.

Rollins returned to the Phillies' dugout. He caught Utley's eye. He had the same look on his face.

It's over.

"I saw the stuff and I saw the swings," Rollins said. "They had no chance. Like, if we get two runs in the first inning, they fold. It's a wrap. You know what I'm saying?"

Victorino scored from third base on a sacrifice fly from Utley in the first inning to take a 1–0 lead. Halladay struck out Rolen on a changeup to start the second. It was an ugly swing on a beautiful pitch (opponents and teammates sometimes called his changeup a "splitter") that Halladay learned to throw for the first time that spring. Halladay got Jonny Gomes and Bruce to ground out to end the inning.

"Everything was in the strike zone," Ruiz said. "The sinker, the cutter, everything was working."

The Phillies scored three runs in the bottom of the second to take a 4–0 lead. Halladay's two-out single to left field scored Ruiz from second base. Victorino's single scored Wilson Valdez and Halladay. Halladay threw nine pitches in the third. Reds relief pitcher Travis Wood hit a sinking line drive to right field with two outs—the hardest-hit ball to that point—but Jayson Werth made a nice sliding catch to end the inning. Halladay scouted Wood before the game because he thought he might hit in a long-relief situation. His sinker got too much of the plate, which allowed Wood to barrel the ball. But when a pitcher squares up a baseball and a defender still catches it, it might be the pitcher's night. Halladay felt it.

Doc threw 12 pitches in the fourth. Phillips struck out looking on a sinker, Cabrera struck out swinging on a changeup, and Votto grounded out to Rollins on a changeup to end the inning.

"I just remember thinking, wow, he's got a really good sinker," Votto said. "I remember seeing his cutter and thinking, wow, he's got a really good cutter. And then he threw his splitter and I remember thinking, wow, he's got a really good splitter too. And then he threw his curveball and I remember thinking, oh, he's got the best curveball I've ever seen. It was just like one after the other after the other."

The Reds led the National League in scoring in 2010, but they found themselves helpless and hopeless. Rolen tried to change their luck with a few words to home plate umpire John Hirschbeck.

"John, if you keep giving him that much off the plate he's going to throw a no-hitter," he said. "You've got to clean it up."

Halladay struck out Rolen looking on a sinker and Gomes swinging on a curveball to start the fifth. Bruce stepped up. He homered and doubled in 12 previous plate appearances against Halladay. He swung over a first-pitch changeup. He swung over a 2-1 curveball to even the count. Halladay missed inside on a sinker to run the count to 3-2.

"The last thing I wanted to do is give him a pitch to give them any momentum," Halladay said. "And if I give him a pitch that he hits [for] a home run on, now they feel good. 'We got to him.' I wasn't trying to do that. I was still trying to make a quality pitch. And if I was going to miss, I was going to miss in my spot. I wasn't going to miss in his spot over the plate. There's times for walks, there's times late in the order you're not going to want to put guys on base to turn the lineup over, but, to me, I felt like that was an at-bat where I had to be careful."

Halladay's cutter was low for ball four. The walk ended Doc's shot at a perfect game. Yankees pitcher Don Larsen threw the only perfect game in postseason history against the Brooklyn Dodgers in Game 5 of the 1956 World Series. It was the only no-hitter in the postseason, but Halladay still had a chance to throw the second. He got out of the inning and threw only eight pitches in the sixth. Ramón Hernández popped out to Werth. Pinch-hitter Juan Francisco hit a ball underneath Halladay's glove that hopped off the mound toward second base. Rollins caught the ball behind the bag. His momentum carried him toward first to throw out the runner. Phillips flew out to Werth to end the inning.

"It could have gone until the next morning and I don't think the Reds would've gotten a hit," Dubee said.

Votto stepped up with one out in the seventh. He needed to try something, so he called timeout in the middle of Halladay's windup before his 1-0 pitch. Halladay stopped his delivery. He brushed the dirt a couple times with his right foot. He looked off toward third base. Fans booed. Votto stepped back into the batter's box. Halladay threw a strike. Halladay started his windup for the 1-1 pitch, and Votto called timeout again. Phillies fans booed again. Votto grounded out for the second out.

"At some point, you need to see whether or not he's going to react emotionally," Votto said. "Whether it's hitting me or maybe you make a mistake because you throw off his rhythm. And I think that fell inside the etiquette of ball. It's a playoff game, we're both trying to go to the World Series. But he ended up keeping a very level head."

Halladay joked with Votto at next year's All-Star Game that he wanted to walk to home plate and choke him to death, but he secretly loved the fact that Votto called timeout twice. It meant the Reds did not know what to do.

"That's when I felt like I had him in my back pocket," Halladay said.

Rolen struck out swinging on a curveball to end the inning. Halladay navigated the heart of the Reds' lineup for the final time. He needed six more outs. Gomes struck out swinging on three pitches to start the eighth. Bruce bounced out to Halladay for the second out and Drew Stubbs struck out looking on three pitches to end the inning.

"My last at-bat I was just up there hacking," Gomes said. "You look up on the board and you see he's thrown only 21, 22 balls by the seventh or eighth inning, so why not hack? But that didn't work for me, either."

The sellout crowd waved its white rally towels as Halladay walked to the mound to start the ninth.

"Let's go, Doc! Let's go, Doc! Let's go, Doc!"

Halladay's wife, Brandy, and their oldest son, Braden, watched from the stands. Braden removed his shirt and whipped it around.

"Ridiculous!" Brandy said, laughing.

Hernández popped out to Utley for the first out. He flipped his bat in disgust. Pinch-hitter Miguel Cairo stepped into the box. Halladay and Cairo knew each other well. They played together in winter ball in Venezuela. They lived near each other in Florida. They coached together. Their sons were friends. He popped out to Valdez in foul territory for the second out. Halladay needed one more out to make history.

The earth shook.

"That's the one thing I remember from the game," Halladay said, "standing on the mound and seeing all those towels. I could feel the field shaking. I could feel the vibration. And to be able to just be calm in that moment was very surreal. I felt like this is where I should be and this is where I'm most comfortable. If I had to go talk to those people, that's where I'm scared to death. I'm not a social guy. But when I felt all that energy and I felt it shaking, I felt I was so comfortable and so relaxed and so confident in the approach and staying in the approach. I wanted to remember it. I wanted to feel it. And I'm glad I did."

But then Doc became Doc again.

"Okay, that's enough," he thought to himself. "Let's go."

Phillips dug his spikes into the dirt and took a first-pitch sinker on the outer half of the plate for a strike. Halladay and Ruiz had been in perfect harmony the entire game. The catcher nicknamed "Chooch" called for a 0-1 fastball up and in, but Halladay didn't like it. He shook off the sign. It was the first and only time he disagreed with Ruiz the entire night.

"You know, elevating is something I'll do on occasion, but it was just something at that point I wasn't comfortable doing," he said. "I felt like I'd rather stay something hard, something away. It was a pitch we hadn't thrown much that night, so to throw the first one or two of them at that point, I wasn't as comfortable with it. You know, I'm sure it wasn't so much the pitch as my comfortableness that I had of throwing it right there. I just felt there were one or two other pitches I'd rather throw first."

Ruiz called for a cutter away. Halladay threw the pitch off the plate, Phillips swung and missed for strike two. The crowd roared. Halladay needed one more strike. Ruiz called for a curveball. Doc came out of his windup and delivered the 104th pitch of his night. The ball broke as it reached the plate. Phillips swung and hit it. The ball dribbled up the first-base line. Ruiz ripped off his mask. Phillips dropped his bat and ran. The ball, drawn to the bat like a magnet, rolled up against it.

Oh, no.

"Is it foul? Is he out?" Rollins said.

Ruiz knew Phillips could run so he hurried. He nearly overran the ball, but he fell to his knees, reached back with his right hand and picked it up.

"I was panicking a little bit," he said. "A no-hitter. If I don't make this play, it's over."

Ruiz had no time to stand and set his feet to throw, so he threw from his knees. It was the only way. Phillies first baseman Ryan Howard, sensing that Ruiz had to make a tough throw from a bad angle, prepared for the possibility that the ball might skip off Phillips' left shoulder. But the arc of the throw carried over it. Howard reached up and caught the ball cleanly. He squeezed his glove for the final out.

History.

Halladay beamed. He opened his arms and spun toward Ruiz, who raced toward him. They embraced. Halladay slapped Ruiz on his side. Ruiz gripped Halladay's head and screamed into his ear.

"What happened?!" Halladay screamed back.

Their teammates mobbed them. Halladay could not believe it.

"What happened?!" he yelled at Werth.

"I don't fucking know!" Werth replied.

They screamed.

AFTERWARD, HALLADAY'S TEAMMATES GATHERED around him in the clubhouse. They wanted him to say something. Maybe something to match the enormity of the moment.

"No speech," he said. "Let's win two more."

They roared. Halladay publicly and privately downplayed the accomplishment. He focused on the job Ruiz did behind the plate. He praised his teammates for the plays they made in the field. He turned the conversation toward winning the best-of-five series. Halladay meant every word. He prepared for this moment. In his mind, he did his job. But in the process, he answered an important question about himself.

"Can I really do it when it matters?" he said. "I had seen my friends in that situation—Chris Carpenter pitching in games like that and having success. I'm sitting there going, 'If they can do it, can I do it? What does it take to do that?' I always wondered what the difference was, how I'd react, would I be able to stand up in a situation like that? I always felt like the greater the challenge the more ready I was. But I wanted to test that. And there couldn't have been a better test than that situation in Philly in that atmosphere. One of the greatest fan bases on the face of the earth. I was at the right place at the right time. I feel like I got struck by lightning, you know?"

It confirmed something else too.

"The fun was in the process," he said. "The fun was in the journey. That's what I enjoyed. I always thought it was about the ring for me. But it wasn't. It was everything you went through to get to those opportunities that made it worthwhile and that made it gratifying. It wasn't a parade or ring or anything like that. I don't think that would've changed anything for me. I think it was the journey, the process, the whole going through it that made it worthwhile."

Later, Halladay checked his email. Dorfman sent him a one-word note.

"Masterful."

| 2 |

The Basement

HARRY LEROY HALLADAY II wanted his son to be a professional baseball player, so when the family moved from Aurora, Colorado, to nearby Arvada before his boy entered the fifth grade, he looked for a home with a basement large enough to make him one.

The basement needed to be at least 60 feet, 6 inches long, so his son could pitch year-round. He found one 65 feet long. He built a portable pitcher's mound, made of plywood and topped with Astroturf. He hung a tire at one end of the basement, which served as a target whenever he could not be there to catch him. He put a mattress against a wall to protect the baseballs from the cinderblock. He got a bucket that held 40 baseballs and a picker that retrieved them. He purchased a pitching machine and built a batting cage, hanging chain links from the support beams, because his son needed to work on his hitting as much as his pitching.

"We started throwing when he was one," Halladay II said. "It just never really stopped."

Harry Leroy Halladay III was born on May 14, 1977. His father considered naming him Merlin after the Rolls-Royce Merlin, a World War II-era aircraft engine, but his father and his wife, Linda, convinced him to continue the family tradition.

"Under protest, I'll do it," he said.

Nobody called Halladay II or Halladay III by their birth names, which was fine because they both hated them. Everybody called them Big Roy and Little Roy. They occasionally joked about their names, but they mostly talked about baseball, flying, and fishing. Dad was a commercial pilot and a licensed flight instructor. He took his son flying for the first time when he was two. They took their first extended trip together when he was four, flying to Boise in a King Air. Little Roy loved his father's job because he loved to fly. His dad got him a logbook to record his flight hours because maybe one day he would be a pilot too. Big Roy trusted his son, but he never let him fly alone. He saw too many instances when young pilots lost focus and made mistakes. Little Roy flew model airplanes on the ground instead. He got his first one when he was four.

"Almost as big as [him], but he could fly it," Big Roy said.

Big and Little Roy restored cars and airplanes together. The family boated and fished. Big lakes scared Little Roy when he was young because he thought there were sharks in the water, but dad wanted his son to ski, so when he refused to jump in he tossed him in. "After that, you couldn't get me out," Little Roy said. He might have been in first or second grade when his father reeled a catfish into the boat. He fell in love with fishing at that moment. If he couldn't fish on a boat with his family, he fished on the shore

16

of the Arvada Reservoir or anywhere else he could drop his line in water.

"He never caught much fishing," his mother said. "A tree, a boot, and once, his sister Heather."

But Little Roy got better because he loved it as much as he loved flying. They later became his escapes. He relished the peace and quiet on the water. "It was you and your friends and your thoughts," he said. He savored the solitude as he sailed through the clouds. "I can leave the world down below for a while," he said.

Little Roy rode mopeds with Heather. They hit golf balls at the driving range. If they bowled, he went early to practice because he wanted to win. He always seemed to be building or tinkering. He built a bike ramp when he was nine or 10 years old. He asked Heather to test it, but she wiped out because she did not pull up on the handlebars as the bike went over the ramp. He built a canoe from scratch, beginning at 13 or 14 and finishing at 16. He and Heather plopped it into a nearby creek for its maiden voyage. It did not sink, but only because they brought buckets to bail out the water leaking into the boat. Little Roy eventually found the leaks, fixed it, and finished it.

"His brain was always constantly going," Heather said. "He was trying to impress somebody and show them what he could do."

Those things came after baseball. Everything came after baseball. Big Roy played baseball growing up. He was a strong-armed outfielder. He thought he could harness his son's abilities to be an outfielder too. They spent hours hitting and throwing, either outside or in the basement. Little Roy played in youth baseball leagues in Aurora and Arvada. Dad coached. He learned quickly that nobody could pitch better than his son, so he started to pitch him more and more. Eventually, the future outfielder became the future pitcher.

"All that time in the basement, that's probably the biggest reason why I'm a big league pitcher," Little Roy said. "It started off as nothing more than a way for us to spend time together. He was a pilot so he was gone a lot. He'd come home and we'd either talk about airplanes or play catch or hit."

Little Roy was pushed hard, harder than most kids, but Big Roy never saw it that way. He believed that the hours practicing and working were a way to help his son achieve his full potential. He believed that they were a way for a father and son to spend time together. But father's expectations could be difficult on his son. Heather wondered if her brother lost out on some of his childhood because of the demands of baseball. He always wanted G.I. Joes, but he never got them. They were dolls.

"He just loved every second of it," Big Roy argued. "We did a lot of things, but he was involved in it. No, he didn't miss out on anything. This kid just had a huge passion for the stuff."

But there were times when Little Roy got yelled at on the baseball field. It was one of his earliest childhood memories. Heather remembers miserable car rides home following games when her brother did not meet their father's expectations. Her brother once snagged a fishing hook into his pitching hand. He feared his father's reaction more than anything. He got the hand stitched up and pitched without complaint.

Heather and their older sister, Merinda, called him "Prince Roy" because he got so much attention from their dad.

"I think he wanted my brother to understand that anything he wanted in life he could make a possibility," Heather said. "But I just don't think he realized to what detriment it was at some point, you know? Because I'm his sister I saw a little bit more than I think a parent would. I was the one hanging out with him.

"If my dad would have looked at it and said, 'I don't think he can do this,' I don't think he would have pushed him. He knew that he could do it, but it's just, was it worth it or not? Only Roy could say that."

Nolan Ryan's Pitcher's Bible hit bookstores in 1991 and Big Roy bought a copy. Ryan, the hard-throwing, seemingly ageless Hall of Fame right-hander from Texas, used the first chapter to tell a story about how his career reached a crossroads in 1972. He struggled with the Mets, who traded him to the Angels. He believed he struggled because he kept running out of gas. He started to train with weights and run. He got stronger and his endurance improved. He pitched better.

The book had pages of photos and illustrations of Ryan's weight-training, core-strengthening, and stretching routines. Big Roy held in his hands a pitching blueprint for his son. He built a bench for the basement and purchased free weights. He studied the book and told his son what Ryan did. Little Roy did it. The boy eventually memorized Ryan's workout routines—he read the book countless times alone in his room—and performed them on his own. Occasionally, he skipped the workouts, which got him in trouble. Heather and her brother finally figured out how their dad knew when he missed a workout. Big Roy put chalk lines on the weights so he knew if they moved or not.

"After we found out about the chalk, we would just move the weights," Heather said.

"We had a little game where I would set little traps for him," Big Roy said. "He'd try and figure out what the trap was, but eventually he did the exercises. We had fun with it."

But Little Roy felt pressure to make his dad happy. He wanted to make everybody happy.

"He grew up wanting to please people," Linda said. "As a mother I was very concerned about him being pushed. Mothers worry. There was pressure to succeed. That's why I think he does so well—he has pitched so long under pressure. If they lost a game, Roy would punish himself."

Her son learned to finish a workout and ask, "When can we do it again?" He memorized motivational sayings that his dad taught him. They recited them back and forth. There might have been 50 in all.

"Stick to your task 'til it sticks to you;
Bend at it, sweat at it, smile at it too;
For out of the bend and the sweat and the smile
Will come life's victories after a while."

They talked psychology. Big Roy once suggested that his son run alongside one of his friends at a cross-country meet—Little Roy joined the team his senior year to improve his endurance on the mound—and asked him if he felt okay because he looked tired.

"Watch what happens," he said.

Little Roy did as instructed. His friend slowed down.

"He saw a lot of examples, things like that, that people would quit if they were told they weren't doing well or didn't look good or something," Big Roy said. "There's a lot of those things, concentrating and thinking about what's going on were all really important to us."

Pitch, hit, run, lift, stretch. It never stopped.

"We had to be careful, because I didn't want to hurt his arm, but we would do something every day," Big Roy said. "It was an hour or two almost every day that something was being done. In the wintertime we talked about it and I said, 'Why don't we make baseball your main sport?' And then we'll do basketball for just pure recreation, just have fun with it. He would do that, then he'd come home and he'd still stretch and do his exercises and things that *Nolan Ryan's Pitcher's Bible* recommended.

"We tried to do things to the best of our ability. We'd start mowing the lawn in front of the house. We'd see who could trim it up the best. I would mow it one day and he would mow it the next. Who had the straightest lines and things like that. Trying to be observant of all things. He had that same philosophy in baseball. I'm going to do it as best as I can. I'm going to concentrate on it. I'm going to do it. There was a little bit of teasing. I'd be like, 'That was 100 balls. You okay?' 'Yeah, can we do some more?' You could tell he would be tired, but he never explained to me that he was tired. He just always seemed to love the game."

Little Roy did love baseball. He loved the competition. He loved his teammates. He loved to play. His eighth-grade teacher asked students to write an essay about what they wanted to be when they grew up. The teacher said that they could pick anything, except something silly like "president" or "professional athlete." Little Roy wanted to be a professional baseball player. He got home and spoke to his father about it. He wondered what he should do. Big Roy called the teacher.

"How can you take away the dream of these little kids," he said, "because that limits their capabilities of what they can become?"

Little Roy's dreams eventually came true. Big Roy's dreams came true too.

"When he was growing up, his friends and his teachers and stuff, my friends would say, do you realize how difficult this is?" he said. "They said, 'So very few people make it. You realize how difficult that really is?' But, you know, looking back on it, it was relatively easy."

| 3 |

Bus

BIG ROY KNEW HIS LIMITATIONS, so he looked for help. He took his son to listen to big league pitchers Danny Jackson and Brian Fisher speak at a local high school in fall 1985. Jackson just helped the Kansas City Royals win the World Series. He attended Aurora Central High School. Fisher went 4–4 with a 2.38 ERA in 55 relief appearances as a rookie with the Yankees. He finished sixth for AL Rookie of the Year behind Ozzie Guillen and others. He attended Hinkley High School in Aurora. Somebody named Robert "Bus" Campbell spoke before the two pitchers. Big Roy was impressed. He seemed like somebody that could help his son take that next step forward. He approached Campbell, introduced himself, and told him that his boy wanted to be a big leaguer.

Could he work with him?

Campbell politely declined, but told the boy to continue to work hard.

"Throw more fastballs," he said.

If you wanted to be a successful pitcher and you lived in Colorado, you knew or wanted to know Bus Campbell. He worked with Hall of Fame reliever Goose Gossage, who needed a tune-up toward the end of his career, and lefty Jamie Moyer, whose career needed saving in the early '90s. He helped Burt Hooton, Steve Busby, Bob Welch, Jay Howell, Mark Langston, Mark Knudson, Cal Eldred, Brad Lidge, Shawn Chacón, Scott Elarton, Jackson, Fisher, and more. He had such an impact on Colorado baseball—more than 100 players he coached reached the big leagues—that he joined Denver Nuggets legend Dan Issel and Denver Broncos stalwart Randy Gradishar in the Colorado Sports Hall of Fame in 1987.

He never got rich from it.

"Don't cheat a kid," Campbell said. "I try not to turn down anybody and I've never charged a kid in my life."

The Mr. Miyagi of Colorado pitching began his coaching career at Denver South High School before becoming a physical education teacher and coach at Littleton High School. He later became the pitching coach at the University of Colorado, the University of Northern Colorado, and the University of Iowa. He remained in baseball, even after retirement. He worked with pitchers on the side, either on a bullpen mound at a local high school or at an indoor baseball facility. He scouted for the Cardinals, Reds, Royals, and Blue Jays.

"What a brilliant baseball guy," Gossage said. "He could spot little flaws in your mechanics immediately. Bus was just one of those kinds of throwbacks, old school and very basic. He knew probably more in his little finger than most guys. Really very, very smart, but very simple. That was the beauty of Bus."

Moyer grew up outside Philadelphia, but after going 34–54 with a 4.56 ERA though five seasons with the Cubs, Rangers, and Cardinals, his career teetered on the brink. He heard about Campbell through his father-in-law. He flew to Denver in December 1991 and spent a weekend talking and working with him. Moyer returned to the majors in 1993. He went 235–155 with a 4.19 ERA over the next 19 seasons. He made the 2003 AL All-Star team; finished in the top six in AL Cy Young voting in 1999, 2001, and 2003; helped the Phillies win the World Series in 2008; and became the oldest pitcher in baseball history to earn a win at 49 years, 150 days old, when he pitched for the Rockies in 2012.

"I was at a time and a place in my career where it was very beneficial to hear somebody different," Moyer said. "What he said made a lot of sense."

Campbell worked with countless kids in between his brushes with big leaguers, tailoring each lesson to the individual, focusing on what he did well and trying to squeeze the most out of his talents. He worked with Cherry Creek High School coach Marc Johnson, who ran a powerhouse program that won eight state championships. Johnson remembers the time a young pitching coach, trying to earn his stripes in professional baseball, worked with a young pitcher in Denver. He talked to him about "horizontal thrust," "vertical reduction," and "pelvic loading." Campbell walked up to the pitcher and said, "Son, just turn your billfold pocket toward the catcher and you'll be fine."

"He was kind of like a Yoda-type sage, the way I saw it," Lidge said. "You'd be throwing these bullpens and he'd be right next to you and he'd be watching you throw and he wouldn't even worry about where the pitch ended up. That was irrelevant. He was just watching the ball come out of your hand and how your body was acting and everything else and just giving you advice based on that. And you might miss a pitch or two outside and instantly, he didn't even know it, he was giving you a correction and then instantly you'd be back to the strike zone."

Campbell had white hair and wore metal-rimmed glasses. He wore a brimmed cap with pleated khakis and a polo shirt. He had a warm smile. He spoke softly. Pitchers often strained to hear him.

Try this.

Do this with your glove.

Why don't you put your middle finger here?

"If I had to paint a picture of the ideal grandpa, that was Bus," Elarton said.

Campbell eventually reconnected with the Halladays. He worked regularly with Johnson, who not only coached Cherry Creek, but the area's top travel teams. Johnson's son Tyler played in the same youth leagues as Halladay, who played on a couple different teams at the same time. Johnson recommended that Campbell give Halladay a look.

"When I first saw him at 10, I think the thing that stood out to me the most was his competitiveness and his willingness to get better," Johnson said.

Campbell asked Big Roy if he still wanted him to work with his now 13-year-old son. Big Roy said yes. They initially worked at a field about a block from Campbell's home. They moved their bullpen sessions to Heritage High School in Littleton, where Bus' son Randy coached. Big Roy caught his son's bullpen sessions in the basement for years. He caught some early ones with Campbell too, but eventually Bus told him to hang up his shin guards, chest protector, and mask. He thought his son might hurt him. Halladay's high school catcher Chad Sigg stepped in.

"Either Roy was calling me and bugging me or his dad was calling me and bugging me," Sigg said. "Like, 'You've got to get over here.' If I had a day off and he knew it, Bus would call me and say, 'Hey, Roy's throwing a pen tonight and I need you to catch him.' Roy would come pick me up or his dad would come pick me up and we'd drive out to Littleton and we'd go throw. It was constantly once or twice a week throughout the winter, doing that for him, catching pens for him. It got to the point where nobody else was going to do it, you know?"

The bond between Campbell and Halladay grew. Campbell saw limitless potential in his star pupil, but it was more than that. He cared for him. Halladay felt the same way. He considered Campbell as much a family member as a coach.

"Roy thought of him as a grandfather," Halladay's wife, Brandy, said. "When Roy and I started dating he would go and do these bullpen sessions with Bus. Bus would record them on a video recorder. I'd sit down there and I'd hold the camera or we'd set it up. He could literally watch you for three seconds and be like, 'Yep, there's your problem.' Half the time he'd be like, 'Stop.' Roy was like, 'I didn't even start.' But he knew. He was so smart, so on it, so sharp."

27

Campbell's work with Halladay catapulted him into the next stratosphere. He was not just a talented local pitcher with a good arm anymore. He was somebody that elite Division I colleges and professional organizations knew. Scouts started to show up wherever and whenever he pitched.

Campbell never took a penny for helping Halladay, although Little Roy repaid him in time. He bought him a grandfather's clock after he got drafted by the Blue Jays in 1995. He installed a satellite dish at his home so he could watch him pitch in the big leagues. And after Halladay threw a perfect game with the Phillies in May 2010, he sent the Campbell family a commemorative watch, even though Bus died in February 2008.

"They were family for us," Brandy said.

Campbell meant so much to them. He meant so much to many. It's a wonder he never coached for a professional organization.

"Trust me, speaking as a big league coach, a lot of times coaching is just opportunity," said Josh Bard, who was a catcher at Cherry Creek High and played 10 seasons in the big leagues before becoming the New York Yankees' bench coach. "There's been a lot of guys in the game, outside of the game, that have been great coaches that have never gotten an opportunity to be a major league coach. You didn't realize it as a kid growing up in Colorado that you had that mind and that teacher and the man that he was. And then you kind of go out and you think that Bus is just another coach or just another scout. But then you start thinking, 'Whoa, this dude was really special.' And you see how much he impacted Roy and how much he impacted other players. Bus is one of my all-time favorites."

Campbell would have downplayed Bard's compliment. He always did.

"I don't feel like I've ever done anything exceptional," he said. "I feel I've done what I wanted to do. Getting fame or glory for any of this stuff is something I don't care to do."

| 4 |

Arvada West

JIM CAPRA STILL HAS the cast in his basement. He brought it home one evening in spring 1995 and his children insisted he keep it because they worshipped Roy Halladay, even as a tall, skinny, awkward teenager at Arvada West High School.

Halladay played four seasons of varsity baseball at Arvada West. He threw a no-hitter in his first start as a freshman against rival Pomona High School. His high school career accelerated from there. He helped AW win a state championship as a junior in 1994. He had the school on its way to a second-consecutive state title as a senior in 1995. Capra just needed his ace to stay healthy. He warned his players that if they ever hurt themselves playing basketball, pickup or otherwise, he would cut them from the team. His persistent warnings sparked an idea. Nobody remembers who came up with it, but shortly before a spring break baseball trip to Arizona, they hatched a plan to scare their coach to death. They wrapped Halladay's prized right arm in a cast before practice, then walked to the field.

"Uh, coach, Roy needs to talk to you," a player said.

Halladay approached Capra and revealed the cast on his arm.

"I tried to dunk one and I lost my balance on the way down and I put my hand down and broke my arm," Halladay said.

Steam shot from Capra's ears. He was livid.

"I warned you!" he said.

Players started to smirk, the smirks turned into chuckles and the chuckles turned into belly laughs. Somebody cut the cast from Halladay's arm. Halladay smiled. Capra and Halladay's high school teammates love that story. It is the first one they tell whenever they talk about him. Capra remembers other things about Halladay.

"He was really good to my kids," he said. "A couple times we went fishing. That was his passion. He was into planes, so he would buy my boys model airplanes. He was in high school when he did that. He was real mature for his age, I think."

PAT GILLICK HAS A plaque hanging in baseball's Hall of Fame in Cooperstown, New York. It's there because he turned the expansion Blue Jays in 1977 into back-to-back World Series champions in 1992 and 1993. It is there because in 27 years as a general manager in Toronto, Baltimore, Seattle, and Philadelphia, his teams won three World Series, made 11 postseasons, and finished 20 times with winning records. Gillick knows talent. He's a winner.

He retired from the Blue Jays following the strike-shortened 1994 season. He said he wanted to smell the roses, travel, and spend more time with his family. But Gillick was a scout at heart and the work pulled at him. He found himself in semi-retirement in Arizona in the spring of '95, scouting replacement players and amateur players. He got a call one afternoon telling him that Arvada West High School from Colorado scheduled a baseball trip to Mesa. The Blue Jays had the 17th overall pick in the '95 draft and they liked a pitcher named Roy Halladay. Could he take a look?

He drove to Mesa. He liked Halladay immediately.

"A very, very physical guy," he said. "At that time he was a straight over the top, a real hard thrower. I filed a report that said he was a frontline prospect and somebody that should be considered."

Gillick watched him only once. He never felt the need to see him again.

"I'm usually a first-impression guy," he said. "If I see somebody and if I'm kind of like, eh, I'll go back. I try to go to games to like somebody. If I like him, you know, that first impression is important to me. If I don't like him, I might go back and say I got him on a bad day. But I got him on a good day and he was an overpowering pitcher."

Halladay made a commitment to the University of Arizona, but everybody knew that he planned to turn pro. He did not throw bucketfuls of baseballs against a mattress in his basement for years to be drafted in the first round and go to college.

"He signed to go to college just to get people off his back," Bus Campbell said. "He was getting letters from everyone in the country, it seemed."

Baseball America ranked Halladay the 27th-best prospect in the amateur draft. Capra heard Halladay could go among the top 10 picks.

"I've got to tell you," Big Roy said, "when he was a junior in high school and the newspaper indicated that he had the potential of being a first-round pick, I was really taken aback by that. Wow, are you serious? I had no idea that that was the potential. I thought maybe he was getting some college interest and stuff. I thought, well, that would be kind of cool because there is a potential for a scholarship. But it kind of graduated as he went further and more and more things happened to him."

The Blue Jays had Halladay covered. Toronto scouting director Bob Engle attended Mesa Junior College in Grand Junction, Colorado. He knew Campbell because he once convinced him to back out of his college commitment to Arizona to join him at Colorado. They became friends. He hired Campbell when the Blue Jays had an opening for a scout.

"We hired Bus not really knowing that a Roy Halladay was going to come along," Engle said. "Bus was instrumental. He recommended Roy. To have any insight into any young player or an extra in-depth evaluation, knowing not only what's happening on the field, but even more importantly what's going on off the field and what type of player you're talking about, I think that gave us certainly—I don't want to say an edge—but it certainly gave us a lot of good information about background and things of that nature."

Moose Johnson, a Blue Jays crosschecker who lived in Arvada, watched Halladay pitch a few times. Fellow crosschecker Tim

Wilken and area scout Chris Bourjos, who is the father of big league outfielder Peter Bourjos, watched Halladay too. Wilken got his only look at Halladay in April 1995. He threw a shutout in front of about 40 scouts. His fastball hit 95 mph, but some scouts had concerns.

"There were some raps against Roy," Wilken said. "Some people called him a one-piece arm action."

It meant Halladay had barely any bend in his elbow when he released the ball. Folks believed that pitchers with one-piece arm action had trouble commanding the baseball.

"I thought there was just enough bend in his elbow at release point," Wilken said. "I kept saying, 'Hey, no, it's not a one-piece arm action.' He had a very coordinated delivery, maybe not the prettiest, kind of upright."

Wilken filed his report. Under the "Summation and Signability" category he wrote: "POWER PITCHER WITH GOOD PITCHING BALANCE AND TWO PLUS PLUS POWER PITCHES WITH GOOD COMMAND AND VERY GOOD ABILITY TO REPEAT HIS DELIVERY. WILL GET STRONGER, COMPETES WELL AND GOOD FEEL. 1ST ROUND."

Toronto had success in previous years selecting high school pitchers Steve Karsay (1990) and Chris Carpenter (1993) in the first round. Team execs wondered if they should take another high school pitcher in the first round.

"This wasn't a slam dunk that this was the guy we were going to take," Blue Jays general manager Gord Ash said. "There was a lot of conversation. I guess that the strongest voice on him was probably Tim Wilken."

Wilken listed him second on his pre-draft list behind right-hander Ariel Prieto, who Oakland selected with the fifth overall pick. Others in the Blue Jays' pre-draft meetings liked high school shortstops Michael Barrett or Jay Woolf with the 17th pick. Wilkens continued to push hard for Halladay.

"I became a little irate and stuff," Wilken said. "I kept pushing the envelope and pushing it. I just really felt that this was going to be something. I was strongly convicted. I lost a friend because of that. When you get in those draft rooms some words can be said and stuff."

EVERYBODY IN COLORADO KNEW about Halladay by the time Arvada West played Cherry Creek in the state championship game in '95.

Cherry Creek had a loaded roster that included future big leaguers Brad Lidge, Josh Bard, and Darnell McDonald. Other kids would play Division I baseball. Halladay did not start the game because he pitched the semifinal game. Capra executed the same plan in '94 when AW won it all.

"Coach was always so nervous that we wouldn't make it to the final that we always had to throw him in the semis because we knew that would at least guarantee that we'd get in, you know?" AW shortstop Brad Madden said.

Cherry Creek held two leads before AW tied the game in the sixth inning, 3–3. Cherry Creek had runners at the corners with no outs when Capra summoned Halladay from the bullpen. He got a fielder's choice, keeping the go-ahead run at third with one out. But Tyler Johnson, the son of head coach Marc Johnson, smacked a sacrifice fly to the warning track in left field. Cherry Creek had a 4–3 lead.

"He had pitched the day before," said Johnson, who played college baseball at Arizona State. "That's important in this whole thing. He had already thrown. It wasn't like he got a ball up and I turned on it. I hit it really well and I legitimately probably hit it where it was thrown. It was kind of an up, somewhat away ball that I just got my bat on. Even with Roy throwing the day before he was still throwing very hard. Much harder than anybody else that we were facing. It was exciting. I had played against Roy growing up. He was like an icon forever. He was one of the only guys that I know that I ever played that was as dominant at eight as he was with the Phillies. He was always known as a beast."

Cherry Creek scored two more runs against Halladay to win 6–3.

"We were definitely stunned," AW second baseman Eric McMaster said. "Late in the game, knowing you have Roy coming in the game, you think, 'Hey, we're going to win back-to-back state championships.'"

Halladay went 10–1 with a 0.55 ERA as a senior. He struck out 105 batters in 63 innings. He surrendered just 24 hits.

"To be honest with you, going into that game, I don't think there was a person in this state that thought they could beat Roy Halladay, including me," Marc Johnson said. "He was just that good. Listen, Roy Halladay was walking away the best pitcher that came out of Colorado. We had some good ones, including Brad Lidge. But in my mind Roy stands out as the best ever."

DARIN ERSTAD, BEN DAVIS, José Cruz Jr., Kerry Wood, and Prieto were the first five picks in the '95 draft. Jamie Jones, Jonathan Johnson, Todd Helton, and Geoff Jenkins were selected with picks six through nine.

The Pirates picked 10th. They kept things close to the vest, but everybody expected them to take high school outfielder Reggie Taylor. Pittsburgh, however, surprised everybody and chose high school shortstop Chad Hermansen. It was an important development. The Phillies, who picked 14th, had narrowed their choices to Taylor and Halladay. If the Pirates took Taylor, they planned to take Halladay. But with Taylor still available they nabbed him instead. Five more pitchers fell off the board before the 17th pick: Mike Drumright, Matt Morris, Mark Redman, Andy Yount, and Joe Fontenot.

Halladay fell into Toronto's lap. The telephone rang at 11:24 AM at Halladay's home.

"Thank you. Thank you. I'm really excited," he told the voice on the other line.

He hung up.

"It's the Toronto Blue Jays!" he said.

Fittingly, Campbell called him with the news. Halladay's high school teammates savored the moment. They had watched Halladay work harder than anybody since they met him in Little League. He made it happen, but he let his teammates know that he appreciated them. He signed a baseball for McMaster, who the Brewers selected in the 68th round: "See you in the big leagues, Roy Halladay." He signed a ball for his batterymate, Chad Sigg: "Chad, thanks for making me look good, Roy Halladay."

"Looking back on it, that's just Roy," Sigg said. "He says stuff like, 'Thanks for making me look good,' but really he was the one making all of us look good, you know?"

"He was just one of the guys," Madden said. "We knew he was great, but at the same time when you look back on it now, it was pretty special we got to play with him. That's still my claim to fame. I got to play with Roy Halladay. I'm a high school baseball coach, so I tell the story every year that if you want to be great you've got to work at it. Roy's always my example."

Back in Toronto's draft room, the Blue Jays believed they got an ace. They were lucky.

"It's funny how the draft goes," Wilken said. "If you look at some of the picks after we took Roy, you can kind of see a thinnish draft."

Halladay finished his career with a 64.3 WAR, according to Baseball Reference. The next 13 picks in the first round, including two sandwich picks, had a combined 0.4 WAR. Eight of them never reached the big leagues. Of the first 18 picks in the second round, before the Royals selected high school outfielder Carlos Beltran with the 49th pick, 14 had a career WAR of 0.0 or less or never reached the big leagues.

Halladay signed an $895,000 bonus in August.

"When he signed later that summer we were practicing at the school and he drove right down the sidewalk to the field in a candy-apple red Corvette," Capra said. "Just proud as heck."

Halladay had another surprise for Capra. He told him to replace the chain-link fence in the outfield with a 10-foot-high wooden fence.

"He just said, 'Buy a fence and I'll pay for it,'" Capra said. "It was something that you just don't expect or anticipate from somebody. You know how kids are as far as their egos, the 'me' stuff. He wasn't like that, which as a coach is most memorable. He didn't care much about, 'I need strikeouts, I need to pitch this game, I need to pitch that game.' Those were never conversations. It was just the kind of guy he was."

Halladay reported to the Gulf Coast League Blue Jays in Dunedin, Florida. He was on his way.

"I finally sign, I get my airline ticket, limo service picking me up at the airport," he said. "Well, it was a limo shuttle. So I'm looking for a big stretch limo and didn't realize I was getting shoved into this little shuttle van. So, I missed my shuttle van and they had to come pick me up. That's kind of when I realized it was going to be a bit of a ladder to lift myself up."

| 5 |

Doc and Carp

DAN PLESAC FINISHED a bullpen session early in the spring of 1997. It was his first spring training with the Blue Jays, but it was his 12th season in the majors. Bullpen sessions are not memorable. Pitchers get on the mound and throw, slowly building arm strength for spring training games, then regular season games. Plesac threw countless bullpens in his life, but this one this spring morning in Dunedin, Florida, remains etched in his mind because of what happened next.

"Hey, Lefty," Blue Jays pitching coach Mel Queen said. "Why don't you hang around and watch the next group throw. You're going to like these three guys."

"Sure," Plesac said.

Roy Halladay, Chris Carpenter, and Kelvim Escobar stepped onto their respective mounds and began to throw. Halladay was 19. He pitched well with the rookie-level Gulf Coast League Blue Jays in 1995 and Class A Dunedin in 1996. He earned an invitation to his first big league camp, and because the Blue Jays planned to start him in Double-A that season, it might not be long before he reached the majors. Carpenter, 21, was selected with the 15th overall pick in the 1993 draft out of Trinity High School in Manchester, New Hampshire. He made 28 starts for Double-A Knoxville in 1996. The Blue Jays believed he could make his big league debut in '97. Escobar, 20, signed with the Blue Jays as an amateur free agent out of Venezuela in '92. He split his '96 season with Dunedin and Knoxville. Like Carpenter, he had a chance to make his big league debut in '97.

Baseball America ranked Halladay as the 23rd-best prospect in baseball. Carpenter ranked 28th and Escobar ranked 67th. Toronto believed the trio could lead the organization back to the postseason, anchoring its rotation for years. Carpenter and Halladay looked like carbon copies as they threw. Carpenter stood 6-foot-6. Halladay stood 6-foot-6. They had similar builds. They both threw right-handed. Plesac watched every pitch.

Wow.

He played golf later that afternoon with a few friends from Chicago at the Copperhead Course at Innisbrook in nearby Palm Harbor.

"Guys, I watched these three pitchers today, but I want you to remember these two in particular—Roy Halladay and Chris Carpenter," Plesac said. "They're both going to be stars. They breathe different air than everybody else."

Halladay and Carpenter impressed more than Plesac that spring. Former Blue Jays slugger George Bell was in camp as an instructor. Bell, who won the American League MVP in 1987, whistled as he watched Halladay throw fastballs during one of his bullpens. "Smoke," he said. During an appearance against the Royals in a Grapefruit League game in March, Halladay allowed one run in three innings, retiring the final eight batters he faced. His fastball hit 95 mph.

"He's just a kid who's not going to spend a lot of time in the minor leagues," Blue Jays manager Cito Gaston said. "He's amazing for the poise he has out there. Halladay and Carpenter give us a bit of a safety valve at [Triple-A] Syracuse. They don't get afraid. They look like they've been there a long time."

Halladay and Carpenter met for the first time that spring, but they bonded later in the season. Carpenter started the season in Triple-A, but joined the Blue Jays in May. Halladay moved from Double-A to Triple-A to take his place. The promotion made Halladay the youngest pitcher in the International League. Carpenter made three appearances with Toronto before he returned to Syracuse.

"That's when we started working out together and really communicated back and forth about baseball," Carpenter said.

They had plenty in common. They grew up in small towns. They liked to fish. They shared similar sensibilities. But more than anything, they were two of the top prospects in baseball and everybody in Toronto expected them to be the next Roger Clemens and Pat Hentgen. It was not easy.

"We were good, talented, young high school kids that didn't have a lot of experience in actual life," Carpenter said. "Emotionally, we were very similar. We probably portrayed ourselves a little stronger and more confident than we were. So I think that that was part of it. Not that we didn't believe in ourselves or our talent, we were competitors, but I think that there were some fears, some little-kid scaredness in there. It's almost like two different guys. We're very similar guys with lots of anxieties and things going on inside that you don't see on the outside. The inside, internal conversation [with the Blue Jays] was that we were going to be the ones who took over every day. We were just trying to survive and get outs."

Carpenter rejoined the Blue Jays in July. He went 3–5 with a 3.86 ERA in 11 starts the rest of the way. Halladay went 7–10 with a 4.58 ERA in 22 starts with Syracuse. They got to spring training in '98 still expected to be Clemens and Hentgen. Halladay was *Baseball America's* 38th ranked prospect.

Carpenter and Halladay set more modest expectations for themselves. They just wanted leather belts and laundry bins. Back then, minor leaguers wore stretchy, elastic belts and tossed their uniforms into laundry bags. The bags got tossed into the wash and the clothes often came back balled up and wet. Big leaguers got leather belts and tossed their uniforms into bins. Everything got laundered properly and placed back in their lockers before the next game.

"At the time, it was awesome," Carpenter said. "You knew you made it."

Halladay and Carpenter spent several springs together. They bought a boat. They spent nights together on a nearby lake wearing headlamps trying to catch fish until one in the morning. They talked about the pressures they felt. It helped.

"I think that's something that made us close," Carpenter said. "Nobody really knew what was going on inside of us because we had to portray ourselves as these confident, first-round guys that were going to take it over and that knew what we were doing. And we really weren't. We were just trying to survive, trying to figure out what it looked like."

"We were supposed to come in and lead this team and be these great pitchers right out of the gate, and I think it was tough for both of us not really knowing how to go about that," Halladay said.

Fortunately, they could learn from the real Clemens and Hentgen. Clemens joined the Blue Jays in '97, following a storied career with the Boston Red Sox. He won the American League Cy Young Award in '86, '87, and '91, but the Red Sox felt Rocket's best years passed him by. He proved them wrong and won the Cy Young in '97, going 21–7 with a 2.05 ERA. Hentgen helped the Blue Jays win the '93 World Series. He won the Cy Young in '96. Both pitchers had reputations as hard workers. Halladay and Carpenter watched every move they made. They attached themselves to Hentgen.

"He was probably the biggest influence on my career as a player," Halladay said. "He respected the game. He respected other players. He taught me so much sitting on the bench. That doesn't happen a lot anymore where a veteran guy takes a younger guy and tells him to quit flicking sunflower seeds; it's not professional. It's just stuff like that that you learn from a guy that I was very fortunate to be around."

"Pat used to say it all the time, 'What are you looking at?'" Carpenter said. "We'd stare at him. Because that's how you'd learn, or it's how I learned anyway. You watch and you learn. Isn't that a thing your parents say?"

Hentgen welcomed his role as mentor. He showed them how to work. He told them how to compete. He recited Jack Morris' mantra about pitching, even without their best stuff: "Put your balls in your cup and pitch as hard as you can until the manager comes and gets you."

Halladay and Carpenter always remembered that. How could anybody forget?

HALLADAY STARTED THE '98 season in Triple-A. He went 9–5 with a 3.79 ERA in 21 starts. He struck out 71 and walked 53 in 116⅓ innings.

His season ended in mid-September, but he hung around Syracuse a couple days because he thought the Blue Jays might promote him once rosters expanded. The call never came. Disappointed, Halladay and his fiancé, Brandy Gates, loaded up the Chevy Tahoe with their cat and dog, hooked up a U-Haul with their stuff, and began a 25-hour drive to Colorado. They reached Cincinnati, where they stopped for the night. Brandy called her mother to let everybody know they arrived safely.

"I'm so glad you called!" she said. "The Blue Jays have been calling. They're trying to find you!"

"What did we do?" Brandy said. "Were we not supposed to leave? Did we do something wrong?"

Brandy's mom gave her a name and number. Halladay picked up the phone and dialed.

"Okay… okay… okay… okay," he said, listening to the person on the other line.

Halladay hung up. He got promoted! He did not have to travel far to meet the team. The Blue Jays opened a two-game series against the Indians the next night in Cleveland. It was a short drive from Cincinnati. They drove the Tahoe with the U-Haul to the team hotel.

"It was the worst first impression for a new team, right?" Brandy said. "We pull in, we park, it was terrible."

Halladay did not have a suit. He needed one. It is not easy finding a nice, off-the-rack suit for a 6-foot-6 guy.

. "We got him the biggest suit we could," Brandy said. "It was halfway down his arm."

The pants were worse, but it did the job. Halladay did not pitch in Cleveland. He left with the team to play two more games in Detroit. Brandy and her mother, who flew from Colorado to Ohio to meet them, drove the Tahoe, the cat, the dog, and the U-Haul back home. Brandy thought she would miss Halladay's debut. She was crushed.

"I drove home hysterical with my mom because I missed it," she said.

ROY AND BRANDY FIRST met when they were kids in Arvada. She was 12. He was nine. Their families met at church and Brandy became friends with Halladay's older sister Merinda. Brandy's family later moved to Chicago, where she graduated high school. She bounced around a bit before returning to Arvada.

"I was having a hard time," she said. "I had quit my job."

A friend recommended they play racquetball one afternoon at the fitness center in town. They went. Halladay was working out. Brandy noticed him as she checked out a racquet.

"I just had that weird feeling like I'm supposed to know who that person is," she said.

Halladay, Brandy, and her friend might have been the only people there under 70. She noticed that Halladay kept walking by. In between breaks in action, she kept peeking around the corner to see if he was still there. He was. Brandy's friend saw him. She recognized him.

"Hey, you know him. Do you remember the Halladays?" she said.

"I do," Brandy said. "I'm going to say hi."

She walked up a flight of stairs to find him. He was walking down.

"I don't know if you remember me, but I used to be friends with your sister," she said.

Halladay thought Brandy wanted to talk about Merinda. He eventually figured out what was going on.

"I know why I'm a loser here on a Tuesday afternoon," Brandy said. "Why are you here on a Tuesday?'"

"Oh, I play baseball," Halladay said.

Brandy thought Halladay played beer-league softball or something.

"Great," she said, "I play racquetball. What do you do for work?"

"No, seriously," Halladay said, laughing. "I actually play baseball. I got drafted by the Blue Jays."

They talked a little longer, Brandy handed Halladay her number and they agreed to go out that night. Brandy had a feeling. She got home and went to her friends' house across the street. She walked through the backdoor and said she came to tell them that she just met the guy she would marry.

Her friends were surprised. Wasn't she just depressed, sitting in her parents' basement and eating nachos the night before? Now she's getting married? "Yes," she said. Halladay and Brandy went out that night and played pool. Brandy won. She never won at pool again. They went out again the next night. The Halladays lived just down the street, so she could see her future husband leave his house, get in his car, and drive to hers.

"And that was that," Brandy said. "It was quick. It was fast."

They were engaged 10 months later. They married in Denver on November 27, 1998. They honeymooned for 10 days in Jamaica.

"I grew up a lot faster than a lot of people," said Halladay, who was 21 when he married. "The whole college experience and that atmosphere is something I didn't miss. The party atmosphere and the going out and stuff, that was never really a part of me. I think I just wanted to settle down very quickly. Those [other] things were just things that I didn't desire."

"He was the one pushing," Brandy said. "He was the one that wanted to get married because I kept saying, 'Let's wait, let's wait, just to make sure everybody is comfortable.' He's like, 'No, I want to get married.' And when we got married he said, 'I want kids.' I said, 'Let's make sure you're legal to even drink yet, you know?' That's what he wanted. He wanted family. He wanted kids. He wanted stability. He wanted home. We always worked very, very hard to make sure we had a home base."

HALLADAY DID NOT PITCH in Detroit. The Blue Jays flew to Tampa Bay to open a three-game series at Tropicana Field. Toronto was competing for the American League Wild Card, but after a poor stretch, including losses in the first two games of the series in Tampa Bay, Blue Jays manager Tim Johnson shelved the idea of starting Clemens on short rest. He chose Halladay to make his major league debut on September 20.

Brandy would not miss her fiancé's debut. Nobody would. Halladay's father's boss let him borrow his plane for the weekend so he could fly his family, Brandy, Arvada West baseball coach Jim Capra, and others to Tampa Bay. Halladay struck out Randy Winn swinging on a 2-2 pitch to begin his major league career. He allowed eight hits, three runs, two earned runs, two walks, and one home run in five innings. He struck out five in a 7–5 win.

"It was pretty exciting because I had been to quite a few of those minor league games," Big Roy said. "Some of them were almost like high school games, you know? I remember Randy Winn was his first strikeout. I remember that and how cool it was. There were so many experiences like that, because we used to watch baseball on TV and the World Series and the next thing you know he's pitching against them. It was pretty exhilarating. When he was about 12 years old—I did this a lot—when he got ready for bed I'd go up and talk to him. I said, 'What would it feel like if you were pitching in the major leagues and you were standing on the mound at Yankee Stadium pitching against the Yankees?' He'd kind of tell me and visualize this in his mind a little bit about what it was like and what he was sensing and everything. Then when it finally happened I called him and I said, 'So how was it? Was it close to what you thought it would be?' He said, 'It was a thousand times better.'"

The Blue Jays flew to Toronto to finish the season. Carpenter was scheduled to pitch the Blue Jays' season finale against the Tigers, but the team told him that it wanted to see Halladay pitch one more time. He understood why. He threw 175 innings with the Blue Jays, going 12–7 with a 4.37 ERA. He had a spot locked up in the 1999 rotation. It might help his friend to enter the spring with another big league start under his belt.

Brandy's family flew from Colorado to watch. Halladay retired the first 12 batters he faced, carrying a perfect game into the fifth inning. Blue Jays second baseman Felipe Crespo committed an error to start the inning, spoiling the perfect game. Halladay retired the next three batters to keep the no-hitter alive. He then retired the side in the sixth, seventh, and eighth innings, carrying a no-hitter into the ninth.

"I had no idea what I was doing," Halladay said. "I was just trying to throw as hard as I could and it was just one of those games when I was hitting the glove. And my curveball was on, which was a big issue for me. I was throwing a different curveball than I was throwing later in my career. And for some reason, it was all just sort of clicking."

Plesac watched Halladay carve up Detroit from the bullpen. He turned to teammate Paul Quantrill and said he was positive Halladay would throw a no-hitter.

"Q, make sure when the game is over and when you run out on the field that you take your jacket off so your grandkids can see down the road that you played with and that you mobbed Roy Halladay on the mound after he threw a no-hitter," Plesac said.

Most of the Blue Jays' veterans watched from the clubhouse. The team had the hokey idea of pulling its veterans off the field throughout the game to give them a nice ovation from the hometown crowd. Tom Evans replaced Tony Fernandez with one out in the first inning. Kevin Witt replaced Carlos Delgado with one out in the second. Kevin Brown replaced Darrin Fletcher with two outs in the second. It continued like that throughout the game.

"As they took all these players out, guys were going to the clubhouse, having a beer, and getting dressed to go home for the season," Fletcher said. "We were all dressed and ready to go. They were like, 'Doc, let's hurry this up dude,' because guys were trying to catch flights and all."

Halladay threw 85 pitches through eight innings. Sixty-six were strikes. He only got into a single three-ball count.

"You see early in the game that the umpire has a liberal strike zone, so you go up there with the idea of swinging at the first pitch," Tigers designated hitter Luis Gonzalez said. "I saw three pitches and swung at all three."

Halladay got Tigers right fielder Gabe Kapler to line out to left fielder Shannon Stewart for the first out in the ninth. Tigers catcher Paul Bako grounded out to Crespo for the second out. Halladay needed one more out to become the youngest pitcher to throw a no-hitter since Oakland's Vida Blue in 1970. Blue was 21 years, two months old. Halladay was 21 years, four months old.

Plesac took off his jacket.

"It's over," he told Quantrill.

Detroit interim manager Larry Parrish sent veteran Bobby Higginson to the plate as a pinch-hitter. Higginson hit .284 with 25 home runs, 85 RBIs, and an .835 OPS in '98. Parrish told him Saturday that he would not play in Sunday's season finale. The 28-year-old outfielder took advantage of the situation.

"Toronto is a good city, you know what I mean?" Higginson said. "You kind of go out a little bit."

He still wanted to break up Halladay's no-hitter. The Blue Jays planned before the game to throw Higginson fastballs down and away because the left-handed-hitting outfielder loved pulling the ball. He almost never hit anything in the air to the opposite field.

Higginson walked to the plate without taking any swings in the cage. Why bother? It wasn't like he could do worse than his teammates. As he stepped into the batter's box, home plate umpire Jim McKean told Higginson that he better swing at anything close, because he planned to call it a strike.

"He was kind of falling in love with the no-hitter because I don't think he had ever called one at the time," Higginson said. "I remember him saying that. He was kind of giving him a wide strike zone."

Brown, who replaced Fletcher behind the plate in the second, called for a first-pitch fastball low and away. Halladay threw it. Higginson expected it and barrelled it. He sent the ball into the jet stream and over the left-field fence for a home run. It was Higginson's second opposite-field homer that season, and one of only seven he hit out of 187 career homers. Dave Stieb caught the ball in the bullpen. The Blue Jays' great threw the only no-hitter in franchise history, but before that he lost three no-hitters with two outs in the ninth.

"This guy's got nothing," Higginson told his teammates back in the dugout. "What's wrong with you guys?"

Halladay told himself late in the game that he would not be disappointed if somebody got a hit. But coming that close, he was.

"I still can't stand that guy," Brown said about Higginson. "I still have nightmares about it. People ask, 'Hey, did you ever catch a no-hitter.' Don't even ask. Don't even start with me. Then, of course, I can't sleep for about two nights. I can still see that pitch."

Halladay retired Frank Catalanotto to end a game that lasted one hour, 45 minutes. McKean told Higginson in the tunnel that he ruined his chance to call a no-hitter. Higginson did not like umpires. He did not care. The veterans in the Blue Jays' clubhouse never said it, but they were relieved.

"Now we're not going to get busted for being fully clothed," Fletcher said. "We would have had to have thrown off our stuff and thrown on some shorts or something to go run out there and tackle him."

Halladay discussed the near no-no in front of his locker afterward. He knew what it meant.

"I'm going to feel that there's a lot of pressure next year, probably some more expectations," he said. "I'm just going to go home, go to winter ball, work as hard as I can, and try and come back and do it next year. I know they're going to expect a few things and I definitely don't want to disappoint them."

| 6 |

10.64

Halladay arrived at spring training in 1999 as the guy that almost threw a no-hitter in his second big league start. *Sports Illustrated* came to talk to him. *ESPN The Magazine* did too.

So, Roy, what do you do for an encore?

He followed his near miss against the Tigers with a 4–0 record and a 1.85 ERA in the Arizona Fall League. He entered camp with a No. 12 ranking in *Baseball America's* top 100 prospects list.

"Those expectations are going to be there for a couple of years," he said. "I just don't want them to become a burden for me."

The focus on Halladay could have been worse, but the Blue Jays grabbed most of the newspaper ink that spring. First, they traded Roger Clemens to the Yankees in February because they had an agreement (or not, depending on who was talking) that they would trade him if they did not increase their payroll to compete with New York, Boston, and Baltimore in the American

League East. The Blue Jays got David Wells, Homer Bush, and Graeme Lloyd in return. Second, they fired manager Tim Johnson in March because he could not recover from the lies he told about his service in Vietnam. Johnson often talked about the war as a motivational tool, but one afternoon at Fenway Park in '98 he tried to motivate Pat Hentgen, telling him that real pressure is 'Nam. He said he accidentally killed a 12-year-old girl because she moved into the line of fire. The truth came out. Johnson never set foot in Vietnam, making his story about shooting an innocent girl even more disturbing. Johnson apologized multiple times, both privately and publicly. Blue Jays general manager Gord Ash hung with him as long as he could, but it became clear that his lies would follow the Blue Jays like a black cloud.

"The unsettledness and the distractions had become the issue," Ash said. "It had become apparent it wasn't going to work."

The Blue Jays hired Jim Fregosi to take Johnson's place.

"They were looking for leadership," Fregosi said. "We've got 18 games. We'll be ready by Opening Day."

Fregosi played 18 seasons in the big leagues. He was the first star player in Angels franchise history, making the All-Star team six times. He managed the Angels from 1978 to 1981, winning the AL West in 1979, and the Chicago White Sox from 1986 to '88, before he replaced Nick Leyva as the Phillies' manager 13 games into the 1991 season. He led the Phillies—a collection of beer-drinking, mullet-sporting rabble rousers—to the 1993 National League pennant, only to watch an exhausted Mitch Williams throw a meatball to Blue Jays outfielder Joe Carter for a World

Series–clinching, walk-off home run in Game 6. Fregosi defended his decision to pitch Williams in Game 6 until he died in 2014.

Fregosi could be loud, brash, and brutally honest. Veteran players on the '93 Phillies loved him. A lot of people did.

The Blue Jays finalized their Opening Day roster. Wells, Hentgen, Chris Carpenter, Kelvim Escobar, and Joey Hamilton made the rotation. Halladay made the bullpen as a long man. It was not the job he wanted, but he got his leather belt and he got his uniform laundered the proper way. He pitched three scoreless innings to earn the first and only save of his career in his first appearance of the season. His time in the bullpen did not last long. Hamilton landed on the 15-day disabled list on April 17 because of a shoulder injury. Halladay started the next day, pitching seven scoreless innings against the Orioles. He was 2–0 with a 0.00 ERA and one save in his first 20 innings as a 21-year-old rookie. He allowed only 14 hits, but he walked 11 and struck out seven. His command issues caught up to him April 29 in Anaheim. He allowed nine hits, 11 runs, three walks, and two home runs in just 2⅓ innings against the Angels.

He got hit hard in his next two starts too. Kevin Brown, who caught most of Halladay's near no-no in '98, caught one of those games.

"At that level, yes, there are mechanical things, but I think that gets in your head, then it's, 'Do I belong here?'" he said. "'Am I ever going to pitch here?' Then you start making one or two small adjustments. You start changing your mechanics. You try to make the ball break more. You're trying to pinpoint it, put it right on the black every time, when all you have to do is hit the outer third of the plate."

Halladay shuttled back and forth from the Blue Jays' bullpen and rotation. He went 8–7 with a 3.92 ERA in 36 appearances (18 starts). He struck out 82, but walked 79 in 149⅓ innings. He showed promise toward the end, posting a 2.70 ERA in six starts before shoulder stiffness ended his season. But he struggled to find consistent success because his over-the-top delivery made his fastball too visible to hitters and he could not throw his knuckle curve for strikes. Carpenter went 9–8 with a 4.38 ERA in 24 starts, although he posted a 6.61 ERA in his final nine starts before having season-ending surgery to remove a bone spur in his elbow.

But Toronto saw enough from Halladay and Carpenter to convince them to trade Hentgen in November. They shipped him and Paul Spoljaric to the Cardinals for catcher Alberto Castillo and pitchers Lance Painter and Matt DeWitt. Hentgen's trade caused some controversy because he was a Blue Jays legend. There was talk that Fregosi did not like his influence on Carpenter and Halladay, which was baffling because both pitchers cite Hentgen as one of the most positive influences in their careers.

The Blue Jays traded outfielder Shawn Green to the Dodgers too. Fregosi would not miss him. "He wanted to be with his girlfriend there," he said. There had been talk that first baseman Carlos Delgado did not want to stay in Toronto because of Fregosi, either. Fregosi changed the coaching staff because he believed some of Johnson's coaches went behind his back and told players what he said about them behind closed doors. He removed popular pitching coach Mel Queen for Rick Langford and made former manager Cito Gaston his hitting coach. He brought in three more coaches. Everybody in Toronto believed that Fregosi pushed for the personnel changes, believing he wanted to squash the country-club atmosphere and give the place a '93 Phillies vibe.

"Everything's ifs, ands, buts, and b.s.," Fregosi said. "Last year, I used a pitcher that I thought was one of the best pitchers on the staff as the long-man out of the 'pen most of the year out of due respect for the other players that were in the rotation at the time. Mr. Halladay needs to start every fifth day."

THE BLUE JAYS HAD high expectations for Halladay in 2000. They signed him in March to a three-year, $3.7 million contract extension. Toronto expected Wells, Carpenter, Halladay, and Escobar to lead the rotation. If everybody stayed healthy, they believed they could compete with the Yankees and Red Sox.

"Those guys are young in age, but that's about it," Blue Jays catcher Darrin Fletcher said. "Halladay, he's got experience. Chris, I almost consider a veteran. It doesn't take long for somebody to get going and I think these guys are going to take off. At least that what we're hoping that they do."

Halladay allowed three runs in seven innings in his first start of the year, a win over Kansas City on April 4, but he got rocked in his next six starts, posting a 13.50 ERA. He allowed 52 hits and 41 runs in 27⅔ innings. He walked 21 and struck out 17. Fregosi sent Halladay to the bullpen after he allowed eight runs in 3⅔ innings against the Indians on May 5. Halladay sounded relieved.

"I think it's a thing where I can go there and figure some things out and not have the same pressure," he said. "It'll be a chance to think about things and not worry so much. Every time out, I've been trying to turn everything around in one outing."

He allowed three runs in one inning in a relief appearance against the Red Sox on May 15. The Blue Jays optioned him to Triple-A, but not before they changed his mechanics. Fregosi and Langford asked Halladay to raise both hands high over his head from the top of his windup, a change they also asked Carpenter to make. It worked for Bob Gibson and Warren Spahn in the '50s and '60s; maybe it would work for them. Halladay rejoined the team in late June. He went 2–3 with an 8.89 ERA in eight appearances (five starts) through the end of July. He walked 18 and struck out 20 in 27⅓ innings. His confidence evaporated.

"Sometimes I question myself and I shouldn't," he said. "If I give up a hit on hard stuff, or I give up a hit on soft stuff, it doesn't matter. I just have to start throwing the pitches I want to. I have to believe in myself. I need to have enough confidence in myself to throw the pitches I want to throw."

Negative thoughts consumed him. Fregosi did not help. He wore out Halladay and Carpenter. Halladay swore as soon as he stepped on the mound that Fregosi put his hand on the bullpen phone, ready to call for help. Then there was the time Halladay turned a corner in the clubhouse and overheard Fregosi ripping him from his office. Halladay asked Fregosi if they needed to talk. Fregosi said no. Halladay walked away not knowing what he needed to do to fix things. He grew up seeking validation from his father whenever he pitched. He wanted it from Fregosi too. It never came. It made Halladay desperate. He continually changed his work in between starts, hoping to find a magic cure. He stretched before he pitched. Then he did not. He skipped bullpen sessions. He threw less long toss. He threw more long toss. He changed his diet. He ate a big meal before he pitched, but if he pitched poorly he ate less before the next one. None of it worked.

"When things are going bad it doesn't matter what psychologists they find to talk to you," said Castillo, who caught Halladay seven times in 2000. "When things are going wrong you're trying so hard to save your life."

"He needed to learn how to fail," Brandy said. "He had always been a big fish in a little pond, then he was a big fish in a little bigger pond. But he finally was just a fish. He wasn't the big fish anymore. He was just a guy trying to figure out what the heck he was doing. So when he got to that point, he had never been taught how to fail. He had never been taught how to handle adversity. He was scared of it. He was terrified to fail. He didn't know how to handle it. He didn't know how to recoup. He didn't know how to keep his head straight. He felt tremendous pressure to live up to what people expected of him and to earn his check and support his family. So when he did struggle it was world-ending for him. He couldn't function. He couldn't think. He was sick to his stomach. He was physically falling apart. He was broken."

The Blue Jays tried everything to fix him. Toronto assistant general manager Dave Stewart was a four-time 20-game winner and one-time World Series champion with the A's. One afternoon he left his office, found Halladay, and introduced his forkball grip to him. A couple days later in late July, the Blue Jays fired Langford and made Stewart the pitching coach.

"I was just asked to do damage control," Stewart said.

Fregosi was not asked. He was pissed.

"They asked me what I thought, but the decision had already been made," he said. "I don't think it was the right decision, and I think it makes for a difficult transition."

Langford was a casualty because Halladay, Carpenter, and Escobar struggled. Carpenter was 7–10 with a 6.89 ERA through the end of July. Escobar was 7–11 with a 5.06 ERA. Fregosi moved Carpenter to the bullpen in July to work on his fastball command. He made one appearance in 10 days before Fregosi swapped him back into the rotation for Halladay.

"We both struggled in the 2000 season," Carpenter said. "A lot of it was the confidence level. I'm speaking for me personally, and he and I talked a little bit about it. I think it was the confidence level of learning the grind of what it took to pitch there. Learning the changes of what it takes. You have to make adjustments and—I don't want to use the word 'grind'—but flying and distractions and money and family, all that other stuff goes on. We just wanted to pitch and not be hit. That hit both of us, and he wasn't able to handle it as well as I was. Not that I handled it a ton better than him, but he just wasn't able to do it and he needed to make some adjustments in his stuff. I had some sink and my curveball I could throw for strikes. He wasn't throwing his breaking ball for strikes and watching his fastball straight over the top. He gave it a good look [to hitters] and all that stuff. He needed to develop his changeup or something different. He just needed to get some deception to what he was doing or he had to be perfect. It was a battle, man. It was a long year."

The Blue Jays optioned Halladay to Triple-A on August 4. Brandy gave birth to their son Braden in Toronto on August 14. Halladay rejoined the team in September and finished the season 4–7 with a 10.64 ERA over 67⅔ innings. He allowed 107 hits, 87 runs, and 14 home runs. He walked 42 and struck out 44. Carpenter went 10–12 with a 6.26 ERA in 34 appearances (27 starts). The Blue Jays fired Fregosi, in part because the pitching failed to develop and in part because his personality clashed with players.

The Halladays and Carpenters went to dinner after the season. They found a restaurant, but they could not get a table inside. They got one on the fire escape in the back. Halladay and Carpenter joked that they were so bad that they could not even get a decent table in a restaurant anymore.

"We sat out there and laughed our asses off," Brandy said.

Halladay's 10.64 ERA remains the highest single-season ERA in baseball history (minimum 50 innings). It might be the most amazing statistic of Halladay's career. More than the 203 wins. More than the 67 complete games. More than the 20 shutouts or 2,749⅓ innings pitched. Great pitchers do not have seasons like the one Halladay had in 2000. Hall of Famers most certainly do not. Pitchers with ERAs like that muddle through mediocre careers. They pitch a few years and vanish. They are forgotten.

The top 10 single-season ERAs in baseball history (minimum 50 innings) show as much:

Halladay: 10.64 (2000)

William Stecher: 10.32 (1890 Philadelphia A's)

Micah Bowie: 10.24 (1999 Atlanta Braves/Chicago Cubs)
Steve Blass: 9.85 (1973 Pittsburgh Pirates)
Sean Bergman: 9.66 (2000 Minnesota Twins)
Andy Larkin: 9.64 (1998 Florida Marlins)
Frank Gabler: 9.43 (1938 Boston Braves/Chicago White Sox)
Alfredo Simon: 9.36 (2016 Cincinnati Reds)
Ed O'Neil: 9.26 (1890 Toledo Maumees/Philadelphia A's)
Reggie Grabowski: 9.23 (1934 Philadelphia Phillies)

Blass is the most notable pitcher in the group, other than Halladay. He pitched 10 years in the big leagues. He went 2–0 with a 1.00 ERA in two starts in the 1971 World Series, helping Pittsburgh beat Baltimore. He went 19–8 with a 2.49 ERA in 1972. He made the NL All-Star team and finished second for Cy Young behind Steve Carlton, who went 27–10 with a 1.97 ERA. But Blass lost the mental capabilities to throw strikes in '73. The yips, Steve Blass Disease, they called it a lot of things, but what they called it didn't matter. Blass made one appearance in '74 and never pitched again. Halladay finished his career with a 64.3 WAR. Combine the career WARs of the next 26 pitchers on that list and it equals 65.3. Seven of those pitchers never pitched again in the big leagues after they had their career-worst seasons. Two of the pitchers—Stecher and O'Neil—only pitched in that single season (oddly, both 1890).

The next Hall of Famer on that list not named Halladay is Lefty Grove, who had a 6.50 ERA with the Boston Red Sox in 1934. That's more than four earned runs lower than Halladay.

"If you really go back and dissect where he was in 2000 and 2001 and where he ended up, I mean, it's pretty amazing," Carpenter said. "It really is pretty amazing. This is a guy who could have packed his tent and went home. So, to just show the determination, the fearlessness, really, because you have to remember that we're already struggling with the fears and lack of confidence. It just shows the character that he has. I think that's something that is overlooked. They talk about his career and how great he was. I don't think anyone understands where he was and how hard he had to work physically and mentally and emotionally to get back to where he was."

Incredibly, Halladay had not hit rock bottom in 2000. The worst was yet to come.

| 7 |

Mel

Halladay attended a Blue Jays minicamp in Dunedin, Florida, in December 2000. There he unburdened himself to new pitching coach Mark Connor.

Connor spent the previous three seasons with the Diamondbacks, which included time with Randy Johnson and Curt Schilling. He knew Halladay's talents and struggles. He wanted to talk to him to see how he could help, if he could help. They found a spot to chat down the right-field line on one of the fields at Toronto's minor league complex. Halladay got emotional as he spoke.

Can I do this?

Can I get big league hitters out?

"He broke up a little bit," Connor said. "You felt for him. But you tried to build him up and build his confidence back up. You tell him it's a process that's going to come about and not everything is going to be perfect."

Halladay entered spring training believing he put himself in a position to succeed, having improved his off-season training and conditioning program. But then the Grapefruit League season started and Halladay's pitches continued to find the barrels of bats. He allowed two runs, two hits, two walks, and two wild pitches in his spring debut against the Rangers in Port Charlotte on March 8. He allowed six runs and six hits in three innings against the Tigers in Lakeland on March 17. Blue Jays general manager Gord Ash's scouts returned with grim reports. Halladay allowed six runs and seven hits in five innings against the Twins in Dunedin on March 23.

"He's just getting his ass kicked," new Blue Jays manager Buck Martinez said.

"It was like the catcher was telling them what was coming," bullpen coach Gil Patterson said.

Halladay came to camp with a chance to win a job in the Blue Jays' rotation. Suddenly, he found himself behind 30-year-old left-handed journeyman Chris Michalak to be the No. 5 starter.

"There was nothing that you could hang your hat on with the stuff," Connor said. "It was generic."

Halladay was a constant topic of conversation within the organization. A few people believed it might be best to trade him and move on. Some suggested he should be released. Ash did not fall into that camp. He could see Halladay's physical talents and he knew the Blue Jays needed to develop pitching if they wanted to compete in the American League East. Besides, what in the world could they get for Halladay in a trade anyway?

"He was not the asset he was," Ash said. "You weren't going to get top value for him."

Martinez felt similarly. He and Connor believed they could help him. But how?

"What are we going to do with this guy?" Martinez said, turning to Connor during one of Halladay's starts. "We've got to do something to salvage this."

"We knew it was in there," Ash said. "We just had to get it out again."

The Blue Jays decided that Halladay would not make the team, but they decided a demotion to Triple-A would not work, either. If Halladay was one step from the big leagues he might feel pressure to perform and not focus on things he needed to be successful in the long run. The Blue Jays wanted the majors to look far away. They decided to send Halladay to Class A Dunedin, where he last pitched as a 19-year-old in 1996.

"Let's get back to square one," Ash said.

"We felt like the best way to do something was to get him out of a statistical environment, where stats didn't matter, where he could just go down and pitch and try to develop some mechanics that would be effective," Martinez said.

They optioned him on March 28. The Blue Jays knew the news would be jarring, so they asked employee assistance program director Tim Hewes to give Halladay a heads up. Hewes called for Halladay, who was shagging balls in the outfield. He invited him into an empty office. Halladay leaned upon a desk as Hewes explained his fate. The meeting might have lasted two minutes. Halladay said little.

"He just had a complete look of shock on his face, like, 'Goodness, what am I going to do?'" Hewes said. "Total shock."

Ash, Martinez, Connor, and others met with Halladay later. They explained their thought process and plan. They said they wanted him in Dunedin because he lived nearby and because it would be most comfortable for him. Dunedin had veteran pitching coach Scott Breeden, whom they thought could help. They wanted Halladay to work on the command of his pitches without the pressures of performance. They wanted him to work on his mental approach and rebuild his confidence. They promised Halladay that he would be promoted as soon as he showed progress. They promised him that they wanted him in the big leagues as quickly as possible.

"He didn't like it," Martinez said. "He was not happy. I don't think he was happy with me for a long time."

Halladay felt more shame than anything. He stepped into a bathroom stall and locked the door. He sat there for hours until everybody left so he would not have to tell anybody what happened.

"I was just... I was so embarrassed," he said. "Having to make the phone calls home and having to tell them, 'Yeah, I'm going to A ball,' and stuff like that. When you're right in the center of it and everybody around you is expecting you to be the next Roger Clemens and you have to explain what's going on, that's pretty rough. A lot of that was extremely motivating for me later in my career."

He left the ballpark and returned to his nearby apartment. He sat on the edge of his bed and sobbed as he discussed the future with Brandy.

Have we saved enough money?

I can still go back to college.

I don't want you to go back to work. Can we live off what we have?

I'm going to do my best. I promise I'll get a job.

Halladay glanced out the second-floor window.

"I would jump, but with my luck I would probably just break my leg and I'd still have to go to the field tomorrow," he said.

Brandy heard enough. She grabbed her car keys and headed for the door.

"It was so unlike him," she said. "He had struggled and he had worried, but he had never quit. And that's what I didn't understand. He had completely given up. To see him like that was terrifying. It was heartbreaking. I said, 'I need some time.' So I left."

She drove to a nearby bookstore. She strolled through the aisles, grabbing books she thought might help her husband. She picked up books from the self-help section. Growing up in the Mormon Church, she believed in the value of keeping a journal. She bought two of them.

"He was very closed, he was very quiet, he was very private," Brandy said. "He didn't share his feelings, he didn't share a lot, getting a real emotional conversation out of him was tough. So I thought maybe having a journal could help him get his feelings out. It helps you express yourself. It helps you deal with something."

Before she reached the cash register, she walked through the baseball section. She figured she would find books about Babe Ruth, Derek Jeter, and Ty Cobb. A random book faced outward. The title caught her eye:

The Mental ABC's of Pitching by H.A. Dorfman.

Brandy chuckled. How many people in the world need a book like this? She added it to the pile, because why not? She bought them and returned home. They finished their conversation. Halladay promised to keep pitching, even if he humiliated himself. He picked up *The Mental ABC's* and flipped through it.

"I opened the book and I swear the guy was following me around, writing stuff about me," he said. "Like, it was my whole life in there. Through that book, it started helping me change the way I thought."

HALLADAY STARTED THE LONG road back in Dunedin, not knowing if he ever would get back. Nothing happened at the beginning. Nothing encouraging anyway. He allowed two hits in two innings against Sarasota in his first relief appearance. He allowed three hits and two runs in two innings two days later in Fort Myers. Halladay went 0–1 with a 3.97 ERA in 13 relief appearances in Dunedin. The numbers might be okay for a middle reliever just out of college selected in the 25th round of the draft, but not for a big leaguer with first-round talent facing batters in the Florida State League.

"As soon as the hitter would take a 94- or 95-mph fastball and foul it straight back, I knew he was in trouble," Dunedin manager Marty Pevey said. "He was giving hitters a very good look at the ball."

Frustrated, Halladay called Bus Campbell.

"Why can't I get anybody out?" he said.

"Your problem isn't physical, it's mental," he said. "You've got to get help."

Halladay started to work on his mental approach. He continued to read Dorfman's book and he spoke to a sports psychologist.

"I really had no comprehension of the mental part of baseball," Halladay said. "I'd get negative things in my head. I just kind of always pitched that way. You kind of let your mind overtake what you want to do. When I thought about it, I figured what I was thinking was the last thing that had anything to do with the way I was pitching. I always thought it was mechanics or not making pitches.

"I knew [management] thought some of the problems were a lot more serious than they were. They were looking at a lot of things: 'Is there anything wrong with his personal life? What happened to him as a kid?' It just had gotten to the point where I couldn't build confidence in myself. I'd never had a doubt from the age of eight to 22. Now for the first time I wasn't getting guys out, and as someone who never had to deal with that kind of adversity, I had no idea how to turn it around. I was thinking about negatives: I can't bounce this pitch or I can't walk this guy or if I throw it over the plate, he's going to hit it 800 miles."

But it was more than just mental. His straight-as-an-arrow fastball remained too tantalizing to hitters and his knuckle curve remained an ineffective secondary pitch because it looked like a curveball out of his hand and he could never throw it for strikes. The Blue Jays needed to try something new, maybe something as drastic as the demotion to Class A. They called Mel Queen.

"He was our fixer," Pat Gillick said.

Queen could do anything in baseball because he had been everything in baseball. He was an outfielder with the Reds in the 1960s, but he made himself a pitcher because he knew he would never play ahead of Frank Robinson, Vada Pinson, and Tommy Harper. Queen went 14–8 with a 2.76 ERA in 31 appearances (24 starts) with Cincinnati in 1967, three years after he made his big league debut as an outfielder. He later turned to coaching and player development. He served as the Blue Jays' pitching coach from 1996 to '99. He eventually became a roving pitching instructor and special assignment scout, which was his role with Toronto in 2001. Queen had juice in Toronto. His opinions and ideas mattered.

"He was a very creative, curious guy," Ash said.

The Jays promoted Halladay to Double-A Tennessee to work with Queen. Halladay flew there immediately after he and Brandy settled on their new home. Halladay wanted to move to Florida full time, not only because it was more convenient, but because he was too embarrassed to return home following his recent failures. He did not want to go back.

"Moving to Florida took a lot of pressure off me," he said. "It was a fresh start. Baseball wasn't my identity there. I could go out and try to be as good as I could be. I didn't have to do it for anyone else. It made it easier for me to put my heart into it and not feel like if I don't do this, I'm disappointing all these people."

Halladay's flight landed in Knoxville. He got to the ballpark and met with Queen in the manager's office. They knew each other. Queen was his pitching coach in '98.

"Hi, how are you doing?" Halladay said.

"You're wasting talent, Doc," Queen shot back.

Halladay never forgot the way Queen greeted him, but it was just the beginning. Queen spoke to a sports psychologist before he got to Tennessee, and the psychologist suggested that he break down Halladay mentally and emotionally. Queen called Halladay naïve. He called him stupid. He called him every name in the book. Halladay took it all.

"You know what?" Queen said. "I wouldn't have blamed him if he had hauled off and cold-cocked me, the way I was talking to that young man. And to his credit, he sat there and took it, and that's what convinced me this guy was ready. He could have easily walked out, the way I was verbally abusing him, but he was more than receptive."

But why? Why did he take it?

"Roy probably took it because he believed it," Brandy said. "I think he took it because he believed it was true. But it's not what he wanted, so he worked hard so that Mel would see that it wasn't who he was. He didn't want to be that anymore. I think that's why he wore it. I think that's why he took it. He did. He felt that way about himself. To hear it was like, 'I know, but what am I going to do about it?' His motivation was to not be those things. Even though he wasn't, that's how he felt. His motivation was: he had a wife and a son and a family and he wanted to make these people in his life proud. And so he said, 'I'll do whatever I have to do to not be those things. Don't leave me here like this.' I don't think he could have been anymore broken or anymore humbled."

Queen told Halladay that unless he made changes—drastic changes—that he would be out of baseball in a year. Halladay said he thought he had been pitching better. Queen said he might be throwing better, but he was not pitching better. He was not missing bats. Hadn't he noticed?

Halladay said he was willing to try anything.

"Off the field, you feel like your whole life is baseball then all of a sudden you're a failure," Halladay said. "And then you feel like it makes your whole life a failure. I'd always felt like I was missing something. And to hear him say that, obviously, it hurt. But I think the most important thing is that, by that point, I was ready to hear it and fix something."

The Blue Jays placed Halladay on the phantom disabled list with a calf issue, which allowed Queen to work with him individually, away from the rest of the team and without interruption. Queen told Ash it would take "vigorous muddling" to fix Halladay, which meant he would try anything and everything.

Queen's No. 1 idea: Kill Iron Mike.

Iron Mike is the name of the old pitching machine. Baseballs fed into a mechanical arm, which slowly rotated upward before it flung the ball to the batter, much like Halladay's arm came straight over the top of his head before he threw. Queen thought it might help to lower Halladay's arm angle to create more deception. The adjustment might be difficult, but they needed to try something because Iron Mike could not get batters out in Class A, much less the big leagues. Halladay's work with a sports psychologist convinced him the change could be good. He said okay.

"The hitters could see the ball coming," Queen explained. "He had no deception. Threw very hard, but his ball basically was very, very straight. Unless he made really, really perfect pitches, they were going to hit him and I think he started realizing that. And then he tried to make perfect pitches and it would be ball one, ball two—and then he'd have to come in and then he'd get hit. I completely redid everything he did, just took the old guy and buried him and created something new."

Queen built a new Halladay with a surprisingly simple suggestion: "Throw sidearm, Doc."

Throw sidearm. That's it. Halladay tried. He dropped his arm angle just a few inches, about three quarters from the top. It wasn't sidearm, not even close, but it felt that way to him.

"It felt like I was throwing from around my belt where in reality it was maybe six to eight inches lower," he said.

His pitches started to move. Queen showed Halladay grips for a sinker and cutter. The ball moved more. Halladay got excited. Could such minor adjustments really change so much?

"I had always thrown a sinker, or a two-seam fastball," Halladay told *The New York Times*' Tyler Kepner in March 2017. "I had always thrown a little bit of a cutter, but they weren't—the cutter was okay, the two-seamer really was ineffective. As soon as I dropped to that lower arm slot... the two-seamer... really started to run for me, and it took so much pressure off having to be so perfect in the strike zone. Before I felt like if I wasn't on the corners, I was in trouble. With the sinker I could basically start it middle of the plate and just let it run. And as a young pitcher not able to really throw the ball anywhere I wanted all the time, it allowed me to throw a sinker on that side that was running to their hands, and then a cutter that was either running away from a righty or in to a lefty.

"Everything was running away from the plate. So it really just gave me so much—it gave me the ability to be aggressive, to go after guys and challenge them, knowing that the ball's moving. Even if I could get it to move three or four inches going either direction, I'm missing the barrel, and that was my only goal. I wanted them to swing at every pitch, I wanted them to put it in play, but I was trying to stay off the barrel. And so that's really where I first started being able to go each to one side."

Halladay had a curveball too, but he made the mistake one afternoon of telling Queen he forgot how to throw it. Queen unloaded on him. He ordered him to throw his breaking ball from 10 feet to get a feel for the pitch again, then slowly work outward from there. Queen explained that his new arm angle would create more horizontal movement, making it more attractive to hitters as the ball left his hand. If Halladay threw the ball toward the middle of the plate, the ball would break to the corner and batters would not make solid contact, if they hit it at all.

Queen also worked on a new windup that tucked Halladay's right shoulder away from hitters, hiding the ball longer and giving him even more deception. They worked hard to get these things right. Halladay threw eight bullpen sessions in 10 days. Tennessee manager Rocket Wheeler watched Queen and Halladay from afar. The first day he said Halladay threw 20 minutes. The second day he threw 30 minutes. The third day he threw 40 minutes. They took breaks in between. They chatted, but they worked. Others remember the bullpen sessions being much, much longer, with Halladay throwing 70 to 100 pitches each time.

"After about the fifth or sixth day, then I knew we got onto something special here, and I knew that he was going to be something special," Queen said.

Josh Phelps caught Halladay in Tennessee. If Doc long tossed, he caught him. If Doc threw in the bullpen, he caught him. He had very little interaction with Queen, other than when Queen asked how Doc's ball moved.

"I had no more influence on him than a caddie," he said. "I wasn't whispering in his ear. I didn't have any great advice. I just sat there, caught him, and reported what I saw. You couldn't have told me in 2001 that Roy was going to be inducted into the Hall of Fame. I was riding buses with him. But the change was pretty instant. Once he figured out how to make the ball move he was a different guy from there on out. It was neat."

Halladay had a cutter, sinker, and curveball. He had deception. He had reasons to feel good about himself again. Of course, he had not faced any batters yet. He made his Double-A debut against the Carolina Mudcats on May 26. He allowed four hits and two runs in five innings. He broke a few bats. He gave up a couple cheap, infield singles. He smiled. He pitched the second game of a doubleheader in Orlando on May 31. Queen poked his head into Tennessee's dugout after a couple innings and barked at Halladay to stop aiming for the corners and just throw the damn ball down the middle. Halladay allowed two hits and one earned run. He struck out nine.

."I was like a kid with a bunch of new toys," Halladay said. "You go out there and you don't have to be as fine. You go out there and throw the ball at the middle of the plate, and all of a sudden it's moving in on the hitters' hands."

His final start in Double-A came in Jacksonville. He finished the seventh inning with about 12 pitches remaining on his pitch count. Wheeler told Halladay that somebody else would pitch the eighth.

"I'm not done yet," Halladay said.

"Look," Wheeler said. "I'm telling you. You've got 12 pitches. And when those 12 pitches are done I'm coming to get you because they gave me a pitch count."

Halladay needed 15 pitches to finish the eighth inning.

"I'm done now," he said.

"That's how determined he was to say, 'I've got this fixed and I'm ready to take off,'" Wheeler said. "You could see him change himself. The look on his face. You could see it."

Halladay went 2–1 with a 2.12 ERA in five starts with Tennessee. The Blue Jays promoted him to Triple-A.

CONNOR GOT A SCOUTING report from Queen. He compared Halladay to Dodgers ace Kevin Brown. Actually, he said he was better than Brown.

It was a hell of a statement. Brown went 211–144 with a 3.28 ERA in his 19-year career. He won 21 games with the Rangers in 1992. He won a World Series with the Marlins in 1997. Brown made six All-Star teams and led the National League with a 2.58

ERA in 2000, pitching for the Dodgers. He finished his career with a 68.2 WAR.

"At that time, Kevin Brown's stuff was filthy, you know?" Connor said. "As much respect as I had for Mel Queen, when he told me he was better than Kevin Brown, I'm thinking, 'Oh boy. I don't know. I have to see it with my own eyes.' Mel was right. I give Mel the credit from the mechanical standpoint. You've got to remember that this is a kid that grew up as one of the top prospect pitchers in the country. He'd been throwing that way since the time he started playing baseball. He just came out, worked at it, and believed. And I think the biggest thing is that the guy has to buy in totally. He's got to trust the fact that you know what you're talking about. This is going to be better for you. What you're doing right now is not working. It's not going to work. He did it. It's a credit to him."

Halladay went 1–0 with a 3.21 ERA in two starts with Syracuse. The Blue Jays promoted him to the big leagues on July 1.

Doc rebuilt himself in just three months.

"There aren't many pitchers out there who could do what he did," Queen said. "But Doc was able to do it because of the special type of individual he is."

| 8 |

A New Roy

BUCK MARTINEZ TRUSTED HIS EYES more than anything, so he grabbed his mitt, squatted behind home plate, and caught Halladay upon his return to Toronto.

The Blue Jays' manager spent 17 seasons as a catcher in the big leagues with the Royals, Brewers, and Blue Jays. He caught pitchers like Dave Stieb, Jimmy Key, Dennis Leonard, and Steve Busby. He knew good pitching. He heard Mel Queen's glowing reports from the minor leagues. He saw Halladay's numbers in Double-A and Triple-A. But Martinez needed to see the proof for himself, from the best vantage point possible. He needed to see how Halladay's pitches looked coming out of his hand and traveling 60 feet, 6 inches to home plate. He needed to see what Derek Jeter, Manny Ramírez, and others would see.

"He had pitches that went this way, he had pitches that went that way," Martinez said, darting his hand back and forth. "They went in both directions. The cutter to the left and the sinker to the right. Everything was in the strike zone. But he also changed his delivery from standing straight up and being right over the top to turning his body, hiding the ball very well, and becoming deceptive."

Toronto planned to break in Halladay slowly, starting him in the bullpen, then moving him to the rotation. But Esteban Loaiza lasted only a third of an inning in his start against the Red Sox at SkyDome on July 2. The Blue Jays needed somebody to pitch, so Martinez and pitching coach Mark Connor brought Halladay into the game. He allowed six hits, six runs, and three walks in 2⅓ innings. He struck out one. He threw 70 pitches. Only 36 were strikes.

"Mark and I are sitting there going, 'Just let him get through this,' because he's had so much success," Martinez said. "He never shied away. He knew we needed some help. He took his lumps and came out the next day and threw on the side [with the] same delivery, same focus."

Halladay made his first start with his new mechanics and repertoire on July 7 against the Expos at SkyDome. He allowed three runs and struck out a career-high 10 batters in six innings. He allowed two runs in six innings in his next start against the Mets at Shea Stadium on July 16. Chris Carpenter barely recognized his friend when he returned. He carried himself completely differently.

"He went out there and made that first start and it was like, yep, he's back," Carpenter said.

Halladay allowed three runs in 4⅔ innings against the Yankees at Yankee Stadium on July 21. It was his worst start of the three, but he made an impression anyway. Yankees catcher Todd Greene played with the Blue Jays in 2000, but never caught Halladay because of a shoulder injury. He caught him the following spring before the Blue Jays released him on March 28, the same day they optioned Halladay to Dunedin.

"You can see it on his face, and you know something is not right, and he knows something is not right," Greene said. "He just seemed lost."

Greene could not believe the transformation since March. He crossed the field the next day to ask Martinez about it.

"What the hell did you guys do to Doc?" he said. "This is not the same animal I was looking at a few months ago."

"He had become a different style of pitcher," Greene explained. "His mentality had changed a little bit. And so when he came back, obviously, he was sinking it and cutting it and using his curveball when necessary. But he just came back with a completely different mentality. That was the biggest thing. You could just look at him and see his presence was different. He had the 'fuck you' he was missing. It's hard to describe, but the players know. You can look at a pitcher and see if he's a dude or not, you know what I mean? His whole presence, everything about him. Not just the stuff and everything else, just his overall demeanor. He's a huge dude and an intimidating figure anyway so it was just a pleasant surprise for me to see him back that way. When he came back he was a freaking beast, man."

Halladay allowed one run and struck out eight in six innings in a loss to the Red Sox at Fenway Park on July 26. The game featured an important moment for Connor, and maybe for Halladay. The Red Sox had runners on first and second with two outs in the fifth inning of a tie game, when Ramírez stepped into the batter's box. It was Ramírez's first season with Boston. He finished the year batting .306 with 41 home runs, 125 RBIs, and a 1.014 OPS.

Connor walked to the mound for a chat.

"Doc, you pitch this guy like you have a 0-2 count on him right from the get-go," he said.

Halladay stared at Connor, perhaps surprised by the suggestion.

"Yeah, you pitch him like you have a 0-2 count on him," Connor said. "You're going to make him hit your pitch. He wants to hit in this situation. He doesn't want to walk. So use that to your advantage."

Halladay attacked Ramírez as ordered. Ramírez struck out swinging on a 1-2 pitch to keep the game tied. Halladay walked into the visitors' dugout at Fenway. He flashed just the faintest hint of a smile.

"I thought that was a turning point for him," Connor said.

Connor marveled at how much Halladay changed.

"The sinker ran arm side," he said. "I guess in today's age with the analytics, the vertical movement on it was probably off the charts. Then when you were looking for the sinker, he'd throw a cutter at the same velocity and it was going to be the opposite direction. And the thing that really made Doc—other than those two pitches—was the ability to drop the curveball in any count, and then throw the nasty ones. Most sinker guys traditionally have trouble with left-handed hitters. Doc, having the cutter to go along with the sinker, the arsenal just went up 100 percent. They couldn't dive out over the plate on it, otherwise he'd be in there and you'd be going in to get a new bat."

HALLADAY FOUND UNLIKELY INSPIRATION along the way. After the Blue Jays traded Roger Clemens following the '98 season and Pat Hentgen following the '99 season, he attached himself to David Wells, who pitched in Toronto in '99 and 2000. They were an unlikely pair because Wells was a self-described "party, out-of-control guy," while Halladay was more reserved.

"He talked a lot to me about his confidence—and his confidence didn't come from working out obviously," Halladay said. "It came from the belief he had in himself and just going out and doing it."

Wells went 20–8 with a 4.11 ERA in 2000, when Halladay posted his record-setting 10.64 ERA. He walked 31 batters in 229⅔ innings. He walked fewer batters than he made starts (35). It resonated with Halladay.

"I remember watching him numerous times," Halladay said. "He wouldn't walk a guy all game. He'd just go after guys. That's the way he did it."

Wells attacked the strike zone throughout his career. It was in his DNA. He averaged 1.88 walks per nine innings in his 21-year career, which ranks 20th in baseball from 1920 through 2019 (minimum 1,500 innings pitched). It ranks behind Hall of Fame pitchers Grover Cleveland Alexander (first: 1.33), Robin Roberts (10th: 1.73), Greg Maddux (11th: 1.80), Carl Hubbell (13th: 1.82), and Juan Marichal (14th: 1.82).

Wells ranks just ahead of Halladay (24th: 1.94).

"If you can pound it on all four corners and in and away, move their eye level, change their feet, strike a little fear in them out there, you can be dominant," Wells said. "You have eight other guys to make plays. You can't get everyone out, so let those other guys make their money."

Wells reinforced his beliefs to Halladay: Pitch with confidence. Don't be afraid to throw strikes.

"Don't be afraid to fail," he said. "If you don't trust your ability, if you don't trust your stuff, if you have no clue what you're doing out there, you're not going to make it. I just poured that into his brain time and time again. I'd have him watch my bullpens, how I prepared in the bullpen. I just knew there was something in there that was really good. Because of his physique, his strength, he just needed a mind."

"Until you actually start doing it and applying it, you miss a lot of what they're telling you," Halladay said.

The Blue Jays traded Wells to the White Sox in January '01. He saw Halladay pitch in person for the first time '02, when he rejoined the Yankees.

"I was like, 'Holy shit,'" Wells said. "He was just a monster."

HALLADAY WAS 4-3 WITH a 2.97 ERA in his first 15 starts in '01. He left three of those games with the lead, only to have the Blue Jays' bullpen blow it. The Blue Jays were thrilled, but they wondered.

He was so bad just a few months ago. Can he keep this up?

"We were cautiously optimistic," general manager Gord Ash said. "I think there was still some concern because we had seen it before and it fell off. We were still a little tentative. We still didn't know exactly what we had."

Halladay made his final start of the season against Cleveland on October 5. The Indians won 91 games in '01, winning their sixth American League Central title in seven years. Their offense included Hall of Fame first baseman Jim Thome, Hall of Fame second baseman Roberto Alomar, Kenny Lofton, Juan González, and Ellis Burks.

Halladay dominated them. He carried a no-hitter into the eighth inning before Travis Fryman hit a line-drive single to center field with two outs.

"Roy wanted to throw a cutter away," said Blue Jays catcher Josh Phelps, who was Doc's self-described caddie in Double-A. "I tried to get him to change his mind, but he shook me off. I wanted sinker in because I watched Fryman move up on the plate. Everybody was just grounding out. He threw cutter away, cutter away, cutter away, sinker away. And then I watched Fryman get closer to the plate. But it was one of those things—you don't run out there late in the game when your pitcher has been dialed in because he shook you off, you know? I knew in my mind what the right pitch was, but he wanted to throw what he wanted to throw. And what I remember about Roy is that he was a pretty determined individual, so I figured it was better he was 100 percent mind made up with what he wanted to throw than maybe 80 percent behind what I wanted to do."

Halladay allowed another hit in the ninth, but he struck out eight for the second shutout of his career. He threw 83 pitches in a game that lasted 1 hour, 57 minutes. It was the second-shortest game in the American League that season.

"It was just like that at Double-A," Phelps said about Halladay's dominance. "It really wasn't any different."

But everything was different. Halladay's numbers from his big league debut in '98 through his emergency relief appearance for Loaiza on July 2 compared to his 16 starts that followed looked like the numbers of two totally different pitchers—one a struggling journeyman, the other a Cy Young candidate:

13–14 vs. 5–3

5.94 ERA vs. 2.71 ERA

1.35 home runs per nine innings vs. 0.26

4.86 walks per nine innings vs. 1.92

5.40 strikeouts per nine innings vs. 8.30

45 percent groundball rate vs. 60 percent

.295 opponent batting average vs. .233

.857 opponent OPS vs. .591

59 strikes percentage vs. 67 percent

"It was almost like a video game, watching him throw a baseball with the movement that he had," bullpen coach Gil Patterson said.

THE BLUE JAYS FIRED Martinez on June 3, 2002. They were 20–33 at the time. Third-base coach Carlos Tosca took his place. Connor resigned two days later. Patterson replaced him. Tosca was Halladay's fourth manager in five seasons. Patterson was Halladay's fifth pitching coach. It was tough.

"There was just so much transitional change in the organization while we were there," Carpenter said. "It was a lot of change. There was a change in ownership. There was a change in general managers. It was just so much change that we didn't know what the hell was going on—except that they expected us to beat the Yankees. That's what we knew."

Halladay was 7–2 with a 3.14 ERA in 13 starts after tossing a two-hit shutout against the Rockies on June 7 in Toronto, his first start following Martinez's firing and Connor's resignation. Thirty-one-year-old rookie Ken Huckaby caught Doc that night. The Blue Jays promoted Huckaby from Triple-A on June 4, his second stint with the team that season. He spent 11 years in the minor leagues, when he made his big league debut with the Diamondbacks in October '01.

"Reporters after the game asked me about my game plan and I said a 12-year-old could have called that game," Huckaby said. "He never missed a spot. That's what I remember about Doc, just his ability to throw the ball where he wanted to with three pitches that were major league, above-average pitches. When he was on he was pretty much unhittable. That's what the Rockies saw that night. I remember the next day that Larry Walker and those guys had made some kind of mention that that was the real deal."

Halladay allowed one unearned run in a complete-game 2–1 victory over the Dodgers in Los Angeles on June 18, the second time Huckaby caught him. He caught Halladay's final 20 starts.

"It was so much fun," he said. "I had caught Randy Johnson before, Curt Schilling, Pedro Martinez. I caught all those guys through my career coming up to that point. But at the big league level I didn't have much playing time going into that season. To catch somebody that good for that long during a season was special. I think I held the bond tighter than he held it, just because it was that special to me. People were like, 'You're catching Halladay?' 'Damn straight, I am. He's a frickin' stud.' It was a sense of pride. I asked him later on in life, between all your catchers, what was the difference? He said, 'You never took it seriously. I did, you didn't. If I was screwing something up and I was pissed off you'd be laughing so I knew it meant it wasn't bothering you and things were okay.' There were times when he'd be yelling at me and I'd be laughing at him."

Like the time Red Sox shortstop Nomar Garciaparra crushed a ball off Halladay at Fenway Park. Halladay was trying to throw a splitter, but it wasn't very good. The inning ended and Halladay screamed at Huckaby as they walked off the field. Huckaby laughed. He could not hear him over the crowd noise.

"Why were you yelling at me?" Huckaby asked in the dugout.

"I was telling you not to call the split anymore!" he said.

Halladay's intensity and desire to win started to come through. He approached third-base coach Brian Butterfield after an inning during a game against the Yankees in Toronto. He had rage in his eyes.

"Butter!" Halladay said. "Don't let Orlando do that anymore!"

"Yeah, okay," Butterfield said, nodding.

Except Butterfield had no clue what Orlando Hudson did. He asked Hudson, "Hey, did you do something to piss off Doc? Because he just picked me up by the lapels and said I should tell you to knock it off." Hudson said yes. He got caught joking with a Yankees player on second base, even though the Blue Jays were losing.

"I noticed when I looked back that Doc was just staring at me," Hudson said. "He wasn't even walking on the mound. He was just staring. I thought he was going to come out there and punch me."

Butterfield loved the intensity. Halladay set the tone in spring training. From the very first fielding drill on the very first day of camp, Halladay snarled as he ran off the mound to make plays. Rookies and newcomers got the message: This is how things are done here. He policed the clubhouse during the season. Patterson went to the video room to look at a pitch during a game. He came back with a disturbed look on his face. Halladay asked what was wrong. Patterson told him that he had two pitchers in the clubhouse hanging out and watching the game on TV.

"I got it," Halladay said.

Halladay went to the back and told them, "You've got your teammates fighting for you out there and you're in here. When you pitch you want them to play well, but when you're not pitching it's okay to go inside? No. Let's go."

Halladay made the American League All-Star team in July. It was an amazing accomplishment, considering where he was more than a year ago, but it caused problems. Doc felt he needed to pitch even better in the second half. As soon as one start ended, he worried about the next one. He constantly stressed.

"The easiest thing for me to do is the physical work," he said. "The weightlifting, the conditioning—for me, that's the easiest part of baseball. For me, the hard part is controlling my emotions, controlling my thoughts in between games. Some of the things you put in your own head are ridiculous. That's my problem, all those demons."

Halladay read *The Mental ABC's of Pitching* six times over the course of the '02 season. In between readings, he met the author. Harvey Dorfman worked previously with Oakland, Florida, and Tampa Bay before he joined The Boras Corporation. Dorfman knew Blue Jays general manager J.P. Ricciardi from Oakland. He knew Tosca from Florida. He visited the Blue Jays one afternoon to work with another player. Halladay and Carpenter introduced themselves. They went into the stands to talk.

"That's what changed our lives," Carpenter said. "Harvey's thoughts and just initiating the mental process, the mental part of the game is what changed both of our careers, I think."

Dorfman recalled his first encounter with Halladay and Carpenter in his memoir, *Each Branch, Each Needle*.

"They went beyond the territorial borders of their profession with their questions," he wrote. "These guys wanted to know whatever could be known. I became almost as excited as they had been.

"That first 'instructional' period provided a 'key'—a trigger word for them. I had asked them both what they thought when a particular game situation arose. After each one gave his answer, I said, 'Jerk!' They laughed heartily. (I then provided the appropriate answer, of course.) 'Jerk' became their key. When they would have a counter-intuitive thought in the dugout or on the mound, they would say the word—and that would help to lead them to a thought that would be productive."

Dorfman recalled later that Halladay would not let him go. He asked if he could continue to talk to him, even though Dorfman worked for Scott Boras and Halladay had other representation.

"I couldn't turn my back on him," Dorfman said. "It would be as if a good musician came to me for help. Hell, what if he turned out to be Mozart?"

He also knew that Halladay needed help.

"The residue from (2001) was so traumatic for him, he still had it with him in 2002," he said. "It didn't go away because he hadn't yet succeeded."

Halladay finished the '02 season 19–7 with a 2.93 ERA in 34 starts. He led the AL with 239⅓ innings pitched. A's left-hander Barry Zito won the Cy Young. He went 23–5 with a 2.75 ERA. Pedro Martinez (20–4, 2.26 ERA), Derek Lowe (21–8, 2.58), and Anaheim's Jarrod Washburn (18–6, 3.15 ERA) were the only other pitchers to receive votes. Halladay deserved serious consideration, but the criteria for Cy Young has changed over the years. Back then, voters essentially looked at three things: wins, ERA, and saves. Halladay pitched more innings than anybody in the league and he pitched the majority of those innings in the AL East. He finished with a 7.3 WAR, according to Baseball Reference. It bested Zito (7.2), Lowe (7.2), Martinez (6.5), and Washburn (4.5).

"Honestly, I think he got hosed that year as far as the Cy Young," said Blue Jays catcher Tom Wilson, who caught eight of Halladay's starts that season. "He should have won it that year. His numbers were ridiculous. And he did it in the American League East."

| 9 |

Harvey

HARVEY DORFMAN CORRECTED anybody that ever called him a shrink. He was not a shrink, he said. He was a stretch.

"I don't diminish. I expand."

He was not Stuart Smalley, Al Franken's soft-talking, cardigan-wearing, self-help character on *Saturday Night Live*. Smalley believed in the power of positive daily affirmations. "I'm good enough, I'm smart enough, and doggone it, people like me," he said, gazing dead-eyed into a mirror. Dorfman was not a psychologist. He did not have a doctorate in psychology, but he knew how the mind worked. He knew people. He believed in honesty and he demanded accountability. After a player told him how he felt, after he expressed his insecurities, Dorfman told him, "It's normal for you to feel that way. It's normal for you to be feeling pressure because of high expectations. That's normal. But you're not fucking normal. You're a major leaguer. Act like it."

"It wasn't picture-yourself-in-the-middle-of-the-lake-feeling-a-cool-breeze,'" said Raúl Ibañez, who played 19 seasons in the majors.

Dorfman was born in the Bronx in 1935. He grew up there. He spent much of his childhood in bed, stricken with asthma. He passed the time listening to Gershwin, Berlin, serials, and baseball. His countless hours alone in his bedroom shaped the way he ultimately viewed the world and lived his life.

"I understand how people limit themselves," he said. "I hitched my wagon early on to that ailing horse, meaning my affliction, and then I started to learn—don't hitch your wagon to that horse; hitch your wagon to the horse you want to be."

Dorfman willed himself to get outside. He later played soccer while he majored in physical education at Brockport State Teachers College in New York. He helped his team win a co-national championship. He earned a degree in education, and a master's in educational psychology. He began his career at Wheeler Avenue School in New York, where he met his wife Anita. They had two children. Dorfman later taught at Burrs Lane Junior High on Long Island before moving to Manchester, Vermont, where he taught at Burr and Burton Academy.

He wrote for the *Rutland Herald*, a newspaper that has published in southern New Hampshire since 1794. His columnist's job there got him an interview with Double-A Pittsfield infielder Roy Smalley. The two became friends. A few years later, Smalley, who played 13 seasons in the major leagues, introduced him to Minnesota Twins coach Karl Kuehl. Kuehl told Dorfman that he wanted to write a book that explored the mental side of baseball because it had never been addressed. Kuehl asked him to help.

"You know psychology, you're a writer—and you know baseball," Kuehl said.

Dorfman said yes. He interviewed countless players in Boston and Montreal. He began to learn how a baseball player's mind worked.

"I was talking to players about their strategies and their deficits, and I noticed that other players were hanging around, eavesdropping," Dorfman said. "I'm talking to Wade Boggs, and as soon as I'm finished, Bruce Hurst says, 'Hey, I heard what you were talking about. Can you spend some time with me?' I sensed there was a hunger; it was suppressed. I knew I was onto something."

He knew baseball players were just like everybody else. They struggled with real life too.

"There are as many causes as there are individuals," Dorfman said. "Don't look at this as something that's in them; it's something in us."

Kuehl became the A's farm director in 1983. He convinced general manager Sandy Alderson to hire Dorfman as a special instructor. Dorfman put on a uniform and took a seat on the bench in his first spring training with the A's. He looked out of place in his baggy jersey and pants. He looked like Mr. Magoo or Sgt. Bilko. His presence startled some. It threatened others. Change is hard in baseball.

"What the fuck are you doing?" A's coach Clete Boyer said. "You're out here wearing a uniform like you're a ballplayer?"

"I'm out here wearing a uniform because I'm part of your team," Dorfman said. "I'm here to tell you how you're not helping the ballplayers you're supposed to help."

Boyer played 16 seasons in the majors, including eight with the Yankees, helping them win the World Series in 1961 and 1962. He had no use for a shrink. Ballplayers played ball. They did not talk about their feelings. Dorfman was undeterred.

"I had to create a persona," he said. "One of not being Caspar Milquetoast. I had to be a credible figure who was aggressive enough to confront athletes who weren't used to being confronted like that. I blended into the woodwork, and of course, it gave me access to the dugout. I could hear everything that they were saying."

Dorfman won over Boyer and they became friends. He roamed the A's system for years, helping countless players along the way. Kuehl and Dorfman published *The Mental Game of Baseball* in 1989. Dorfman left Oakland and joined the Marlins in 1994, working in Miami through their 1997 World Series championship season. Rich Dubee was the Marlins' Triple-A pitching coach in '94 and their minor league pitching coordinator from 1995 to '97. He marvelled at Dorfman's ability to read a player.

"He's done," Dorfman would say, watching a pitcher from the dugout.

"What do you mean, Harv?" Dubee said.

"Look at his body language right now," Dorfman said. "Look at his shoulders. Look at his eyes right now. He's lost."

A group of Marlins minor league pitchers participated one afternoon in pitchers' fielding practice (otherwise known as PFP).

One of the pitchers had low self-esteem, and often acted out to get attention. He kept screwing up the drill. His teammates busted his balls. Dubee joined in. A few hours later, Dorfman found Dubee in the coaches' room.

"What the fuck are you doing?" Dorfman said.

"What do you mean?" Dubee said.

"There you are, adding fuel to the fire out there when you're supposed to be building his self-esteem and his confidence," Dorfman said. "You're allowing him to get his satisfaction by goofing around and not doing things properly and you're bashing him with the rest of the group."

"Oh my God, Harv," Dubee said. "I didn't even realize what I was doing."

"Well, you have to realize what you're doing," Dorfman said. "You have to be accountable to get these guys better and you can't fall into those traps."

Nobody was safe with Dorfman. If you screwed up, he told you.

"Harvey was the Doc of mental skills," Dubee said. "He was at a different level. He could pat you on the back, he could chew you a new one, he could show you the love, he could show you the tough love. He was so good."

Dorfman worked for Tampa Bay in '98 before joining The Boras Corporation as a full-time sports psychology consultant for mega-agent Scott Boras. He worked with Boras until he died in 2011.

"Our agreement was, he just did this for our clients, unless he thought it was a necessity of life-saving dynamic," Boras said.

"But the reality of it is, do what you need to do in life that you feel is most necessary to be who you are. And so basically there was no restriction. Harvey's restriction was self-imposed. He handled the ethic of that."

Players flew to Dorfman's home in North Carolina for help, mostly in the off-season, but occasionally in season. Dorfman requested only one thing from his players: You have to tell me the truth. He got it from Greg Maddux, Alex Rodriguez, Mark McGwire, Jamie Moyer, José Canseco, Bob Welch, Al Leiter, Ibañez, Halladay, and others.

"For some of these guys, this is the first time they have had to admit they are not the world's greatest expert on themselves," Dorfman said. "This is their first recognition of their own humanity. They've been coddled their whole lives, worshipped in every setting, told they were exceptional, and all along, they were deficit."

Dorfman believed players needed to develop tools and behaviors to overcome their fears, rather than sit on a couch, find the root cause of them, and discuss them. He found that most players struggled because they got ahead of themselves. They dwelled on the enormity of the moment. Sometimes those thoughts and feelings paralyzed them.

"Your muscles convene at night and have a couple beers," Dorfman said. "They say, 'If the freakin' guy would leave us alone, we'd be fine.' They've been doing this since you were a little kid.... You want a composite drawing of the guys it happens to? From my experience, wonderful guys—sensitive, caring, good people. Guys insensitive to the judgment of others generally don't have this problem."

It was Halladay's problem.

"I would go into a game and be thinking, 'Okay, I need to go seven innings, I need to give up three runs or less, I have to walk away with the win,'" he said. "All these big-picture things that have nothing to do with how to get there. They were all end-result goals. They had nothing to do with how I'm going to get there. I had no idea how I was going to do it. I just knew what I had to do."

"Self-consciousness will fuck you up," Dorfman said.

Dorfman wanted players to stop thinking big. He asked players about their finances and what they would do if they could not play baseball anymore. Would they be okay?

"Now look in the mirror," he said. "You're a nice-looking kid. You're a good kid. You're certainly smart enough to get along in this world. You have a good family. If I were a doctor and said, 'Son, you're never going to pitch again. You've got something terribly wrong with your arm,' would you kill yourself?"

"No," the pitcher said.

"So there it is," Dorfman said. "What are you worried about? Your life will go on if you never threw another pitch. So now let's see how good you can be."

HALLADAY WANTED TO BE good. He took an important step when he read *The Mental ABC's of Pitching*. He took another step when he asked Dorfman to work with him. He took another step when he committed to the work.

"It's something that you have to become," he said. "You can't just read the book, you can't just talk to him once, you have to become it. He's the one who said, 'Put all the other distractions aside, put the media aside, put the thoughts of what your coaches think, what your parents think, what your peers think aside, and focus on your job.' And that took so much pressure off me to the point that I could go out and just worry about making one pitch and that was it. It simplified it. It gave me a whole new perspective on the game and on myself and made it so easy to go out and feel prepared and feel confident based on the things that I had learned from him."

Three of Dorfman's tenets resonated with Halladay the most: preparation, aggressiveness, and control. He made them part of his belief system.

Dorfman believed preparation preceded confidence and success. "Confidence" and "success" are abstract terms, Dorfman said. There is nothing abstract about being prepared to pitch. Either a pitcher is prepared or he isn't.

"Pitchers who wish to be consistent must make a commitment," Dorfman wrote. "First, they should formulate goals, which will help them determine what it is they need to work at. Then they should develop a program or routine, which will allow them to habituate behaviors, so that these behaviors will become 'second nature' to them. Learned instincts. They then must have the mental discipline and stamina to follow these routines, irrespective of how they may be 'feeling' at a given moment or on a given day."

Halladay started to set goals and establish a routine. It involved conditioning, weight training, sleeping, eating, hydrating, studying, focusing, and visualizing. He started to write down everything he did in notebooks so he had records of his work and his feelings about it.

"It was part of his have-to," Carpenter said. "Doc could eliminate all the other junk that goes on in that mental part of it and know that if I prepare myself consistently every single day the way I'm supposed to, there's no excuse, right? So it's like, okay, I did this, I did that, I did this, I did that, so now I can go compete and execute. And when I'm done, no matter the results, I can't look back and be like, 'Oh, I half-assed it on Tuesday and didn't run,' or, 'I half-assed it in the gym on Wednesday.' No. You did everything you could. It gave us relief of the pressures."

Dorfman believed that pitchers needed to have a "readying place" and a "readying procedure" before they pitched. Some pitchers preferred to socialize. Others, like Halladay, went into isolation mode. As first pitch approached, he believed every pitcher should be in his "quiet place," where he internalizes mental keys and maybe visualizes the opponent's lineup.

Halladay did it all. He became a living, breathing version of the book.

"Throughout my career, the night before I pitched, I'd eat dinner, go to bed, and [Brandy would] say, 'We'll see you after the game,'" Halladay said. "And even though I'm leaving at noon the next day to leave for the field, she knew that's when my preparation started, the night before. I wanted to go through the lineup in my head. I kind of wanted the game to play out in my head before I even touched the field. And that would start the night before. Getting to the field, same thing, I would go through the hitters in my head over and over. I'd go through the lineup over and over. And I felt, by the time I got to the bullpen, I was so prepared that I could just flip off that switch and let my body take over and do it. It was more ingrained in me at that point to where it was more natural. I didn't have to go out there and think as much during the game because it was just natural. I thought about it so much before, planned it out, knew what I was going to do the whole time that I didn't have to think as much during the game. I could be aggressive, put my tempo in place, and I could command the game, which was something Harvey and I talked about."

Dorfman taught Doc about aggressiveness. Pitchers thrive when they let loose with their best stuff early in the count, throwing strikes and forcing the action. It is being proactive rather than reactive.

Hitters can smell a reactive pitcher.

"Talking to Harvey, our definition of a perfect game is 27 pitches and 27 outs," Halladay said. "Not 27 strikeouts. I wanted to throw 27 pitches and get 27 outs. That's a perfect game to me. And I wanted them swinging and I wanted them hitting the ball. The percentages when they have to swing early in the count are in my favor. And when I'm ahead in the count, they're in my favor. So, really, it's in my court. When I get ahead, when I go after them, everything in baseball will tell you that your chances are better.

"It's not like boxing. You don't go out and feel out your opponent in the first inning. You go out and knock them out in the first inning. If you go and dance around and see what they're going to do, you're going to be on your back real quick. And I wanted to come out swinging. I wanted to come out letting them know that I was going to be throwing punches. And to me, the aggressiveness, the pace of the game, throwing strikes was important right at the get-go. I wanted to establish that. The key for me is throwing your strike, throwing your pitch where you're taking the sting out of the bat, but it's still a strike. And even with two strikes. There's a lot of philosophies out there that you don't throw them a strike with two strikes. They shouldn't make contact with two strikes. I never bought into that. I felt like every pitch, I wanted to get an out on. Even with two strikes, I wasn't concerned with striking guys out. I wanted to make a quality pitch in my spot and I wasn't going to waste anything. Every pitch, I wanted to have a purpose and I wanted to get an out on. And I think that's what kept me out of the deeper counts, it kept me out of getting back into even counts, letting them into the count. By not trying to let them expand and always go for strikeouts it was, 'I want them to hit it. Let them hit it. If you're going to beat me, it's going to be with your bat.'"

Of course, a pitcher can prepare and attack and bad things still happen. Control is critical in these situations. Dorfman looked at aggressiveness and control as the accelerator and the brake in a race. Without the accelerator the race cannot be won, he wrote. Without the brake, the race cannot be completed.

"A pitcher 'in control' is a pitcher in control of himself," Dorfman wrote. "It may appear that he is in control 'of the situation,' as pitchers have said to me when things were going their way. But a pitcher cannot control a 'situation' or results." That is because a batter is involved. Sometimes they hit good pitches. Sometimes fielders drop pop flies, let a ball roll between their legs, or make bad throws. Sometimes umpires call a strike a ball. Strike three becomes a full count. Rain, wind, and poorly manicured fields come into play. All those things are out of a pitcher's control. The only thing a pitcher can control are his thoughts and his body. He can control the next pitch. The next pitch is the only thing that matters.

"I saw a quote, I think it was a female tennis player, and they described it as competitive indifference," Halladay said. "You give everything you have but you're indifferent to the results. The results don't matter as much as my execution, as much as the pitches I make. I'm judging myself. I'm not judging the results. You have to have a little bit of indifference. You can't hang on every pitch. You can't beat yourself up over every mistake. So, I had to have a little bit of that indifference where it didn't matter if I gave up a hit. I had to have that. And it got to the point where I was like, 'You have to get four hits to score,' because I'm going to make them all on the ground, I'm going to minimize the damage and not give you a free base. So you're going to have to put the ball in play and find a hole four times. And that made it a lot easier to pitch in those games. There was no stress, there was no anxiety. It was just keep going out and attacking."

EVERYBODY TOOK SOMETHING FROM Dorfman. The people that knew him speak reverentially about him. They miss him.

"Harvey helped us sort stuff out about life," Ibañez said. "I tended to be a people-pleaser. And when you're a people-pleaser, you care about what other people think. And when you're caring about what other people think, you're not performing. You're not focusing on what you need to be doing. Harvey really helped me with that because he taught me to only care about what the people who really care about you deeply think—your family, your loved ones—and focus on being the best version of yourself every day, which was being true to yourself, being true to who you are, focusing on what you can control, executing your plan, and becoming a master of your craft, and being disciplined and vigilant with your thoughts. Never allowing yourself to make an excuse for anything that you do. One thing is to never let an excuse come out of your mouth, but Harvey taught us to never let yourself make an excuse in your own mind."

Moyer learned how powerful the mind can be too. It's a weapon.

"One pitch at a time," Moyer said. "When there were tough times for me on the mound, sometimes I would call timeout, go behind the mound, and untie my shoe. I actually acted like my shoe came untied but I double-knotted by shoes so they never came untied. But I untied my shoes on purpose because either I had lost my focus, my thoughts and my mind were out of control, or I was just pissed off at myself. And there were times when I would yell at myself out loud. Most of the times were out loud. I didn't care who heard it because I was in my space, my work space, and I had to recollect myself. So, what Harvey taught me was to get off the mound, you've got that tractor-trailer making circles inside your head and you can't get it out of the way so let it take its course. Find a way to get rid of it. So, for me, that was timeout, untie my shoe, scream and holler at myself, whatever I had to say. But when that bow got tied and that second bow got tied in my shoes, it's over. And now it's time to refocus on the next pitch or the next task at hand. And that's to execute the next pitch."

| 10 |

Cy Young

Thwack.

Thwack.

Halladay fired baseballs through the drywall at the Blue Jays' minor league complex in the fall of 2001, just weeks after his promising return from Dunedin. Blue Jays closer Billy Koch, minor league strength and conditioning coordinator Donovan Santas, and rehab coordinator Jay Inouye were the only other souls at the antiquated facility, which would be bulldozed in a few months to make way for more modern amenities. Halladay and Koch took advantage of the building's final days, drawing targets on the walls and chucking fastballs at them.

Thwack.

"I don't know how much training we did, but we had so much fun literally destroying the place," Santas said.

Santas joined the organization that July. He knew nothing about Halladay when he met him, other than he was trying to save his career.

"He was just a guy, honestly," he said.

But after Halladay won 19 games and made the AL All-Star team in 2002, he returned to a sparkling new complex in the fall—this time without Koch, who had been traded to Oakland the previous December—as the Blue Jays' ace. Santas found himself in a new role too. The Blue Jays made him the major league strength and conditioning coordinator, which meant he worked closely with Halladay as he developed the fanatical routine that famously defined the rest of his career.

Halladay always worked hard. He trained daily since elementary school. But Harvey Dorfman preached the importance of preparation and routine. Halladay believed if he prepared better and maintained a routine he could take another step forward in 2003.

"If the record was five, then Roy did eight, you know?" Brandy said. "If the goal was 10, then Roy did 15. It was never enough. He just developed that maniacal work ethic. He was never again going to let himself get beat. He was never going to go through that again. I think that that 10-year streak that he went through, so much of that was that fear of failure. He never wanted to go back to that place again. So he worked his ass off to make sure he didn't."

Dorfman told a story about Hall of Fame right-hander Tom Seaver missing a start in Montreal because of bad weather. The Mets flew home that night and arrived in Queens after midnight. Seaver got to Shea Stadium, got a security guard to turn on the lights in the Mets' bullpen, set up a screen behind home plate, grabbed a bucket of balls, and threw. Seaver had a routine, and he planned to keep it—game or not, catcher or not, middle of the night or not. Years later, Halladay lost an opportunity to throw on the road because of bad weather. The Blue Jays returned to Toronto around two in the morning and Halladay asked Blue Jays pitching coach Gil Patterson to play catch with him.

"There really was not much watchdog from me," Santas said. "It was like me or somebody in the field giving him the directions, giving him the expertise, and he would take it and do it. A lot of times, athletes say they want or need to improve on something, but then when they get the information it's like, 'Okay,' but they don't follow through. He was meticulous. 'We're going to add this to my pregame prep. We're going to add this during the off-season. We're going to add this the day after I pitch.'"

Halladay's running program started to become legendary by 2003. He and Santas ran outside for 20–30 minutes every afternoon the day after he pitched. Halladay never ran on a treadmill because he wanted to keep things interesting and he wanted to challenge himself. They ran a regular course alongside Lake Ontario in Toronto, which ended back at SkyDome. They ran a regular course along the Inner Harbor in Baltimore. Occasionally, they ran inside ballparks, including Yankee Stadium in the Bronx. They ran the concourses there, ascending the ramps as they completed laps until they reached the top.

The intensity of the runs correlated with how well Halladay pitched. If he pitched well and the team won, it was challenging but reasonable. If he pitched poorly and the team lost, it was punishing.

"I knew that that run was going to be hell," Santas said.

Everyone else knew it too. Santas received sympathetic looks from colleagues during the game or before the run.

"Damn, Dono. Sorry."

Then there were the other runners. Halladay and Santas ran their loop in Toronto, which is a popular trail for casual runners and competitive runners, for runners looking to burn a few calories, and for runners looking to train for the next marathon. Occasionally, people recognized Halladay as he ran. Occasionally, as Halladay and Santas neared the end, a serious runner bolted past them.

"All hell broke loose," Santas said.

Halladay did not allow anybody to pass him. He could not be beat. He ran down the runner, who had no clue what he or she had just done.

"They're running like a five-and-a-half-minute pace because they're a marathon runner, and he would sprint," Santas said. "He would run them down and pass them. He would not let them beat him. Of course, he'd peel off and run into the stadium while they'd probably keep going for another 10 miles. But that wasn't the point. The point was that they weren't going to beat him in whatever distance he had left to run. They were not going to beat him."

This happened everywhere. It happened constantly in Boston, where they ran along the Charles River.

"They're all marathon runners," Santas said. "We're going along and I would know I'm screwed. I'm screwed because I know that people were going to pass us. And we'd sprint that whole thing. That was awful."

Halladay continually looked for ways to challenge himself, especially when there weren't runners to beat. He allowed seven runs in 6⅓ innings in a start against the Red Sox on June 1, so Santas knew he was in trouble when he showed up at old Busch Stadium in St. Louis to open the next series. They ran laps around the concourse before they reached the top level of the ballpark, which had an unobstructed view of the field below. Halladay purchased a watch that measured distance. It was probably one of the first GPS watches of its kind. Doc loved gadgets.

"I want to run a six-minute mile," Halladay said.

Wait, what?

Santas never ran one before. He never tried. He never even thought about it.

"This is the perfect trail," Halladay insisted.

Halladay and Santas jogged one lap around the concourse, determining that two-and-a-half laps were exactly one mile.

"Are you ready?" Halladay said. "Let's go."

Halladay took off. Santas ran behind him the entire way, chugging as hard as he could, trying to keep up. Santas thought he was going to die, but he finished. Halladay sprinted the whole time.

"It was the hardest thing I've ever done in my life," Santas said.

"I just wanted to see if I could do it," Halladay said.

They ran along the waterfront in Seattle, which presented its own challenges. One time a taxi, flying down a side street, never came to a complete stop at an intersection. The driver never saw Halladay as he crossed.

Boom!

The cab crashed into Halladay, who slid across the hood.

"Oh my God! Are you okay?! Are you okay?!" Santas said.

"Yeah, I'm fine," Halladay said.

Santas' personal and professional life flashed before his eyes. He was pretty sure he would be fired and never work in baseball again once he became known as the guy that got Halladay hit by a car in Seattle.

Halladay finished the run.

Back at the ballpark, the work continued. Halladay did a heavy lower-body lift, which included Romanian deadlifts, squats, and more. The workout probably lasted an hour. Occasionally, Santas convinced him to decrease the intensity, based upon his response to a simple question.

"How are you feeling today, Doc?" Santas asked.

"I feel like 10 pounds of shit in a five-pound bag," Halladay occasionally replied.

That was a common expression for Halladay. Whenever Doc said he felt like 10 pounds of shit in a five-pound bag, Santas knew he needed to dial down his workout.

"Cool, let's make some adjustments then," Santas said. "You want to ride the bike today instead of run?"

"Fuck no," he said. "Let's go."

"Okay, fine," Santas said. "We can run, but when we come back we're going to scale back the lift."

Halladay relented.

"It was part of him," Santas said about the running. "Sometimes he would be like, 'I need to do this.' But for the most part it was just a box he needed to check. It was either a set course, it was a distance, it was a time, but it was something. It was a box he needed to check to just know that he had done it."

Santas and Blue Jays head athletic trainer George Poulis each developed close relationships with Halladay. They continually looked for ways to take his performance to the next level. Poulis frequently offered suggestions, like little tweaks to his program. Sometimes Halladay liked them. Sometimes he did not.

"Quit trying to reinvent the wheel, George," Halladay said.

Santas and Poulis quickly learned where they could find Halladay every day, just by looking at the clock. At five o'clock on the nights he pitched, Halladay would be at his locker, working on a puzzle that sharpened his focus. Halladay took a 10-square-by-10-square laminated grid with randomly distributed numbers. He had to locate each number in sequence: 00, 01, 02, 03, until he reached 99. Halladay crossed off each number with an erasable marker. He carried multiple grids with him so he could not memorize the patterns. He once said he needed 25 minutes to finish the first time he tried. But as time passed he honed his focus and set a personal best at two minutes, 35 seconds. Once it became easier, he blasted the TV in front of him or the music in his headphones to test his focus.

"He really started to lock everything down," Santas said.

At 6:00 PM, Halladay returned to his locker to chug the two shakes that Santas prepared and placed on his chair. Santas made the same shake every time: strawberries, bananas, milk, orange juice, protein powder, and ice.

At 6:15 PM, Poulis stretched Halladay's arm.

"Doc, have a good one," Poulis said when he finished.

Poulis said that every time: "Doc, have a good one." Halladay eventually incorporated Poulis' well wishes into his routine. If Poulis forgot to wish him luck, Halladay waited. A few times an assistant athletic trainer noticed Halladay waiting in the trainer's room after Poulis walked away.

"George," the trainer said, motioning to Halladay.

"Doc, have a good one," Poulis said.

HALLADAY WONDERED HOW HE would follow his 2002 season. The Blue Jays wondered too. They talked about a contract extension, but he was only two years removed from Dunedin and Mel Queen.

"We want to see if you can do it again," Blue Jays general manager J.P. Riccardi said.

Halladay had no problem with that. Then the season started about as poorly as he could have imagined. He was 0–2 with a 4.89 ERA through six starts in April. He blew a five-run lead against the Red Sox at Fenway Park on April 20. He said afterward he ran out of steam. The Blue Jays believed Halladay's off-season throwing program had him in a "dead arm" period to start the season.

"His program is something we're going to have to look at when the season's over," Blue Jays manager Carlos Tosca said. "We may have to tinker with it a bit."

Halladay earned his first win on May 1 against Texas, allowing four runs in seven innings in a 7–6 victory at SkyDome. He allowed five runs in seven innings in a win in Texas on May 6. Halladay's arm started to rebound. He went 6–0 with a 3.22 ERA in May, striking out 35 and walking three in 44⅔ innings, and 5–0 with a 3.15 ERA in six starts in June, striking out 36 and walking eight in 45⅔ innings. Things were going well, but Halladay wanted more. He allowed one run in eight innings against the Pirates on June 11, but lamented the fact that his changeup remained ineffective.

Doc threw a changeup every spring, but he rarely threw it once the season started. It was his fourth-best pitch and getting beat with his fourth-best pitch never made sense. Blue Jays catcher Tom Wilson learned that the hard way. He thought Halladay's changeup looked good in the bullpen before a May 22 start against the Yankees in New York.

"Doc, your split is really good today, dude," Wilson said. "Can we fire it in there?"

"Yeah, totally low leverage," Halladay said.

Wilson found the perfect spot. Halladay got Yankees left fielder Hideki Matsui in an 0–2 count with one out in the first inning and nobody on base. Wilson called for it. It tumbled as it entered the zone, but Matsui dropped the barrel of the bat on it and fired a rocket into the left-center-field gap for a double.

"Don't you ever fucking put that down again," Halladay said, back in the dugout.

"God damn, the split was fucking nasty," Wilson said.

"He knocked the shit out of it!" Halladay said.

Wilson stuck with the standards the rest of the game. Halladay allowed two runs in seven innings for the win.

"I just had to sit there. I just wore it," Wilson said. "I'm like, 'My bad.' It *was* a good pitch. But as a pitcher, good pitches don't get fucking whacked, you know?"

Halladay won his 11th consecutive start on June 22 against the Expos, allowing two unearned runs in eight innings while pitching on short rest for the first time in his career. The streak set a Blue Jays record and tied him for the third-longest win streak among American League starters since 1949. He won two more starts before the All-Star break, although he snapped the consecutive-start win streak with a no-decision on June 27 against Montreal. Still, Halladay was 13–2 with a 3.41 ERA when he made his second consecutive All-Star team. He was 15–2 with a 3.29 ERA at the end of July, throwing two more times on short rest.

Halladay had an opportunity to make history on August 1 in Anaheim. He had a chance to win his 16th consecutive decision as a starter, which would set a new single-season franchise record. The Philadelphia A's Lefty Grove won a major league record 21 consecutive decisions as a starter in 1931. (He had some relief appearances in between, like many starters in that era). Twelve pitchers had winning streaks of 16-plus decisions in a single season as a starter. According to Elias Sports Bureau, only two won 16 in the modern era (since 1961): Roger Clemens with the Yankees in 2001 and Jack Sanford with the Giants in 1962.

Halladay allowed five runs in 6⅔ innings against the Angels. He shouted an expletive from the mound as he uncorked a wild pitch that allowed the fifth run to score in the seventh inning. The streak was over. He fell one short of Clemens and Sanford, but he tied five other starters with 15 consecutive wins by a starter in the modern era: Clemens with the Blue Jays (1998), the Indians' Gaylord Perry (1974), the Phillies' Steve Carlton (1972), the Orioles' Dave McNally (1969), and the Cardinals' Bob Gibson (1968).

Halladay lost three of his first four starts in August. He allowed seven runs in three innings in Oakland on August 17. Rookie Kevin Cash caught him five days later for the first time. Cash got called up earlier that month. He'd caught five games, but none with Halladay.

"I wasn't allowed to catch him," he said. "I was catching a lot of other guys and then he basically gave the approval after watching a time or two through the rotation. He said, 'All right, he can catch me.'"

Halladay's no-nonsense reputation preceded him. Cash was more nervous to catch Halladay than he was hitting for the first time. But Cash did okay. Halladay allowed three runs in six innings that night. The Blue Jays won. Cash caught Halladay the rest of the season.

"He was sinker, cutter, curveball. That's it. No changeup, none of that," Cash said. "And the sinker went to one side of the plate and the cutter went to the other side of the plate and he threw the curveball basically middle. And he had this long notepad with a substantial-sized paragraph on every hitter and he would go into detail with it. It was a lot of listening. I wasn't talking too much."

Halladay threw 99 pitches in a 10-inning shutout against the Tigers on September 6. He carried a no-hitter into the eighth inning when former Blue Jays prospect Kevin Witt hit a 1-2 curveball off the center-field wall for a two-out double. The Blue Jays scored a run in the 10th inning to win the game 1–0.

"I feel like I had at least two more," Halladay said.

The game lasted two hours, three minutes. It was the first extra-inning shutout in the big leagues since Jack Morris in Game 7 of the 1991 World Series. There has been only one in the big leagues since: Mark Mulder's 10-inning shutout in 2005.

"If it did happen today, it would have to be someone like him or [Kyle] Hendricks on the Cubs," Cash said. "A guy who is so efficient that can just roll up ground balls. But the thing with Doc was he got his strikeouts and he was efficient. And he did it all the time. It was just remarkable sitting back there. Everyone asks me for the best pitcher you ever caught and it's tough not to say him. As far as command and stuff, his stuff was just ridiculous. Hitters would come up and say, 'You get to face our pitcher today and we have to come up and face this mess.' They were defeated and for good reason. They knew that, if he was on, it was going to be a quick game but it was going to be a quick 0-for."

Halladay won his 20th game on September 11 in Tampa Bay. Halladay handed Poulis a signed baseball the next day.

George, thanks for not reinventing the wheel. Thanks for everything, Roy Halladay.

The ball sits on Poulis' desk.

Halladay finished the season with a complete-game win over the Indians to finish 22–7 with a 3.25 ERA. He and Santas flew back to Tampa after the season. He leaned over to Santas with a satisfied look.

"I did it," he said.

"What did you do?" Santas said.

"I had more starts than walks," Halladay said.

"What?" Santas said "Are you serious? How is that even possible?"

Halladay made it one of his goals before the season started. He started 36 games. He walked 32 batters in a major league leading 266 innings.

Halladay won the American League Cy Young Award in November. He received 26 of 28 first-plate votes from the Baseball Writers' Association of America, finishing with 136 points. The White Sox's Esteban Loaiza (21–9, 2.90 ERA) finished second with 63 points. Pedro Martinez (14–4, 2.22 ERA) finished third with 20 points. The Halladays got the news in Hawaii. They were there on Nike's annual baseball trip. Reporters and photographers were not allowed at the resort, so Brandy took a picture of Halladay celebrating. The Associated Press distributed the photo on its wire service.

"It was so cool to celebrate with the best of the best," Brandy said. "They're like, 'You deserve it, we're so happy for you.' It was a huge celebration. It was so cool just because the last few years had been so tough. You didn't take anything for granted. You knew it could end the next day. It's like every day was a bonus. So that year, I really think, was the best year. Everything was exciting. It was still so new. To go from nothing to anything is amazing, but to go from I'm-not-going-to-have-a-job-anymore-are-we going-to-be-okay? to I-just-won-the-Cy-Young-Award-in-the-toughest-division-in-baseball? Wow. Talk about highs and lows."

The Halladays celebrated again in January, when the Blue Jays signed him to a four-year, $42 million contract extension. Ricciardi told Doc the previous spring that he wanted to see him do it again.

"He told me to prove it to him, so I did," Halladay said.

| 11 |

The Arsenal

To GET A BASEBALL TO RISE, sink, cut, break, knuckle, or "fall off the table," a pitcher holds the ball in a specific way with his fingers and thumb before he throws it.

A pitcher can throw a four-seam fastball if he separates the index and middle fingers and places them across the widest part of the seams. The rotation from the four seams hurtling through the air creates backspin. If there is enough backspin, it creates the illusion that the ball is rising before it crosses home plate. But place the fingers elsewhere; move them closer together or further apart; run them along or across different seams; grip the ball more firmly or more delicately; move the wrist a certain way while the pitch is thrown; and the ball will move differently.

The possibilities to throw and shape pitches seem endless, but most pitchers only master a few. Halladay threw a sinker, cutter, and curveball throughout his peak from 2001–11. He finally found a changeup he liked in 2010.

Sinker

The sinker is also called a two-seam fastball (or two-seamer, for short). Pitchers typically place their index and middle fingers along the narrowest point of the seams. The two seams catch the air (the opposite of a four-seamer) when thrown. The sinker is popular and effective because the ball rotates downward as it reaches home plate. If it is thrown by a right-handed pitcher like Halladay, it runs in on the hands of right-handed hitters. If the pitch is located down in the strike zone hitters typically beat it into the ground. Groundballs are good.

"Early on, at least from when I faced him, he would pitch at about 95 and they were very, very unique, almost Wiffle ball-like sinkers," said Rocco Baldelli, who played seven years in the big leagues and became manager of the Twins in 2019. "So the ball would start up and it would dive hard, down and in on you. So you had to look for the ball up. That was the only chance you had. You had to look for the ball way up because the one that was way up may really dive into your path. It didn't fall. There was nothing subtle about what the ball was doing. You kind of had to guess as to where the ball was going to end up because it was coming in too hard and moving too abruptly."

Halladay placed his index and middle fingers almost together and mostly along the narrowest seam on the left, overloading the left side of the ball. His thumb faced out, underneath his index finger on the bottom seam. He saw mostly the right half of the ball as he held it.

"That's how I knew I was going to get that run," he said.

Doc showed up one spring and started to throw the ball to his glove side (or left side of the plate). He moved from the right side to the left side of the rubber to make the pitch easier to throw.

"The ones where it's a ball, it looks like a ball out of your hand and finishes as a strike, are *really* tough for hitters," Halladay told *The New York Times*' Tyler Kepner in 2017. "It's a great two-strike pitch, because guys are expecting the ball to be off the plate, so you start with something off that's coming back on the plate with two strikes and you're getting so many called strikes just because they've given up. They're expecting it out of the zone, it *looks* out of the zone, and then it comes back in. So then I was able to get that to where I could throw sinker pretty consistently both sides."

Sinkers in on lefties are sometimes called "dicknickers" because, well, they nick the extremities of the left-handed hitter before they come back over the plate for a strike.

"Most of the time you're trying to trick a guy," said Brad Arnsberg, who was the Blue Jays' pitching coach from 2005 to '09. "You're not going to use that in a 2-1 count. You're going to use that in a 1-2 count when you maybe cut a lefty batter in and then cut him in again. And now you dicknick him. It goes the other way."

Cutter

The cutter is not a slider. There is a difference. A slider is a power breaking ball that has a downward tilt to it. A cutter is a fastball that breaks on the same plane. Halladay loved the cutter because of its sharp, late break as it approached the zone. It looked like a fastball then—*boom*—jammed hands and broken bats.

"I don't know why it took so long for people to come up with it; anytime they tried to throw something other than a fastball it was always four-seam or two-seam, you never heard anything else," he said. "It'd be a slider or a curveball. Nobody was trying to throw anything hard that had just a little bit of movement. For some reason that cutter, right as I came in, they were teaching it to everybody on the planet when I came to the organization. I mean it's literally one of the first things I remember being taught in the minor leagues was how to throw a cutter."

Sometimes the cutter backed up on Halladay, meaning it did not break like he needed it. He allowed 17 runs in 10⅓ innings in back-to-back starts in early May 2007, just before he had an emergency appendectomy. As he recovered from surgery, he thought about his cutter and how it failed him the last few times he pitched. He stood in the outfield one afternoon, alongside Blue Jays catcher Sal Fasano, who spent the final few months of the 2006 season with the Yankees. Fasano loved to know what made each pitcher great, so he asked Yankees closer Mariano Rivera how he threw his cutter. Fasano told Halladay what Rivera told him.

In Halladay's first start following his appendectomy, he allowed six hits and struck out seven in seven scoreless innings in a 2–0 win over the White Sox. It was the 100th win of Halladay's career.

"It actually broke the way he wanted it to," Fasano said. "It was like, now we have it. He was a coachable, tenacious competitor. But, son of a gun, he applied it right out of the chute."

Of course, it was one thing to hear about Rivera's cutter secondhand from Fasano. When Halladay had the opportunity to spend time with Rivera at the 2008 All-Star Game, he asked the man himself.

"I had this belief that so much of it had to do with my thumb position and where my thumb was on the ball. When I got a chance to talk to him, sure enough, he told me that one of the keys for him was making sure he wrapped his thumb under and got it on the opposite side of the ball," he said.

A TV camera caught the entire session between Rivera and Halladay. Halladay held a ball in his right hand as he asked Rivera about the pitch. Rivera took the ball from him and gripped it. Halladay's head dropped as he focused on the way Rivera held the baseball. Halladay shifted his body to get another look from a different angle. He moved the ball in Rivera's hand to see exactly where he placed his fingers on the seams. Rivera mimicked the movement of the ball, exaggerating how it broke hard to the right. Halladay nodded. Rivera chuckled and smiled. He gave the ball back to Halladay, who had a look on his face like, "So *that's* how one of the greatest pitchers in baseball history throws one of the nastiest pitches in baseball history."

The Yankees fined Rivera in kangaroo court once they saw the video on TV. They could not believe a teammate helped Halladay, who went 3–0 with a 2.74 ERA and one complete game in three starts against the Yankees after the All-Star break.

"That's just me, that's just me," Rivera said. "If I had to do it over again, I would do it again."

Yankees shortstop Derek Jeter had 25 or more plate appearances against five current Hall of Fame pitchers in his 20-year career. He had a .962 OPS in 28 plate appearances against Greg Maddux, a .936 OPS in 38 plate appearances against Mike Mussina, a .925 OPS in 39 plate appearances against Tom Glavine, and a .789 OPS in 121 plate appearances against Pedro Martinez.

He had a .571 OPS in 104 plate appearances against Halladay.

"Toughest on me? Halladay, that sinker and cutter," Jeter said in the book *K: A History of Baseball in Ten Pitches*. "I tried to just guess which way it's gonna go—and I always guessed wrong."

Halladay overloaded the right side of the ball with his fingers when he threw his cutter, so he mostly saw the left half of the ball as he held it. His index and middle fingers ran across the wide part of the seams. He bent his thumb at the knuckle and tucked it underneath the ball. His thumbnail was even with his middle finger. If he kept his thumb there, the pitch broke like he needed it. If his thumb moved toward the outside of the ball, it blocked the ball's spin and it backed up on him.

He pulled straight down on the cutter as he threw it. He did nothing with his wrist.

"You know a lot of people had concerns about arm injuries with it, and I think the thinking was kind of like the slider, if you're twisting your wrist, that could be damaging ..." Halladay said. "If you throw it right, you don't have to do that. If you throw it right, it's just overloading the ball, finger placement, and you're just pulling straight down through it like you would any other pitch. I think there were a lot of people trying to create it without understanding that it may have caused issues and maybe giving it some negative tags connected with it. But anybody who ever threw it right—obviously Mariano never had any health issues and it was all of his finger placement and the way he finished the ball."

But even knowing that his thumb position meant everything, Halladay still lost the feel for the pitch from time to time. One day when the cutter felt nasty, Halladay took a baseball, grabbed a ballpoint pen and traced his fingers and thumb over it. He took the ball with him wherever he went. If he lost the feel for it again, he picked up the ball and looked to see where his thumb was. Sure enough, the thumb crept toward the outside of the ball.

"It was a pitch that you really had to monitor where you were, how you grip it, because you could get in bad habits just from long tossing. It's just an odd place to throw a ball," Halladay said.

Halladay eventually started to throw his sinker and cutter to both sides of the plate, creating the "X" effect—two pitches moving two ways on each side of the plate. Eric Hinske played with Halladay in Toronto from 2002 to '06 before playing for six other teams. He faced Halladay 45 times, more than any other pitcher in his career.

"He'd come inside hard with two strikes, like that hip-shot that comes back over the plate," Hinske said. "He would basically throw the ball right at my ass cheek, it would be coming at my hip, and then it would move six inches to the right over the plate for a strike. You'd jump out of the way of it and it'd be a strike. Then, all of the sudden, he showed up with a cutter. And he'd play that X-game with the inside half: comeback sinker, cutter in over the hands. And then he started, for whatever reason, throwing a backdoor cutter. After pounding you in with both of them, he'd start with that cutter over that white chalk away from you and it would come back in over the plate. And there's no way that's a strike in my mind. I'm like, 'There's no way that's over the plate.' And then I go back and watch the video and, sure enough, it hits the white part of the outside half. He won the Cy Young in 2003. He was already the nastiest thing. But that cutter changed his whole life."

Curveball

Halladay had a good curveball, but it got overlooked at times. He grew up throwing a knuckle curveball, which he learned when he was 10 or 11. He threw the knuckle curve through high school, the minor leagues, and early in his big league career. Every curveball he threw in his second big league start, when he almost no-hit the Tigers, were knuckle curves.

"It's the safest curveball you can throw for a young kid, all you're doing is flipping it," Halladay said. "And it was sharp, it was hard and sharp. The only problem was I couldn't ever control it. Like it was either sharp, most of the times it was down, I had a hard time throwing it for strikes, it just wasn't a consistent strike pitch for me."

Halladay asked Chris Carpenter in Triple-A how he threw his curveball. He showed him and Halladay started working on it. He threw the ball repeatedly against the wall, trying to get a feel for it. He came back to Carpenter again and again.

How do you hold it?

What do you do with your hand when you release it?

"That's when I first saw his drive to be great," Carpenter said. "He had to figure it out. He wasn't going to fail, even if it meant blowing his elbow out."

Halladay eventually got it. He could soften it up to get a strike or he could pull down harder on it to get more break.

"Let's say we're at the mound looking at home plate and there's a clock," said Gil Patterson, who was Halladay's pitching coach with the Blue Jays from 2002 to '04. "Probably the old curveball was more 12 to six. The new one was probably more two to eight. So not only did you have to worry about depth, you had to worry about it going from right to left. You had to worry about two things. He could start that thing off the plate against a lefty like five or six inches so they think it's six inches outside—*whoop*. It had teeth too. It means it's got some bite. He was able to do that. Nowadays you can see how many swings and misses a guy he gets. I would love to see what his swing-and-miss and groundball rate were with all his pitches."

Halladay ran his middle finger down the middle of the ball between the wide seams, on the leather. Many pitchers place a finger on a seam because it helps them pull down on the ball, but Halladay preferred to throw the pitch without it. He held the ball with his middle finger, pinching it into his palm. His index finger and thumb rested gently on the baseball, only so hitters could not see what pitch was coming. He lightly tapped his index finger and thumb to make sure they stayed loose. His hand was pronated as he threw the pitch.

"The big thing was just pulling straight down, letting it come off the top," he said. "I'd shorten my stride a little bit and just pull straight down. Get my arm as high as I could and pull straight down with it. And that's where I'd get the most break. I really felt like I had to have two pitches I could throw for strikes in any count. I could throw a fastball for a strike in any count, whether I was cutting it or sinking it, and then I was able to throw a curveball in any count, whether it be 3-2, 3-0, 3-1. If I could throw it in any count knowing it was gonna be for a strike, that played so much into a hitter's head, knowing they can't sit on any pitch, ever, 100 percent convinced it's gonna to be a fastball. And the tough part about having two was there's times my curveball wasn't there."

Gregg Zaun caught Halladay 75 times from 2004 to '08. He witnessed his share of frustrated hitters walking away from home plate following one of Halladay's curveballs.

"I used to giggle at some of the turtles he used to get on his breaking ball," he said. "Guys were so aware of just getting their knuckles hammered all the time, it made that curveball terrifying. Because when it came out of his hand you thought it was the two-seamer at your neck. So guys would turtle up on his curveball all the time because the sinker was so good. It was a good curveball, but it wasn't like Mussina's curveball. He had a nasty hook. It was good, but man, that sinker made it elite because they were terrified. He used the sinker the way it's supposed to be used: down and away to lefties and boring in on the knuckles of right-handed hitters. Guys would just take uncomfortable at-bats against him. It was funny to watch. They just knew. It was like facing Mariano, except you were facing him two or three times in a game. They take their bad wood up there. They're not taking their good bats up there against him."

Rod Barajas caught Halladay 50 times from 2008 to '09. He remembers Halladay's curveball getting similar reactions. Hitters were defeated before they even dug their spikes into the dirt.

"Please don't throw that pitch to me anymore," they asked Barajas. "I don't know what pitch it is. It's coming down the same tunnel, same angle, same starting spot. I don't know if it's a cutter. I don't know if it's a sinker. You can't see the spin on the ball."

Barajas chuckled.

"All of these guys were kind of in awe of what he could do with a baseball," he said.

Changeup

Halladay tried for years to throw a changeup. He tried different grips and techniques. Nothing ever worked.

"Every camp! Every camp!" Arnsberg said, recalling Halladay's desire to throw one. "He always wanted to pitch until he was 35, 40 years old, and I said, 'You're going to thank me someday.' I was never able to show him a grip that he liked, but god dang it he worked on it. He was so relentless with it. It would just get hammered or he'd just throw it horribly. He'd look at me. It was so funny because his first couple starts in spring training he'd go two innings and three innings and he'd throw nothing but sinkers and changeups and oh my god, did he just battle. I think he worked harder in those games than he did in the nine-inning shutouts. He worked so hard at being the best in the world. He always, always asked me, how he could get better."

Doc finally found a changeup he could throw in 2010 with the Phillies.

"It's not a split," Halladay said.

A true splitter has a pitcher's index and middle fingers almost on opposite sides of the ball in the middle of the ball. But Halladay separated his index and middle fingers just outside the narrowest seams on the ball with his thumb on the side. He kept a loose grip.

"Super light," Halladay said. "I wanted it to come off the tips of these fingers. Throw it as hard as I could and spin it off this way. I could have as much arm speed as I wanted and still get action on the ball."

But it wasn't just that Halladay had three or four effective pitches. He threw each of them for strikes too.

"He was around the plate," said Curtis Granderson, who had a 1.319 OPS in 18 career plate appearances against Halladay. "Look at the hitters' chart that's broken into nine squares. You have your hot zones and your cold zones. A lot of those zones are pretty cold, so as long as I can get it around there I don't need to waste a pitch. I think that's what Halladay was trying his best to do. 'Hey, I know he struggles with the ball on this part of the plate or at this height or at this speed. So let me just do that.' Why waste a pitch? If I waste a pitch there's a chance he might not swing at it. But if I throw it around the plate he has to swing at it, and I know he typically hasn't done very well with it."

| 12 |

The Machine

LONG BEFORE HALLADAY and Jimmy Rollins became teammates in Philadelphia, they met on one of those Nike trips. It might have been in Hawaii or Mexico. Maybe it was Aruba. Wherever it was, Rollins woke up one morning and made his way to the hospitality suite for coffee and breakfast. He passed Halladay on the way. Doc was soaked following an early-morning workout.

"Roy, you know this is the Nike baseball vacation," Rollins said.

"Yeah, I know," Halladay said. "I have to do something."

Rollins shook his head. The stories were true. Here is Halladay, on vacation, in November, finishing a workout while some of the best baseball players in the world were waking up with one thought on their mind: What kind of omelet should they have today?

"It made you look at yourself," Rollins said. "I'm like, 'I don't work out until after Thanksgiving. Maybe I need to start a little earlier.' But that was Doc. That was just him. That's how he functioned. That's what made him go and he felt that's what made him great and obviously who's to argue against that? I'm going to the hospitality suite to see what's for breakfast and he's sweating, towel, ready to go back to his room."

Halladay returned from Hawaii with 2004 on his mind. He consulted with Donovan Santas and George Poulis about his off-season training program. They looked for ways to follow his Cy Young season with another one. Halladay's endless pursuit of excellence was the drumbeat of his career.

"He wanted to keep getting better," Santas said. "He was taking steps, but he never threw positive things away that he did before. If he added a good routine that made him feel better, he didn't throw that away for something different. It was, in a lot of cases add, add, add. And that's where his program—especially in the off-season—his program would get to be so long and so involved. Guys would come to spring training and, yeah he'd be here, ready to go at 5:00 AM and getting through his program at 5:00 AM. Guys would roll in at 6:00 or 6:30 and he's dripping sweat. They're like, 'Oh man, I could never do all that work.' And it's like, 'Well, he didn't start the first day of the off-season doing all this. He built up to this.'"

Halladay wanted to add 10–12 pounds of muscle in the off-season to maintain his strength through next season. He drank multiple protein shakes a day, which is not unusual for a professional athlete. But Halladay took one additional step. He set his alarm for one in the morning. He woke up, walked to the kitchen, chugged a shake, and returned to bed. He did that every night.

"He could have gotten up in the morning, but I think his idea was, he already feels like he's eating a high-calorie count during the day," Santas said. "This is just another opportunity. Here are eight or 10 hours where I'm doing nothing. I'm just going to throw some more calories in there. I'm like, 'All right, man, as long as this is not destroying your sleep cycles then this is totally fine.' This is extra calories. And so there was nothing wrong with it. Could he have gotten the extra calories without doing it that way? Of course, but this was just another way of him holding himself accountable so that if he missed during the day, if he missed his opportunity to have a shake or whatever, or didn't want to drink it right before bed, this was just a way for him to know that he always got it in. His own checks and balances."

Brandy kiddingly called her husband "Captain Overkill" because he did everything to the extreme.

"Amazing people have odd tendencies," she said. "Roy had a very addictive personality. He would fixate on something and he couldn't let go."

Halladay needed to be the biggest and best at everything. It meant buying the best bass boat. It meant snatching up the best fishing poles, lures, and gear. If he saw a golf gadget on TV, he bought it. If he learned about a new set of irons, he bought them. Golf balls, tees, chipping nets, chess sets, model planes. He sometimes bought multiples of the same thing, just in case something happened to the first one.

"He had to have all the gizmos and gadgets because then he felt like he was prepared to be the best fisherman ever," Brandy said.

Halladay laughed at himself when he realized he had every gadget, but still could not claim to be the world's greatest fisherman. It never stopped him from continuing to try.

Halladay pushed himself hard, so hard sometimes that the Blue Jays' front office expressed its concerns. It worried that Halladay might suffer from burnout. It worried that he might hurt himself. Santas reassured everybody that Halladay could handle the work. He reminded everybody that Halladay *needed* the work to feel prepared and be successful.

"He works hard enough for himself," he said. "He works way harder than everyone else and very few other people on the team would be capable of doing what he's doing—and that's fine because they're different. But this is what he needs to know that he's fully prepared and ready to go. And this is what he would draw upon in the seventh, eighth, ninth inning. He would know that he's pushed himself far beyond any of that crap, you know what I mean? He would know he could make 36 starts a year because of it. He just knew."

HALLADAY GOT HIT HARD on Opening Day 2004. He allowed seven runs in 6⅔ innings in a loss to Detroit. The Blue Jays wanted to make the day a spectacle, so they turned off the lights while he and Kevin Cash warmed up in the bullpen. There were go-go dancers in the windows of the hotel above them. Their silhouettes covered the ground below. There was a single spotlight on Halladay and a single spotlight on Cash.

This was not part of Doc's routine.

"He is seething pissed," Cash said. "I'm sitting there trying to catch him in the dark and it was ridiculous. And that pissed him off so bad I think it affected the outing."

Maybe it was an omen. Halladay got scratched from an early-June start and landed on the disabled list for the first time in his career. The Blue Jays called it "right shoulder discomfort." He returned a couple weeks later, but landed on the DL again after he allowed 11 runs in 10 innings in back-to-back starts in July. This time the Blue Jays called it "right shoulder fatigue." Halladay hated the word "fatigue." It meant tired. It indicated weakness. Halladay told Poulis to never use the word "fatigue" when he spoke to anybody about his health. He used words like "inflammation" or "tightness" instead.

"They all kind of work together," Poulis said. "Heck, the reason there's tightness and inflammation is they might be fatigued. They might be overworked in one certain area. I guess you just choose the terminology."

But Halladay made only 21 starts in '04 because of shoulder problems. He finished 8–8 with a 4.20 ERA. Four days after the season, Brandy gave birth to their son Ryan in Dunedin on October 7.

Halladay threw a combined 505⅓ innings the previous two seasons, 27 more than second-ranked Tim Hudson. Halladay's shoulder issues probably stemmed from a combination of innings pitched, plus the fact he did not scale back his off-season workouts. He learned from it. He modified his off-season throwing program before '05 to keep his shoulder strong. Red Sox ace Curt Schilling recommended fewer bullpen sessions before camp opened.

Halladay typically threw off a mound 15 times before spring training. He cut the number to six. It helped.

Halladay was 12–4 with a 2.33 ERA in his first 18 starts in '05. He was pitching better than '03, when he won the Cy Young. Red Sox manager Terry Francona planned to name him the AL starter for the All-Star Game, which would have been special because the NL named Chris Carpenter as its starter. But in a game in Texas on July 8, Rangers left fielder Kevin Mench crushed a line drive off Halladay's left leg in the third inning. The impact sounded like two pieces of wood smacking together. Halladay dropped to the ground. The ball fell next to him. He picked it up and fired a strike to first base. Mench was out. Halladay grimaced. He rolled to his side.

"We're like, 'Get up, get up, get up,'" Santas said.

He could not. Poulis and others jogged to the mound.

"Doc, let's get the cart," he said. "Let's get the cart and go get an x-ray."

"No," Halladay said. "I'm walking off. I don't want anyone to see me get carted off."

Brandy watched everything on TV.

"His leg stayed sideways," she said. "They came out, they talked to him for a minute. The next thing is he jumped up and walked off as fast as he got up. He was up and off. And I'm watching him walk and I'm watching him kind of flick his foot. It looked like it hurt. I watched him flick it. I think he was pulling himself because he couldn't move his leg. And when he got into the clubhouse—it's really creepy—when he got into the tunnel he collapsed and he's like, 'Help me.' And they carried him out the rest of the way."

Santas and Poulis could not believe he made it that far.

"He needed to make a point walking off," Santas said.

"There were times on the mound when stuff like that would happen and I would just get choked up and it would almost be hard for me to talk because I just loved this guy so much it was crazy," Poulis said.

The Blue Jays did a tap test in the clubhouse to check Halladay's leg. He almost flew off the table. The x-ray showed a non-displaced fracture in the tibia. It also showed the stitches from the ball on the bone.

"The doctor told him that was only the second time in his career that he'd ever seen a fracture take the shape of what caused it," Brandy said. "It just crushed into the bone."

The next afternoon, Halladay, leaning on crutches with his leg in a boot cast, said he hoped to begin playing catch in a week and be back on the mound in a month. Poulis knew how much a speedy recovery meant to him, so he told him about the potential benefits of a hyperbaric chamber. He said he could get one, but he might have to rent it because he did not have the money in his budget. Halladay bought one himself. He spent hours in there.

"He healed the fracture in three weeks," Brandy said. "It was ridiculous. He had the hyperbaric chamber. He was doing these cow-blood treatments and platelet therapies. It was crazy."

Santas and Poulis tried to keep Halladay's arm in shape while keeping weight off the leg. Poulis recommended that he sit on a chair on the foul line in the outfield and play catch with him. Halladay pictured what that would look like.

Not a chance in hell, he said.

"How about one knee?" Poulis said.

"I'll think about the knee, but I ain't sitting in no chair," Halladay said.

They compromised. Halladay sat on a chair inside the batting cage and played catch—out of sight of cameras and reporters. Santas, meanwhile, found swimming pools on the road to do water workouts. Halladay was set to rejoin the rotation August 2 against the White Sox, but it got pushed back to August 7 against the Yankees. Then it never happened at all. The team announced later that month that his season was over. Halladay's eyes welled up when he learned he would not pitch again in '05.

"What didn't show in the first x-ray is that when it hit, it actually spiderwebbed the back of his leg," Brandy said. "We never knew about any of the fractures behind the bone. So he healed the front part, but there were microfractures and it looked like a spiderweb in the back of the bone. That's why he couldn't weight bear it."

Angels right-hander Bartolo Colón went 21–8 with a 3.48 ERA to win the AL Cy Young Award. He finished with a 4.0 WAR. Halladay, despite not pitching the final three months of the season, finished with a 5.5 WAR. He was that good. Seven pitchers received AL Cy Young votes. The only pitcher with a better WAR than Halladay was Minnesota's Johan Santana, who went 16–7 with a 2.87 ERA in 33 starts. He had a 7.2 WAR, but finished third.

"I still think if he could've gotten another month he still would have won the Cy Young," Blue Jays pitching coach Brad Arnsberg said.

RAÚL IBAÑEZ AND GREGG Zaun were teammates in Kansas City in 2001. Ibañez later joined the Mariners, while Zaun joined the Blue Jays. The Mariners and Blue Jays played each other in a series in Toronto in July 2007. Zaun caught Halladay one night, while his old buddy Ibañez hit for Seattle. Halladay dropped a first-pitch curveball on Ibañez for a strike in the first inning. Ibañez glanced at the mound. Halladay looked pissed. Focused, but pissed. Ibañez looked back at his former teammate.

"Zauny, is this guy having any fun?" he said. "If I had stuff like this, I'd be having a blast on the mound."

Zaun is not a shy guy. He can strike up a conversation with anybody anywhere.

"Eh," he said quietly. "I don't know."

Ibañez wondered why Zaun seemed tongue tied for the first time in his life. Then he looked back at the mound. Halladay was staring down Ibañez. He wanted him back in the box. He wanted to throw his next pitch.

Get in there, dude.

"It was like, way too intense," Ibañez said. "And it's funny because the next day I saw Zauny and I talked to him about it briefly and he was like, 'Yeah, when he's up, I don't talk to the hitters when he's on the mound.'"

Twenty-two different catchers caught Halladay in the big leagues. He had 16 catchers in Toronto, including Zaun. All of Halladay's catchers speak reverentially about him.

"This is the way I felt about Roy," Rod Barajas said. "Because of all the preparation, all the work that he put in, I did not want to disappoint this man. He had his book, he had everything written down. We would have our meeting early. It wasn't really a conversation, he was telling me what he was going to do. He watched every pitch he threw to every single hitter in the lineup. He had a plan and knew exactly how to attack them. He wasn't going to deviate from that plan unless the catcher saw something. I was so paranoid. I'd go [into the clubhouse] right before BP, I'd see his book, I'd go over there and read it again. Before the game, I'd go over and read it again. I did not want to let this guy down. I wanted to make sure I was out there doing exactly what he wanted to do. I knew the game plan like the back of my hand. There was no chance I was going to let this guy down behind the plate."

Halladay kept detailed notes of every hitter in a series of notebooks. He studied video religiously, following a recommendation from Schilling. Doc had a Plan A, Plan B, and Plan C for everybody.

"His Plan A was going to get rammed down your throat until you beat him," Zaun said.

These were not guidelines, either. These were rules.

"He'd go through each guy," said Brian Schneider, who caught Halladay five times with the Phillies. "He might say, '[Giancarlo] Stanton, I'm going to go sinker both sides, I'm going to cutter in, I'm not going to go cutter away. Split, I'll throw split. We'll go curveball away, we're not going to front door it.' Roll with that.

"Now, think seventh inning when you're 90 pitches into it. Stanton is up and you call a frontdoor curveball and it's not what he went over four hours ago. He just steps off and looks at you like, 'I told you four hours ago I'm not going to throw that pitch.' He'd step off and you'd go, 'Oh, fuck. Sorry, my bad.' He knew exactly what pitches. He told you. It was easier in the game because he already told you what he was going to do. Not like, 'Oh, let's go sinker in here.' No, he already said no. Why am I going to call that? It was so down to the point. This is what I'm going to do because he's done all the work in the days previous. The last thing you want to do is disappoint a guy like that. He's the best of the best. It's not that there's pressure, but you want to... he's so damn good that you don't want to screw up. You want him to be the best he can be."

It is not to say Doc never allowed his catchers to improvise. He did. Halladay told Barajas before a game against Tampa Bay that he did not want to throw B.J. Upton sinkers away under any circumstances. He wanted to pound him inside. But as the game progressed, Upton fouled off a few of Halladay's sinkers inside. Upton stepped back into the box, but moved his feet just a hair away from the plate. Barajas noticed that he was trying to cheat so he could barrel the next sinker inside.

Barajas looked at Halladay, gestured toward Upton's feet and called for a sinker away. Halladay understood. He threw the pitch, it hit Barajas' glove on the outside corner and Upton struck out.

"He was fine with you ad-libbing as long as there was a reason for it," Barajas said. "If he trusts you as a catcher behind the plate, he'd roll with you. Back in the dugout, you give him a little shake of the head, chest is puffed out a little bit. And I explained it to him and he was like, 'Yeah. Any time you ever see that, man, you just let me know and we'll go with it.'"

Barajas spent parts of nine seasons in the big leagues before he met Halladay. He felt comfortable making a suggestion like that. It wasn't always easy for younger catchers. Halladay once told rookie Kevin Cash that he had two rules: Do not come to the mound and talk to me. Do not sugarcoat anything.

"Always be honest with me," Halladay said.

Cash, who became manager of the Rays in 2015, caught Halladay 19 times in 2003–04. He found being honest easy. He found not visiting the mound hard. It came to a head when Halladay struggled in one of their first games together. Doc gave up a string of hits and looked gassed. Cash knew he should go to the mound, but he remembered the rule.

"I knew I should've gone out, I wanted to go out, but I didn't," he said. "So I just stayed there."

The inning ended. Halladay walked up to Cash and unloaded on him.

"How could you not come out there and give me a breather!?" he said.

"Doc, you're the one who sets these rules," Blue Jays pitching coach Gil Patterson said, defending Cash. "You need to follow them or not."

"We called that the little island out there," said Tom Wilson, who caught Halladay 20 times in 2002–03. "The mound was the island and nobody wanted to go to the island when Doc was on the mound. It was all business. I got told, 'Get off the mound,' one time. Yeah, he said, 'Get the fuck out of here. Get behind the plate.' He was so well-conditioned. This guy was the toughest, hardest competitor I've ever played against or played with. He was so intense about what he was doing. It's just unbelievable."

"I think the first time I ever went out there, he looked at me and said, 'What the fuck are you doing out here?'" Zaun said.

"If I ever made a trip to the mound I wouldn't say anything," said Ken Huckaby, who caught Halladay 30 times in 2002–03 and '05. "I would just stand there. I would just walk out to the mound and stand there like I was talking, but he knew why I was there. He would take his second to get his breath back and then he'd look at me and he'd just stare at me and that'd mean this is over and I'd just turn around and jog back. He was working with Harvey Dorfman, so I knew he had a little wheel. He'd do it every time. That way the previous pitch wouldn't affect the next pitch. So he'd reflect, he'd make his adjustment, and then he'd execute. If that wheel got off, he could reset that wheel and then get back on. But that was Harvey."

Dorfman wrote about "The Circuit" in *The Mental ABC's of Pitching*. It was *approach*, *result*, and *response*.

"A pitcher's approach, remember, is entirely within his control," Dorfman wrote. "Result is yet to be determined. It is not within the pitcher's control. A pitcher's response is pivotal. How he acts after the previous 'event'—the result of a delivered pitch, a batted ball, an umpire's call, a fielder's error—will often dictate the quality of the pitchers' next approach. Meaning that if a pitcher's response is a poor one—loss of poise, loss of purpose, loss of focus—he is likely to take that distraction into his next approach. The next pitch, therefore, will not be executed with maximum effectiveness, to say the least. The pitcher has complete control of his response."

HALLADAY WENT 16-5 WITH a 3.19 ERA in 32 starts in 2006, 16–7 with a 3.71 ERA in 2007, and 20–11 with a 2.78 ERA in 34 appearances (33 starts) in 2008. He finished third, fifth, and second in Cy Young voting, respectively. He threw the second 10-inning complete game of his career in a 2–1 victory over Detroit on April 13, 2007. Halladay is the only pitcher in baseball to have two 10-inning complete games since 1990.

"It was actually quite comical at the end," said Zaun, who caught Halladay that day. "You could see just how uncomfortable guys were. I think that's what I remembered the most about it. The look in their eyes, similar to facing Mariano [Rivera] in the ninth. You know you're beat before you step in the box. There's just this uncomfortable hesitancy to stepping in there. Roy was intimidating. Not only was he a good pitcher, but he was a big guy. He wasn't a guy that laughed and smiled out there on the field. He wasn't a guy that ever let his opponent feel a moment of comfort. I loved it. That's one of the things that made me giggle the most was how awful the contact was. He was blowing guys up left and right."

Halladay's legend kept growing. He threw a complete game to earn his 20th win in his final start of the '08 season, allowing two runs and six hits in nine innings against the Yankees.

"You look forward to the challenge, but you'd rather be facing somebody else," Yankees shortstop Derek Jeter said.

Halladay became more confident in his beliefs and processes every year. He believed strongly in what helped him succeed. He opened up and told his teammates about Dorfman. They could unlock their potential too. He could help. Halladay handed out copies of the *Mental ABC's of Pitching*. He highlighted chapters or passages that meant something to him. He gave one of those highlighted copies to A.J. Burnett, who signed with Toronto before the '06 season. During their first season together, Halladay and Burnett did contrast sessions in the hot and cold tubs. One sat in the hot tub, while the other sat in the cold tub. Then they switched. It was during one of those sessions that Halladay asked Burnett something nobody asked him before.

"So... what's your approach?" he said.

Burnett's mind raced. Is there a correct answer here? Is there a wrong answer here?

"Umm... I just try to throw heaters by guys," he said. "And if I get ahead, I throw my curveball as hard as I can."

Halladay laughed. But the conversation started something. Burnett began to transition from hard-throwing right-hander that pumped fastballs by everybody to bona fide pitcher. He started to throw inside more. He started to use offspeed pitches earlier in counts. He worked both sides of the plate. He developed a routine and prepared better.

"I quickly came to realize the difference between doing enough to get by, and pitching at the highest possible level," Burnett wrote in a tribute to Halladay in the *Players' Tribune*. "Before long, I noticed myself spending more time preparing, and doing the same thing day in and day out, regardless of what happened the previous time I pitched. And I'm definitely proud to say that one of the things I stole from Doc was locking in early every fifth day and being that serious, don't-eff-with-me, man-with-a-plan as soon as I got to the ballpark. I stole that approach from Doc, and I kept things that way no matter what team I played for after that.

"And you know what, anytime I was kind of scuffling a little bit... heck yeah I'd pull out that Dorfman book in a heartbeat and go over some of that stuff."

| 13 |

Time To Move On

HALLADAY FLEW HOME to Florida feeling frustrated following the 2008 season. The Blue Jays won 86 games, but finished 11 games out of first place in the American League East and fourth behind the Rays, Red Sox, and Yankees.

"It's hard to keep doing the same things each year and it's hard to not see a progression," he said that July at the All-Star Game. "I don't think you ever go out there and kind of take that route of, 'Here we go,' but it's definitely hard to see. You want to see things go in the right direction, but you don't want to take on the self-pity thing. You want to try to help do something to turn things around. That's the hardest thing. We sit down every spring training and we talk about the same things and it's almost like a little bit of Groundhog Day. That definitely gets frustrating, you want to talk about why we're succeeding, what we've done to help us get to the point of where we're at, and we just haven't done that. It's hard to keep talking about the same thing."

It would continue to be the same thing in Toronto. Halladay looked at the Blue Jays' roster, looked at the payroll and saw that their chances to win in 2009 looked no better. In fact, they looked worse. Rogers Communications owned the Blue Jays and it told general manager J.P. Ricciardi to shed payroll, even if A.J. Burnett exercised the opt-out clause in his contract and signed elsewhere. It put Ricciardi between a rock and a hard place. He knew he could not count on starting pitchers Dustin McGowan (who was recovering from right shoulder surgery) and Shaun Marcum (who would miss the entire season following Tommy John surgery). If Burnett departed, it left Halladay and Jesse Litsch as the only returning members of the '08 rotation. Ricciardi needed to find legitimate replacements, but Rogers told him to find a way without its help.

Ricciardi opened the off-season saying he would trade "anybody," if it meant improving the club. As expected, Burnett opted out and signed a five-year, $82.5 million contract with the Yankees. As expected, the Blue Jays did not make the moves they needed to keep up with the Rays, Red Sox, and Yankees. They opened spring training in 2009 with low-cost acquisitions, including pitchers Matt Clement and Mike Maroth, catcher Michael Barrett, and first baseman Kevin Millar.

"I thought we were going to... hopefully bring A.J. back, maybe add something else," Halladay said.

Maroth got released before the end of camp. Clement retired when he did not make the team out of spring training. Barrett, whom the Blue Jays once considered drafting over Halladay in 1995, played seven games before tearing a muscle in his right shoulder. He never played in the big leagues again. Millar posted a .674 OPS in 283 plate appearances in the final season of his major league career.

The Blue Jays opened the season with Halladay, Litsch, David Purcey, Ricky Romero, and Scott Richmond in the rotation. Halladay made 255 career starts before Opening Day. Litsch (48), Purcey (12), Richmond (five), and Romero (zero) started a combined 65. The Jays were 43–41 and fourth in the AL East on July 6. Ricciardi called Phillies general manager Rubén Amaro Jr. to say he was ready to talk about Halladay. Ricciardi made the news public, when he told Ken Rosenthal from Fox Sports.

"I'm not saying we're going to shop him," Ricciardi said. "But if something makes sense, we at least have to listen. We're more toward listening than we've ever been."

Rosenthal wrote that Toronto probably wanted to strike a deal similar to the one the Indians made for Bartolo Colón and Tim Drew in 2002, when they got Brandon Phillips, Grady Sizemore, Cliff Lee, and Lee Stevens from the Expos. In other words, Halladay would not come cheap.

Reporters swarmed Halladay in front of his locker the next day at Tropicana Field, where the Blue Jays opened a three-game series against the Rays.

"I love Toronto," he said. "I want to stay here, but I want to win as well. That's becoming more and more of a goal for me. I think when an organization is kind of thinking that maybe we kind of want to go this direction, and it's a situation that suits the team and yourself, then you have to evaluate that and say, 'Maybe this is the best thing.' I'm really not in that situation yet."

Halladay had the final say, because he had a complete no-trade clause. He would not accept a trade to a middling team hoping to win a Wild Card or a rebuilding team hoping to contend in a few years. Ricciardi knew that, though. They talked.

"I just went to Doc and said, 'Look, you've been nothing but great. We are not going to do anything here until we talk to you,'" Ricciardi said. "'They want us to go backwards now and that's not fair to you. You signed an extension to stay here and you're committed. If you want to be traded you just let me know. No. 1, we will try to trade you. No. 2, we're not trading you to any place that doesn't have a chance to win and any place you don't want to go.' We kept him totally involved with every possible scenario in regards to trades."

FROM THE MOMENT RICCIARDI hung an "Open for Business" sign around the neck of the best pitcher in baseball, the talk never stopped. It reached a fevered pitch at the All-Star Game in St. Louis. American League manager Joe Maddon named Halladay the AL starter, which meant he had to appear at a press conference with Maddon, NL manager Charlie Manuel, and NL starter Tim Lincecum. Bob Costas emceed. He introduced Halladay as "representing, at least for the moment, the Toronto Blue Jays."

"You would like to be, you know, three games up in first place and not have to deal with this," Halladay said.

He answered more questions in the clubhouse before the game. He was asked about the Cardinals, Phillies, Yankees, Dodgers, and more.

"I don't want to name places out of respect for Toronto," he said. "I hate to put the cart in front of the horse."

George Poulis joined Halladay at the All-Star Game as the AL's athletic trainer. He brought his family, which meant extra rooms and airfare. The Halladays picked up the tab.

Poulis stretched Halladay's arm on the training table before the game, like he had for years. He knew how much the start meant to him because both Braden and Ryan could watch him pitch. Poulis choked up. He thought how it might be one of their final days together. He thought about how far Halladay had come to get here. He sniffled.

Halladay's right eye slowly peeled open.

"What are you sniffling about?" he said.

"Hey, man," Poulis said. "It's just me. You know me."

"What?"

"Man, I'm stretching you in the All-Star Game. This is like a dream for me."

A moment passed.

"Man, you're weird," Halladay said.

Poulis finished. Halladay stood up.

"Doc, have a good one," Poulis said.

"You really have issues," Halladay said. "Thanks, I appreciate you."

HALLADAY PITCHED TWO INNINGS in the All-Star Game and rejoined the Blue Jays in Toronto to begin the second half. He pitched a complete game 3–1 victory over the Red Sox on July 19. Former Blue Jays general manager Pat Gillick watched from the stands. He once recommended that Toronto draft Halladay after watching him pitch in a high school game in Arizona in 1995. Now he served as a special advisor for the Phillies, who were Halladay's top pursuer. The game felt like it could be Halladay's final start in Toronto. Fans down the left-field line stood and cheered as he left the bullpen before the game. His teammates gave him a head start before they ran onto the field in the first inning so he could receive an ovation from the crowd. Brandy gave an emotional interview during the Blue Jays' radio broadcast.

"This could very well be our last homestand," she said. "We're leaving on Monday. If something happens before the trade deadline, I won't be back. That's difficult. That's more than difficult."

But no trade. Halladay allowed two runs in nine innings in a 4–2 loss to the Rays in 10 innings on July 24. Fans down the left-field line stood again and cheered as he left the bullpen. As the deadline drew closer, however, some fans soured on the idea that the Blue Jays would trade their iconic ace. Some brought signs that begged them to reconsider.

"Don't trade Roy! Don't trade Roy!" fans chanted in the fifth inning.

"Trade J.P.! Trade J.P.!" chants followed.

Ricciardi announced a July 28 deadline to trade Halladay because he did not want him to pitch with distractions when he pitched in Seattle on July 29. Of course, if he got an offer he could not refuse five minutes before the July 31 deadline he would accept it. But perhaps a soft deadline would put more pressure on teams to move.

The Phillies wanted Halladay the most. Amaro replaced Gillick as the Phillies' general manager following the 2008 World Series. A short time later, he sat in the office of Phillies president David Montgomery, talking about the future, the players they had on the roster and the players they wanted in the future. Amaro said that if he could get anybody, he wanted Halladay.

The Phillies and Blue Jays went back and forth multiple times with various packages for Doc. Amaro called Ricciardi with their final offer on July 26: left-hander J.A. Happ, right-hander Carlos Carrasco, infielder Jason Donald, and catcher Travis d'Arnaud. They said they would replace either Carrasco or Donald with outfielder Michael Taylor, if Toronto wanted him.

Happ went 12–4 with a 2.93 ERA in 35 appearances (23 starts) in '09, and would blossom into a 20-game winner with the Blue Jays in 2016. Carrasco was the Phillies' No. 2 prospect and the No. 52 prospect in baseball, according to *Baseball America*. He developed into a top-of-the-rotation starter for the Indians. D'Arnaud never lived up to the hype as the Phillies' No. 7 prospect, but he was a replacement-level catcher for years with the Mets and Rays. Phillies manager Charlie Manuel once compared Donald to Craig Biggio. Donald, who was the Phillies' No. 4 prospect and the No. 69 prospect in baseball, played three seasons as a utility infielder for Cleveland.

The Blue Jays rejected it. They wanted Happ, outfielder Domonic Brown, right-hander Kyle Drabek, and outfielder Anthony Gose. Brown was the Phillies' No. 1 prospect and the No. 48 prospect in baseball. Drabek was the son of 1990 NL Cy Young–winner Doug Drabek and the Phillies' No. 5 prospect. Gose was another promising talent in the Phillies' system. The Phillies said no. They refused to trade Brown or Drabek. They expected Brown to replace Jayson Werth in right field following the 2010 season. They thought Drabek and left-hander Cole Hamels could anchor the top of the Phillies' rotation for years.

"Rubén, you're going to get *Roy Halladay*," Ricciardi said. "They're going to have a parade for you coming through town. They're going to have a parade to get me out of town."

Ricciardi reminded Amaro that even the best prospects are just prospects. Most of them disappoint.

"In three years, they'll be serving me my breakfast at Lenny's," he said, referring to a popular Clearwater, Florida, diner.

Amaro was not swayed. They reached an impasse.

"He wasn't going to budge and neither were we," Phillies assistant general manager Scott Proefrock said.

The Phillies executed Plan B on July 29. They traded Carrasco, Donald, catcher Lou Marson, and right-hander Jason Knapp to the Indians for Cliff Lee and outfielder Ben Francisco. It was a solid package of prospects, but none were as highly regarded as Drabek and Brown. The Phillies kept Happ too.

Halladay learned about the deal before he pitched on an oppressively humid afternoon in Seattle. He allowed three runs in seven innings in a 3–2 loss to the Mariners. He looked drained and defeated afterward. He disappeared to a back room before finally emerging and dressing at his locker. His teammates had boarded the bus to the airport. Halladay turned to address reporters, including a couple scribes from Philadelphia. Halladay could not hide his disappointment. The past three weeks were a slog. He answered countless questions and not just from reporters.

"It's family, friends, acquaintances," he said. "You're constantly getting phone calls."

He believed he would be in a Phillies' uniform before the end of the month. Instead, he boarded the Blue Jays' flight to San Francisco, where they would stay while they played a three-game series in Oakland.

The team's buses rolled up to Hotel Nikko on Mason Street. In a cruel twist, the Phillies checked into the same hotel for a three-game series against the Giants. Phillies director of team travel and clubhouse services Frank Coppenbarger ran into Halladay in the lobby. Coppenbarger, like everybody else, thought the Phillies would get Doc. He even made a jersey with Halladay's name and number on the back, which sat at the bottom of a trunk in the visitors' clubhouse at AT&T Park. Nobody knows what happened to it.

"I was really hoping you'd be on our bus," Coppenbarger said.

"Well, I'm not," Halladay snapped. "I'm glad I'm not there."

Halladay deflected because he was hurt. He brushed past Coppenbarger and walked away.

The trade deadline passed without a deal. Toronto reportedly came close with the Angels. Toronto wanted Jered Weaver or Joe Saunders, plus shortstop Erick Aybar and outfield prospect Peter Bourjos. The Angels said no. They wanted Aybar. Halladay was crestfallen. Brandy was heartbroken.

"I liked being where I was," Halladay said, "but I was ready to go somewhere where we had a chance. Going through that month with nothing happening—it kind of sucks it all out of you. It was disappointing, but at the same time, a weight was gone."

"I didn't go back to Toronto for three months," Brandy said. "Roy was so loyal to a fault. We renewed contracts there multiple times. We loved Toronto so much. We still love Toronto. Our son [Braden] was born there. We consider that a home for us to this day. He just wanted a chance to compete. Three different contracts they signed it was, 'We're going to rebuild, we're going to rebuild. We're starting over, we want you to be a big part of it.' It just never quite happened. And we knew that we did not want to go through another rebuild at that point in his career. He didn't have the time. You only play for so many years. You only have so much time to make things happen and be relevant in this game. He wanted a chance to win."

The July drama sapped him. Halladay went 2–4 with a 4.71 ERA in six starts in August.

"It was just a little quieter Roy than what you'd normally get, especially on the days when he didn't pitch," catcher Rod Barajas said.

Halladay snapped out of his funk in September. He went 4–1 with a 1.47 ERA in six starts to finish 17–10 with a 2.79 ERA. He threw shutouts against the Yankees, Mariners, and Red Sox, and one complete game against the Twins. He finished fifth in AL Cy Young voting behind Zack Greinke (16–8, 2.16 ERA), Felix Hernandez (19–5, 2.49 ERA), Justin Verlander (19–9, 3.45 ERA), and CC Sabathia (19–8, 3.37 ERA). Again, Halladay deserved stronger consideration, putting up his numbers on an inferior team in the best division in baseball. His 6.9 WAR ranked second only to Greinke's 10.4, according to Baseball Reference.

THE BLUE JAYS FIRED Ricciardi on the second-to-final day of the season. They replaced him with assistant general manager Alex Anthopoulos. He was in his new role less than a month when Halladay and his representatives requested a meeting. Late in October, as Lee and the Phillies charged toward their second consecutive National League pennant, Blue Jays president Paul Beeston, Anthopoulos, the Halladays, and Halladay's agents scheduled a dinner at Roy's Restaurant, a Hawaiian fusion joint in Tampa. Anthopoulos canceled at the last minute because he fell ill, but he talked to Halladay beforehand. Halladay repeated the same message to Beeston.

"Look, if you guys are rebuilding, my clock is getting short," Halladay said. "I don't know how long I have and I don't want to go through another rebuilding process. I would love nothing more than to win a World Series championship in Toronto, but I don't know that I have that time. So, I would really prefer that you guys would push me to one of these two teams."

He wanted to play for the Phillies or Yankees. Anthopoulos understood.

"As far as I was concerned he was six months away from being able to choose where he wanted to play," he said, referring to free agency. "I didn't begrudge him at all. And he earned his no-trade clause. He gave the club plenty of hometown discounts, and he also did a lot in the off-season to try and recruit. He really wanted to win in Toronto. He really cared about it. I remember, in any off-season, we would call and say, 'Hey, can you come up? We're bringing up Gil Meche,' or, 'We're bringing in A.J. Burnett.' Done, he was there. I remember one time in the winter, we may have been going to a Leaf game. I was in the car with him, he was saying at the time, 'I wouldn't want to play in Boston or New York. This is where I want to win. This is what I want to do.' He really legitimately cared about the organization.

"This point's to Roy's class. I remember when he first talked to me and Paul when he requested the trade. He said, 'If there are any concerns for the organization, PR, optics, I understand.' He wasn't being arrogant about it, but he said, 'Look, I understand. I'm a name here. I'll wear it. Put it all on me.' Which, I've got to tell you, was pretty amazing. 'Put it all on me. I'm driving this. I'm doing this.' This is 100 percent, I'm accountable. This is my responsibility. I do not want the organization to suffer. We didn't even bring it up, 'We're concerned,' this or that. None of that. It didn't even come out of our mouths. He just volunteered."

Amaro reconnected with Anthopoulos at the GM meetings in November. Amaro, Proefrock, and other Phillies' officials were stepping onto an elevator when Anthopoulos approached. He asked to speak to Amaro. Before the elevator doors closed, Amaro stepped off. Amaro reiterated to Anthopoulos that he wanted Halladay, even though he had Lee.

"We're interested in doing something," he said.

Anthopoulos mentioned the names that would get the ball rolling again: Brown and Drabek. The Phillies pushed back. Anthopoulos tried to line up something with the Angels, White Sox, and Rays. His efforts proved futile. Halladay insisted on the

Phillies or Yankees. They were two World Series–caliber teams that trained close to his home outside of Tampa. The Phillies won two consecutive National League pennants, including the '08 World Series. They held spring training in Clearwater, a 15-minute drive from the Blue Jays' facility in Dunedin. The Yankees just beat them in the '09 World Series. They trained in Tampa.

The Blue Jays started to push the White Sox and Angels, but both teams trained in Arizona. It was not going to happen. Halladay's agents became frustrated. They exercised some leverage. Jeff Berry, a partner at CAA who worked with Halladay's long-time point man, Greg Landry, spoke with ESPN's Buster Olney.

"Once Roy reports to spring training as a member of the Blue Jays," he told him, "from that point forward he will not approve or even discuss any potential trade scenario. This will eliminate a repeat of the distracting media frenzy of 2009 for both Roy and his teammates, and will allow Roy to focus on pitching at the exceptional level Jays fans have come to expect."

It was a clear message to Anthopoulos: forget about the White Sox and Angels and get something done with the Phillies or Yankees. If not, Halladay leaves after 2010 and Toronto receives only draft picks as compensation.

"That was authentic," Berry said. "That wasn't a bluff. Roy was genuine and they knew that. I remember going to his house to meet with him in person and we were meeting with him to discuss how we were going to approach the trade. You walk up to his house and we go upstairs and walk past the Cy Youngs and the All-Stars, and Roy's in jeans and cowboy boots, larger than life as always, and very calm. He had thought a lot about it. Those are the two places he thought about going."

The winter meetings arrived. There were rumors the Rays could send outfielder B.J. Upton and prospects Wade Davis and Desmond Jennings to Toronto. Amaro asked Anthopoulos if the reports were true. He would not say.

"It was an impossible market," Anthopoulos said. "Every time I asked about other teams it was just like, 'No.' Which was fine. I don't begrudge that he had it, but from there I've never given out a no-trade clause. We were caught in a tough spot. He made it very clear, 'I'm leaving. There's nothing you can do to talk me into staying. I can't emphasize this enough. You can't extend me. You can offer me all the money in the world. I need to win. I want to win.' You're weighing everything against two draft picks. The line would have to be significantly better than two picks."

Anthopoulos wanted Drabek, Brown, Gose, and d'Arnaud, essentially the same deal as the one in July, except d'Arnaud replaced Happ. The Phillies agreed to include Drabek. Things were progressing, although the Phillies worked on Plan B just in case. They were negotiating with Lee about a contract extension, but their feelings soured at one point. Players traded in the middle of a multiyear deal can request a trade. Lee's agent, Darek Braunecker, indicated after the Phillies acquired him that they would not seek compensation from the Phillies as a goodwill gesture to not exercise their right. Then they did.

"That sort of set everybody off," Proefrock said.

The Blue Jays made another offer: Drabek, d'Arnaud, Taylor, and Joe Blanton. It seemed more palatable to the Phillies, but they did not want to trade Blanton. He went 12–8 with a 4.05 ERA in 31 starts in 2009. He was not a top-of-the-rotation starter like Halladay, Lee, or Hamels, but he could pitch every five days and throw six innings. There was value in that.

"Blanton still had some thunder in him," Amaro said.

The Phillies convinced Toronto to remove Blanton, giving them a framework for a deal: Drabek, d'Arnaud, and Taylor for Halladay.

Now the hard part. The Phillies needed to accomplish three things before they crossed the finish line: 1) Halladay needed to agree to a contract extension, 2) he needed to pass a physical, 3) the Phillies needed to trade Lee. Montgomery told Amaro that he needed to trade somebody to restock the farm system. Nobody could fetch talent like Lee, who made only $9 million in 2009.

"It's something I didn't necessarily want to do," Amaro said. "That was kind of part of the deal. If you're going to keep dumping some of this talent out of the system, you better replenish. We had to answer to some people. It wasn't that we didn't want Cliff on our club and it wasn't that I didn't want a super rotation."

Back in Florida, Halladay, Brandy, and the boys boarded their boat at a nearby marina. They ordered pizza, made popcorn, and watched movies. They spent the night talking about the future. They wanted to play for the Phillies or Yankees, but if it could not happen, maybe they could play for the White Sox. The Sox won the AL Central in 2008 before losing 83 games in '09. But they loved Chicago. Brandy went to high school there. She knew people there. Could it work? Yes, they said. They could play for the White Sox for one year, then hit free agency, and choose where they wanted to play.

"It was just kind of the start of a transition," Brandy said.

The Halladays decided they would call Landry and tell him that they would accept a trade to Chicago. Halladay's phone rang first. Toronto had an agreement in place with the Phillies. They had a 72-hour window to agree to a contract extension. The Halladays flew to Philadelphia. Landry, Berry, and fellow CAA partner Brodie Van Wagenen joined them there.

"We landed, they took us off the back of the plane in a black car and drove us off the tarmac," Brandy said. "I'm like, 'Is this the CIA? What is this?'"

The Halladays pulled up to the Ritz-Carlton in Center City, checked into their room, and did not leave for two days. (If anybody called the hotel looking for him, they probably would not find him. Halladay frequently used the alias "Jim Nasium" when he stayed in hotels.) Landry, Berry, and Van Wagenen shuttled back and forth from the hotel to Citizens Bank Park, where they met with Amaro and Proefrock in a conference room outside Amaro's office. They negotiated with the Phillies for about an hour or so, then returned to the hotel to talk with the Halladays. They probably made four trips to the ballpark in two days.

CAA wanted Halladay to sign an extension that matched any potential contract he could sign if he hit free agency following the 2010 season. They looked for a five-year, $90 million extension (or $18 million per season), on top of the $15.75 million he would make in 2010. The Phillies said no. First, this was not a free-agent situation. Second, they had a policy of not signing a pitcher to more than three years. Amaro countered with a three-year offer worth about $54 million. CAA rejected it.

"There were choke points," said Van Wagenen, who left CAA to become the New York Mets' general manager before the 2019 season. "From the agent's perspective, you're working on trying to accomplish the goals for the player and the family. Now I have a perspective from a team's standpoint of negotiating on the other side of that. When you get to that point, you want the player. You want that player to be a part of your history. But it's high stress because you don't know the outcome. Everyone wants the same outcome at that point because you don't get that far if both sides don't want to make it happen. At the end of the day, from the agent's perspective, when you have two parties that want to make something happen, I always viewed that it was our job to make sure that happened."

Negotiations stalled and the Phillies became pessimistic. Proefrock suggested to Amaro that he circle back to Braunecker to heat up extension talks with Lee. Halladay sensed the stall too. He told his agents to forget the extra years and make something happen with three.

"When John Wayne wants to see this happen, you want to make this happen," Berry said.

Amaro made concessions. The extension had to average $20 million per season. The Phillies offered three years and $60 million. Halladay agreed. He passed his physical. The Phillies then rushed into a trade, shipping Lee to Seattle for prospects Phillippe Aumont, Tyson Gillies, and J.C. Ramírez. The deal flopped. Aumont had a 6.80 ERA in 46 career appearances in the big leagues. Gillies never reached the big leagues. Ramírez had a 4.71 ERA in 142 career appearances with five different organizations from 2013 to '19.

"My only regret is that we didn't take the appropriate time," Amaro said. "There was a feeling that if we allowed this to drift, the fans would have a tough time accepting it. Why would you now move this guy? So we had to make it sort of look like it was a three-way deal."

It was a bittersweet moment for Anthopoulos.

"Roy did everything," he said. "Whatever he needed to do, he tried and tried and tried and tried. For me, I look back on having generational talents like Roy Halladay and Carlos Delgado. We were never able to get to the playoffs. The shame of it for me is when you think of Roy Halladay and his greatest moments, you're thinking playoffs with the Phillies. It's not his fault. We never got those guys to that stage. When you talk about the legacies of players, it's just rare that you have a chance to have these guys. I'm really happy for him that he got his opportunity. You wish it would have been for a longer period of time at an elite level, but he had that opportunity on the big stage to do it and dominate and everybody appreciated how great he was."

On December 16, Halladay pulled on his Phillies jersey and cap at Citizens Bank Park. He smiled.

"This is where I wanted to be," he said.

| 14 |

Philly

RICH DUBEE THOUGHT A LOT about the questions he might ask Halladay when they met for the first time at the Phillies' spring training complex in Clearwater, Florida. After all, what does a pitching coach ask the best pitcher in baseball?

How can *he* help *him*?

Dubee figured that might be the best place to start.

"Okay, what do you need from me?" he said. "What can I do for you that you haven't been able to achieve?"

"I've never been able to elevate a fastball," Halladay said. "And I have no changeup."

Dubee had a jumping off point. They talked about Halladay's thought process when he tried to elevate a fastball. They discussed his past attempts to throw a changeup. Halladay estimated he threw no more than 50 changeups in any season, although data shows that he threw anywhere roughly 100–150 per season from 2006 to '08. Dubee mentioned that Phillies right-hander Kyle

Kendrick found success learning a split-changeup, spreading his fingers just beyond the narrowest seams of the baseball and throwing it with a loose hand and wrist. Kendrick learned the changeup because he was a one-pitch pitcher in the early part of his career. He needed an offspeed pitch to survive. Halladay, of course, had three elite-level pitches. He just wanted a fourth one.

"Okay, when I get throwing here we'll try it," Halladay said.

Spring training arrived in February 2010 and Halladay tried the grip that Dubee suggested. The pitch cut a little bit in the beginning, so Dubee had Halladay put more pressure on his index finger.

Halladay threw the pitch for a few days. He fell in love with it immediately.

"Hey," Halladay said. "I'm going to be able to do this."

"Doc," Dubee said, "you haven't even thrown it off a mound yet."

"No, I'm telling you," Halladay said. "I'm going to be able to do this."

"It wasn't like that deep split," Halladay told *The New York Times*' Tyler Kepner. "[José] Contreras threw a deep split, but for me it was just a comfortable split and I got right there with it and I was basically just pulling right down through it. We came over here and it was probably my second or third bullpen throwing it, all of a sudden, it was like…"

The ball tumbled.

"It was a lot like the one [Roger] Clemens was throwing later," Halladay said. "I think his was deeper but I remember him starting to throw it in New York. I didn't remember him having it that much in Toronto, so I picked it up late, I came over here and started throwing it and it was working in like the third bullpen. Once I took that into the season, it was a revival almost. I wasn't always as on when I was when I was younger, and it gave me more room for error, because I felt I always had at least two pitches that I could throw for a strike, and on the good days I had three and then I felt like I really had an advantage."

Halladay's attempt to elevate the fastball did not last as long. He tried to throw one in one of his earliest spring starts. A batter ripped the belt-high pitch for a double.

"That's it," Halladay said, returning to the dugout. "Elevation is out the door."

Dubee chuckled. Halladay was so good locating his pitches down in the zone and on the edges that he did not need to elevate his fastball, especially if he had a fourth pitch to keep hitters confused and frustrated.

Halladay's arrival sparked a buzz in Phillies camp, even for a team that won the 2008 World Series and 2009 National League pennant. Halladay had a presence about him. Even a clubhouse full of stars wondered if the stories about him were true. Phillies second baseman Chase Utley arrived at the ballpark early every morning. On his first morning of camp with Halladay, he walked into the clubhouse to find Halladay soaked in sweat.

"Was it raining when you got here?" Utley deadpanned.

"No," Halladay chuckled, appreciating his dry sense of humor. "I just finished my workout."

Halladay's early-morning workouts were not news to anybody that followed his career in Toronto, but playing in Canada meant playing under the radar, much like West Coast teams in the United States play in relative obscurity to East Coast teams. Shoot, president George W. Bush, who once owned the Texas Rangers, issued a qualifier in 2008, when Politico asked him about the pitcher and player he would build a franchise around.

"Roy Halladay from the Toronto Blue Jays is a great pitcher," Bush said. "He's a steady guy, he burns up innings."

Roy Halladay… from the Toronto Blue Jays.

Oh, *that* Roy Halladay.

It jumped out to folks in Canada, although to be fair, Bush said Utley "from the Philadelphia Phillies" would be his franchise position player.

"That's cool," Halladay said about Bush's endorsement. "Any time the leader of a country acknowledges you, it's cool."

Yeah, because that happens all the time.

Kendrick did not need the president to tell him about Halladay. He felt a connection to him before he arrived. KK joined the Phillies from Double-A Reading in June 2007, when the Phillies were desperate for starting pitching. He went 10–4 with a 3.87 ERA in 20 starts, helping the Phillies win their first National League East title since 1993. He threw mostly sinkers. It caught up to him in '08, when he went 11–9 with a 5.49 ERA and failed to make the postseason roster. Kendrick opened the '09 season in Triple-A. He knew Halladay's Dunedin story. He hoped he could help.

"What time do you get to the field?" Kendrick asked one morning.

"Probably around 5:30 or 5:45," Halladay said.

"Okay, can I start working out with you?" Kendrick said.

"Sure, no problem," he said. "Just get here early."

Kendrick did. He beat Halladay to the ballpark a couple times, which bothered him enough that he started to arrive earlier.

"You're not going to beat me," Halladay said.

He wasn't joking.

"It wasn't about getting there early," Kendrick explained. "It was just the time I got to be with him. It felt like our time. I could just pick his brain and talk baseball with him and just watch him work outside of being on the mound. It was something. I was excited to get to the field and see him work and just be with him. He came off as not a very talkative guy, outgoing guy, but he really was in those moments, in that time with me that we had. We talked about being sent down. We talked about pitching.

"Roy was always big on just being aggressive and strike one. Roy was always throwing strikes. He was always around the plate. I'm like, 'Roy, it's not that easy. Your stuff, you throw 95 and your stuff is always moving. I throw 88–90 and you're telling me to be aggressive.' He laughed. He's like, 'Well, you've got to pitch with what you have.' But he's right. You've got to be aggressive. When I was younger, I didn't trust my stuff as much as I probably should have. It's hard, you know. It's easy when you go out there when you have Roy's stuff. I had big league stuff, but it was mediocre. I wasn't an ace or Cy Young. He was like, trust your stuff, be aggressive, read swings, read hitters."

The Phillies were learning from Halladay, and Halladay was learning from them. The give and take included his work in the Phillies' training and weight rooms. Phillies strength and conditioning coordinator Dong Lien knew Halladay's reputation beforehand. He grew up in Winnipeg, Manitoba, and graduated from the University of Manitoba in 2003. Lien, like Dubee, met with Halladay before camp started. Halladay walked into the weight room with a thick binder full of notes that detailed his workouts with the Blue Jays. The papers went back years. Lien had never seen anything like it.

"I was absolutely impressed by it and as I think back to what he had in there, it shows how important it is just documenting things that go on regularly," he said. "Writing things down. How do you feel in each performance? What did you do leading up to it? Just preparation. He prepared better than most are able to."

Lien told Halladay to continue his routine, but in time he hoped to compliment or make subtle changes.

"If we need to add or subtract, we will along the way," Lien said.

Lien adjusted his schedule to make sure he arrived at the ballpark before Halladay. After all, somebody had to let him into the building. Even then, Halladay beat him there.

"I got up early and I didn't want to wait so I just headed over," Halladay explained.

"Now you look back and you think about the mindset and his focus for accomplishing amazing things," Lien said. "I learned a lot from that. Just taking care of his responsibilities, first and foremost."

Halladay considered one of his most important responsibilities to pitch deep into games, even when he did not feel his best. Lien watched Halladay build for those moments as soon as camp started. He watched him do lunges in between his first "up-down" bullpen session. The up-downs are meant to create the break a pitcher gets between innings. He is up when he is pitching, he is down when he is not.

"Doc, what's with the lunges?" Lien said.

"I want to mimic how my legs will feel in season," Halladay said.

Essentially, Halladay was turning his legs into Jell-O so he knew how to push through that feeling during the season.

"That's a mindset," Lien said. "That's through experience. That's through numerous spring trainings. He knew his body. He knew how his legs would feel in season. He understood how he would feel in season, and he was already applying it in spring training to make sure that he was not only physically able to get through it, but mentally get through it and perform well. And this was just throwing an up-down."

Phillies head athletic trainer Scott Sheridan went through the same process as Dubee and Lien. He met with Halladay before camp opened. They talked about the past. They discussed a plan of attack for the future. Sheridan offered suggestions based upon what he saw in Halladay's medical reports. He noticed a change in Halladay's posterior shoulder. The shoulder weakened over the years. It was nothing unusual or alarming, especially for somebody his age that had thrown as many innings as him, but Sheridan wanted to implement ways to keep Halladay's shoulder strong.

"He was really very responsive to that," Sheridan said. "I thought he would totally be like, 'Screw you guys, I'm Cy Young. You can't tell me anything.' But he was really open to us, just kind of talking to him. I think he was appreciative that we were willing to approach him. Some people wouldn't approach Roy, right? Even a pitching coach might be like, 'I'm going to mess with Roy?' But I can just remember making those changes and kind of being impressed with how he embraced it. I never had to go back and say, 'Hey, why aren't we doing this?' He was like, 'You said I need to do these. I'm going to go with this.'

"He knew how he would feel at every time of the year. He could tell you, like, 'Hey, in May I usually get this and I'm going to start to feel something here.' He just kind of had an idea of how his body was going to respond to 180-some games. He was just so in tune with his body. I don't know if everybody kind of had that ability to just know what's going on with their body. But then you're really thinking about, how do we get other guys to take part in what he's doing? How do you get them to value what we do? Then you see people buy in, like Kendrick. It's kind of like that fishtail that happens. People start to hear that Roy Halladay has this workout thing and people want to know what that is. Minor league kids are asking and they're talking to our trainers. And they're asking, 'What does he really do?' They really wanted to know, 'Is it true that he's in at that time?' Yeah, it is. So I think that whole persona came with it and I think it probably changed the culture of maybe somebody else in the minor leagues."

Halladay quickly settled into camp with his new teammates and new surroundings. His new clubhouse carried World Series expectations, but he embraced it. It was why he came, wasn't it?

"For me, the pressure part of it is what you perceive it to be," he said.

Halladay got asked about postseason hero Cliff Lee and Mets ace Johan Santana, who declared himself the best pitcher in the National League East. Could he be better than Lee? Did he know that he *needed* to be better than Lee? Lee had been amazing in the '09 postseason, and the Phillies traded him to Seattle to make room for him. If Halladay made the postseason with the Phillies, he needed to be better.

"I think that's what baseball is," Halladay said. "I think everybody is always comparing different players. I think that's how they decide who is the better player. That's always been the case, whether it's guys on the team being compared to you or other teams. That's part of it. It's nothing that, fortunately, I have to pay attention to."

And Santana's claim at being No. 1?

"I think it was a Lou Holtz quote, 'Well done is always more important than well said,'" Halladay said. "I've always tried to take that philosophy. I try to stay out of those things as much as possible."

Actually, famous Philadelphia resident Ben Franklin said that. Halladay spent only a few days in Philadelphia in December. He had been in a Phillies' uniform only a few days too. He had time to learn his new city.

PHILLIES CATCHER CARLOS RUIZ approached Halladay just before 10:00 AM on April 5, about three-and-a-half hours before the Phillies faced the Nationals on Opening Day at Nationals Park. Halladay had his headphones in. He was reading his notes on the Nationals' lineup. Ruiz told him that it was time to meet with Dubee to discuss the afternoon's plan of attack. Halladay did the talking, like he had for years with Toronto. He told Ruiz everything that he wanted to do. Chooch just needed to remember it. He did. Halladay allowed one run in seven innings in an 11–1 victory.

Halladay never shook off Ruiz.

"Not once," Ruiz said.

Halladay and Ruiz developed a rapport in the spring. Halladay was scheduled to pitch in a minor-league game against the Yankees in Tampa. Ruiz offered to drive. Halladay said okay.

"I want you to know how much I care about your success," Ruiz said. "I want you to succeed more than I want myself to succeed."

Halladay was floored. He had his guy.

"We had this mutual deal where he didn't want to let me down," Halladay said. "I didn't want to let him down, and it just kept growing. There were times when Charlie [Manuel] would come out to the mound and Chooch would come out and say, 'Don't let him take you out. Don't let him take you out.' And Charlie would get out there and say, 'How do you feel?' And I'd say, 'Charlie, you're not taking me out.' And Charlie would turn around and walk back and Chooch would go, 'Atta boy, let's go. Let's get 'em.' He was so inspirational and I felt like we were really one person working toward the same goal which is rare in a lot of teams.

"I had other guys who I trusted. I never had a guy where I felt like he was so much on the same page, so much thinking the way I was. And what was strange about him, compared to the other guys, is we would sit down and talk about a game plan. The other guys would stick to the game plan throughout the game. Carlos would stick to the game plan for the first four or five innings and then all of the sudden, he'd start changing things up. And that's where teams really got confused. And that, I think, is what led to most of the games I had there. He'd start calling pitches. He knew what I felt confident in that day and he would start doing things that we had never done before even in bullpens and knew that I trusted him. We were almost on the same page to the point that I felt like we didn't even need signs at times. And I would come up with a crazy thought and, sure enough, he would put down the finger. It was unbelievable. I'd never had that. They always stuck to the game plan, stuck to the game plan, stuck to the game plan. Chooch stuck with it and got creative. And that's what made him different."

Halladay allowed one unearned run in a complete-game 2–1 victory over the Astros at Minute Maid Park in Houston on April 11. Halladay returned to the visitors' dugout after the eighth inning having thrown 102 pitches.

"All right," Manuel said, indicating that Halladay was finished.

Halladay walked past Manuel with a look in his eye that said, "I'm finishing this game." He retired the Astros on nine pitches in the ninth.

"Okay, I see you," Manuel said.

"It's moments like those that made you realize we had all been around greatness," Phillies relief pitcher Chad Durbin said. "It was different with him to the point that, when you knew he was out there that day, as a sixth-seventh inning guy, there's really a good chance I don't throw that day unless it's extra innings. You couldn't bring that mentality in, but you found yourself letting your foot off the gas for just a second because he's good. It's rare that he didn't throw seven or eight innings. He was just that guy."

Halladay allowed two runs in eight innings in a win over Florida on April 16, his first start in Philadelphia. He threw a shutout in Atlanta on April 21. Manuel sent him to pitch the ninth with 101 pitches. He never considered pulling him.

"There wasn't nobody up," Manuel said. "They were all down there eating peanuts."

Durbin echoed Manuel's version of the story.

"There's not much to do but put the voicemail on the [bullpen] phone," he said.

Halladay was 6–2 with a 1.64 ERA in his first nine starts with the Phillies. He threw a shutout against the Mets on May 1—his second shutout in six starts—and allowed two runs in a complete-game loss to the Pirates on May 18. He threw 132 pitches in the loss, the second-highest pitch count of his career. Halladay threw 118 or more pitches in four consecutive starts. It was the first time in his career Halladay had done that. He was not concerned.

"I've learned to make the adjustment on my work days in between," he said. "If I throw more, I'll cut down on my bullpens. You've just got to know your body, and know when you need to step back."

Halladay followed those four starts with a heavy workload with his worst start with the Phillies. He allowed seven runs in 5⅔ innings against the Red Sox on May 23 at Citizens Bank Park. It snapped a streak of 17 consecutive starts of six or more innings. It was just the second time in his career that he pitched five or more innings with only one strikeout and it was his shortest start since August 19, 2009, against Boston.

It wasn't all Halladay's fault. Phillies third baseman Greg Dobbs let an inning-ending double play roll between his legs with the bases loaded and one out in the fourth inning, which allowed two runs to score.

"I just missed it," Dobbs said. "He made his pitch, I let him down."

Halladay allowed four more runs in the sixth before being pulled. Naturally, questions afterward centered around his recent workload. Maybe it had something to do with his struggles?

"Not a damn thing," Manuel said.

Halladay got upset at the suggestions too. He typically spoke in an even-keel manner after games, but not this time.

"Obviously, I've had games before when I haven't pitched well," Halladay said sarcastically. "It's a matter of getting back to what you do. And I didn't feel like we were far off today. It's part of the game. Those things happen. I'm pretty sure over the rest of my career, it's going to happen again."

Halladay took the loss personally. As he exited the game that afternoon, Halladay covered the dugout camera and looked into Manuel's eyes.

"I'm better than that," he said.

| 15 |

Four More Days

HALLADAY LEFT THE PHILLIES' dugout on May 23 and walked into the trainer's room to begin his post-start arm care. He never skipped this, even if he lost. He would feel unprepared for his next start if he did.

Phillies head athletic trainer Scott Sheridan waited for him. Halladay entered—often red-faced because he pushed his body to the limit—laid on the table, and waited for Sheridan to work on his shoulder and arm.

"If he took the 'L' it was the most miserable set of arm care you had to do ever," Sheridan said. "You couldn't talk to him. You didn't know what to say. You couldn't say, like, 'That sucked.' With Cliff [Lee] or somebody you could make a joke. Like, 'Man, you really sucked tonight.' Or like [Kyle] Kendrick would come in and mess with Cliff. Roy just came in and did his stuff. You could tell that he was still processing whatever went on in the game. He was still thinking about something."

Occasionally, Sheridan asked, "We're still doing 10 reps?" Other than that, nothing. Halladay wasn't an asshole about it. But following a start like the one he had against the Red Sox, he stewed. Sheridan finished his work, Halladay got up and he went through his normal routine with cuff weights and elastic tubing.

"It never really stopped for him," Sheridan said. "Like, for some starters it was—breathe—I've got four more days to get ready. This is no big deal. But it never really ended. There was never really that stopping point, you know? I'm going to grind through this."

Halladay visited strength and conditioning coordinator Dong Lien. If the start went well, Lien might ask, "How did you feel tonight, Doc?" Halladay might say he felt great or that his legs felt tired halfway through, so they needed to work on that before the next one. The conversation never lasted long. If he lost, it never happened.

"Once you've worked with the person, in spring training, each time he goes to battle, you learn his habits," Lien said. "If he's fuming, I'm going to start that conversation probably the next day with regards to how he felt. He doesn't like to lose. He took it to heart. He took every start to heart. The win was for the team. If he lost, he took accountability because he let the team down, even though a lot of things were out of his control. He took accountability and responsibility."

Phillies video coaching services manager Kevin Camiscioli emailed Halladay's notes on the hitters he expected to face in his next start. He downloaded video to Halladay's iPad. Camiscioli

Halladay faces the Yankees in a spring training game in March 1998. He made his big-league debut that September, nearly throwing a no-hitter in his second start. "I had no idea what I was doing," he said. (Scott Halleran/Allsport/Getty Images)

Halladay poses during spring training photo day in Dunedin, Florida, in February 1999. He entered the season with high expectations. "I just don't want them to become a burden for me," he said.
(Vincent Laforet/Getty Images)

Halladay makes the 2002 American League All-Star team. More important, he meets his mentor Harvey Dorfman that year. "That's what changed our lives," Blue Jays teammate and friend Chris Carpenter said. "Harvey's thoughts and just initiating the mental process—the mental part of the game is what changed both of our careers, I think." (Matthew Stockman/Getty Images)

Halladay pitched seven scoreless innings against the Orioles in Toronto on July 27, 2003. Afterward, he talks to his son Braden in the Blue Jays' dugout.
(Kevin Frayer/The Canadian Press via AP Photo)

Roy and Brandy smile during a January 2004 press conference in Toronto that announces his four-year, $42 million contract extension. He won the AL Cy Young Award in 2003. "That year, I really think, was the best year," Brandy said about 2003. (Aaron Harris/AP Photo)

Halladay asked Yankees closer Mariano Rivera to show him his cutter grip during the 2008 All-Star Game at Yankee Stadium. Rivera obliged. Halladay later traced his grip on a ball, so if he ever lost the feel for the pitch he could find it again.
(Rich Pilling/MLB via Getty Images)

Halladay's cutter. "You really have to monitor how you grip it," he said.
(Courtesy of MLB Productions)

Halladay's changeup, which teammates and opponents often called a splitter. "It's not a split," he said. (Courtesy of MLB Productions)

Halladay's curveball. "The big thing was just pulling straight down, letting it come off the top," he said. (Courtesy of MLB Productions)

Halladay's sinker. "The ones where it's a ball—it looks like a ball out of your hand and finishes as a strike—are really tough for hitters," he said. (Courtesy of MLB Productions)

Halladay pitches a complete game against the Royals on May 23, 2008, in Toronto. He had established himself as the best pitcher in baseball. "You look forward to the challenge, but you'd rather be facing somebody else," Yankees shortstop Derek Jeter said. (Mike Janes/Four Seam Images via AP Photo)

Halladay hugs Carlos Ruiz following the final out of his perfect game on May 29, 2010, in Miami. "After the game was over, it was gone," Halladay said. "After that game was over, was like, 'I just want to go home and sleep.'" (Wilfredo Lee/AP Photo)

Halladay hugs Ruiz following the final out of his no-hitter in Game 1 of the 2010 National League Division Series. "The fun was in the process," Halladay said. "The fun was in the journey. That's what I enjoyed." (Rob Carr/AP Photo)

Jayson Werth pours champagne over Halladay's head after the Phillies clinched the 2010 National League East title. "It's only going to get funner," Halladay said. (Evan Vucci/AP Photo)

Halladay poses with his 2010 National League Cy Young Award at Citizens Bank Park in April 2011 (Matt Slocum/AP Photo)

Halladay, accompanied by Brandy, Braden, and Ryan, is honored during a pregame ceremony in August 2010, celebrating his perfect game against the Marlins. (Matt Rourke/AP Photo)

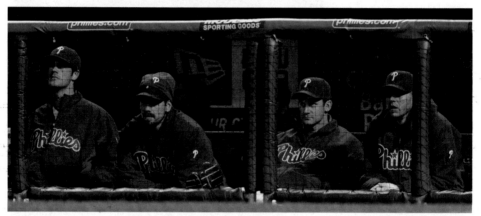

(L-R) Cole Hamels, Cliff Lee, Roy Oswalt, and Halladay in 2011 made up one of the greatest rotations in baseball history. The season ended in stinging defeat to Chris Carpenter and the Cardinals in the NLDS. "That was the start of the end," Brandy said. (Miles Kennedy/Philadelphia Phillies/Getty Images)

Halladay announces his retirement during the winter meetings in Lake Buena Vista, Florida, in December 2013. Brandy, Braden, and Ryan attended. "They're starting to strive for their dreams," Halladay said about his boys, "and that's something I want to be a part of." (John Raoux/AP Photo)

Brandy wipes away tears at Halladay's "Celebration of Life" service at Spectrum Field in Clearwater, Florida, a week after he died in a plane crash on November 7, 2017. "We miss him," Brandy said. "But we still have so much of him." (Yong Kim/ *The Philadelphia Inquirer* via AP Photo)

(L-R) Braden, Ryan, and Brandy walk onto the field at Rogers Centre in Toronto for a ceremony to honor Halladay on March 29, 2018. The Blue Jays retired Halladay's No. 32. (Nathan Denette/The Canadian Press via AP Photo)

Brandy speaks on her late husband's behalf at the Hall of Fame's induction ceremony in Cooperstown, New York, on July 21, 2019. "I think that Roy would want everyone to know that people are not perfect," Brandy said. (Hans Pennink/AP Photo)

Halladay leaves the National League's dugout before the 2010 All-Star Game in Anaheim, California. "I love the saying, 'Men don't differ in their desire to win, they differ in the price they are willing to pay in order to have a chance to win.' Just a chance. So what's the price you guys are willing to pay to have a chance to be in the big leagues, to win at the big-league level, to be an All-Star, to have a long career?"
(Michael Zagaris/Getty Images)

never knew when Halladay might want his notes and videos. He made certain he never asked.

"It was almost like the last out of the game—boom—send," Camiscioli said. "It was kind of funny, just knowing how he was. That start's over, what's next?"

Halladay had an extra day before his next start against the Marlins in Miami on May 29, but his five-day routine was a thing of beauty. Halladay knew those days like the back of his hand. Everybody else knew them too.

"It was like clockwork," Phillies center fielder Shane Victorino said. "The day after he pitched I [knew] where I could find him at 12:38 and 30 seconds. Wherever we were, he was going to be in whatever facility doing his exercises."

Day 1

"That was the killer day," Lien said.

It had not changed much since Halladay's Blue Jays days. He arrived at the ballpark between noon and one and ran, but not like he had with Donovan Santas. Halladay was older. He managed his body differently. Lien convinced Halladay to scale back the frequency, distance, and duration of his runs. Halladay still took Lien on road runs. He could not wait to show him his trail in Toronto. They ran together along the waterfront in San Francisco. Toward the end of the run, on the way back to the ballpark, a runner surprised Halladay and sprinted past him.

"It set him off," Lien said.

Halladay ran him down.

"You're the rabbit and I'll try to keep up with you," Lien said.

Halladay ran ballpark ramps and stairs, like he had in the past. He liked to tell Lien how Roger Clemens did lunges up stadium ramps on game days. But some days Halladay just rode a bike or used the elliptical, depending on how he felt. They added frisbee into his routine. They took an Aerobie, picked a spot on the field, and counted their throws to that spot, like golf. They ran between throws. They played 30–40 minutes.

"There was always some competition," Lien said. "He'd always say, 'Do you think we could throw the frisbee from one side to the other side of the ballpark? From the highest point? Can we get it across?' We'd try. It took away from the monotony of training, but it was still training. If at any time he didn't feel like it was enough, then he'd go out and run. Not extra on top of the frisbee, but it would be, 'Hey, today I'm going to run,' or, 'Today I'm going to bike because I need to scale back.' It's always what's best for his body and in preparation for his start."

Halladay lifted weights, initially working off the exercises in his binder from Toronto. The sets and reps were based upon how he felt. If he felt strong or tired he adjusted. He did abdominal work.

Part of the reason Halladay arrived so early to the ballpark in spring training and in the regular season is because he preferred to work alone. He wanted an empty weight room, so he would not wait for a machine or have to talk to anybody.

"He wanted to work with intensity," Lien said.

Sheridan worked with Halladay on Day 1 too. They did shoulder stretches, manual therapy and soft tissue work. Halladay used a Bodyblade, a device that uses oscillation to strengthen the rotator cuff. He performed ball-hold exercises to strengthen his forearms, dropping an unweighted ball from different positions and catching it. He exercised with a dowel rod, which worked his forearms. Everything was meant to strengthen the shoulder, forearms, wrists, etc.

Halladay long tossed to keep his arm loose.

Day 2

Halladay had his bullpen session. It started with long toss around 3:30 PM, for a 7:00 PM game, although he always seemed to be on the field 10 to 15 minutes early.

Halladay's bullpens amazed Phillies pitching coach Rich Dubee. Doc had the ability to repeat his delivery with the precision of a surgeon. Halladay's first step off the rubber with his left foot and the spot the foot landed after he delivered the pitch hit the same spots every time.

"You know how fine it is to put a spike in the same hole? That's how precise he was," Dubee said. "A lot of pitchers, they're missing by a couple inches and missing out in front in where they land. His spike marks, when he was locked in and he had his steps right and his rhythm right, you could basically clean the bullpen mound with a toothbrush. I mean, really, you could fill those holes with a toothbrush instead of a rake."

Halladay's first step back off the rubber got too long against the Red Sox. It threw off his balance and rhythm. He liked to keep his weight over the rubber. But because he stepped back too far, everything shifted. His shoulders went back. His head went back. He lost his balance. Phillies left-hander Jamie Moyer noticed the problem. Halladay and Dubee cleaned it up.

Often, Halladay figured out his problems on his own.

"He was his own best pitching coach," Dubee said. "He knew himself, he had learned himself, he had body awareness and feel. He had the ability to understand when something wasn't right and the ability to put it back together and get it working again. He was probably the toughest challenge to watch warm up. You're trying to watch a guy's delivery and watch where he is and everything and there were times that he was so flawless that you'd become mesmerized just watching him. Just watching the execution, you'd say, 'Holy cow.'"

Phillies bullpen coach Mick Billmeyer caught Halladay in the pen. He squatted behind the plate and practically fell asleep because the ball hit his glove every time. It was easy.

Halladay started his session from the windup. He threw his sinker to both sides of the plate, his cutter to both sides of the plate, and his changeup to both sides of the plate. He threw his curveball too, but sometimes he skipped his breaking ball to reduce the reps and strain on his arm. He then threw from the stretch: sinker to both sides, cutter to both sides, and changeup to both sides. He finished from the windup with a sinker to his arm side and a sinker to his glove side.

Finished.

"It's something that good players develop," Dubee said. "They develop a regimen and a routine. You know younger pitchers might panic if they're not getting a fastball to a certain location. Doc never really panicked. He'd knew he'd find it. He'd work his way through it."

If Halladay threw a lot of pitches in his last start—or if he had two or three long starts in a row—he might play catch on flat ground and skip the bullpen entirely.

"When I talk about a pitching coach's dream, he wasn't only aware of his schedule and everything, he was aware of how his body felt," Dubee said. "If he felt like, 'Okay, I can cut back a little bit, I'm pretty locked in, I can preserve some bullets here and I don't really need to get out on a mound and start grinding after going so long in other starts.'"

Halladay ran after he threw in the bullpen, but it was lighter than Day 1. He did an upper-body workout. Its intensity depended on his bullpen session. If he did not feel great, he skipped the dumbbell free weights, choosing elastic tubing instead.

He always worked out to music. Halladay requested music by decade, depending on his mood.

"How about some '70s today?" he said.

Imagine Halladay pumping iron to Player's "Baby Come Back" or 10cc's "I'm Not In Love."

"It might be the saddest love song, but he was so locked in that it didn't matter," Lien said.

Day 3

Halladay played catch. He did agility work in the outfield.

"I'd feel bad sometimes for the grounds crew because we'd beat up the grass," Lien said. "But it needed to get done. He's Doc. This is one of the best."

Halladay's agility work, like everything else, served a purpose. He not only wanted to pitch well, he wanted to field his position well. Lien and Halladay mixed up the agility workouts. It might be a ladder drill. It might be a box drill. It might be a "5-10-5," which had Halladay moving laterally and changing direction. Lien either rolled or threw a ball to him. It put Halladay through the physical demands of lateral movements and changes of direction, while concentrating on catching a ball.

"He's constantly pushing himself from a physical and mental standpoint," Lien said.

Halladay ran 10 long strides from a foul pole to center field, mixing in the frisbee more and more.

"It forced me to throw well," Lien said. "If he's going to run 100 yards, I better throw it to him dead on. If it's not, you're making him do extra running. That is pressure."

Halladay started to penalize Lien for bad throws: 10 pushups.

"Accountability there too," Lien said.

Halladay did shoulder work, the Bodyblade, and wall dribbles, which was tapping a ball across a wall. The Phillies identified when they got him that his right shoulder was a touch lower than the left. They hoped the exercises could improve that. Halladay talked to people these days. He loved talking about his passions: family, flying, fishing, and food.

"He had a spot in Media," Sheridan said about the Philadelphia suburb. "Wimpy's. He'd go get a Wimpy's burger. Of all the things you'd think would excite somebody, a Wimpy's burger for Roy Halladay. But that was his thing. He always had some gadget he was messing with, flying around in the training room. I remember he had one of those big-ass helicopters in the training room and it's blowing the ceiling tiles up."

Halladay always had model airplanes or helicopters at his locker. He flew them at ballparks for years. One afternoon in Toronto he tried to get two planes in the air at the same time. He handed the controls to one of the planes to Donovan Santas, who never flew one before.

"I don't know what I'm doing," he said.

"Just keep it in the air. Just keep flying circles," Halladay said.

Santas kept flying circles, but the plane kept flying higher each lap around the ballpark, which had its retractable roof closed.

"Doc, I'm losing, I'm losing, I'm losing it," Santas said.

"Turn it! Turn it! Turn it!"

Santas flew the plane straight into a metal grate that hung in front of the Jumbotron. Santas sheepishly retrieved the remnants near a tour group that watched the entire thing happen. One afternoon in Philadelphia, Frank Coppenbarger and Halladay attached Ryan Howard's pay stub to the bottom of his helicopter. Howard signed a five-year, $125 million contract extension in April 2010, and Coppenbarger liked to have fun with it. Sometimes he put the check on a cart and pretended to struggle to push it. Halladay flew the check into the food room, where Howard was sitting at a table eating lunch. He landed it there.

"Airmail," Howard said, laughing.

Day 4

Halladay played catch, sometimes with Lien.

"That day was lighter for most people," Lien said, "but he didn't want it to be. He just wanted to make sure that he was moving around. Nothing long duration, short duration. A last-minute check to see how his body is feeling that day. There's a checklist. My legs are a bit tight, then I need to do more stretching. Making sure he's hydrated for the next day's start. He's fueling with food, hydration. He taught me a lot. Things we may not have considered at the time, but just the importance of being mindful. A day before my start, just making sure that I've addressed nutrition needs, hydration needs, recovery needs, video preparation. It was strategic."

Halladay spent time in his hyperbaric chamber, but he spent most of Day 4 in the video room. Many times it was just Halladay, Chase Utley, and Camiscioli.

"What was funny was it became Doc and Utley kind of going head to head, staring at the monitors and looking for anything and everything mortals can't see," Camiscioli said. "They were two students of the game with a tremendous amount of respect for the game."

Halladay and Utley typically worked in silence, which surprised nobody that knew them. But occasionally one of them asked a question about something they saw on their screen.

"Hey, Chase," Halladay said.

"Yeah?"

"What do you think about this?"

Utley's ability to uncover how pitchers tipped pitches was legendary. He could spend hours in the video room looking for a subtle movement that would give himself and his teammates an edge. When he found something, he froze the image on the screen, stood up and walked out of the room.

"We would talk about giving away pitches from a hitter's standpoint, what a hitter could see on him," Utley said. "So we talked about that a lot. He was always picking my brain on things he could do to essentially keep from tipping his pitches."

Halladay had been throwing his changeup only a couple months, when he prepared for his start against the Marlins. Utley picked up something early.

"His split, he would tip," Utley said. "His glove would change shape a bit early on, but he cleaned it up."

"Those two guys, I mean, there will never be guys like that," Phillies right fielder Jayson Werth said. "What I've seen—and I've played with a lot of guys on a lot of teams—preparation-wise, no one comes close to Roy Halladay and Chase Utley. They were the most prepared guys on the field every day. You try to have a conversation with those guys and forget it. But you put them in the video room and they can't shut up."

Halladay might spend 90 minutes to two hours in the video room. He took breaks to get lunch.

"Or who knows? Maybe run 10 miles or something," Camiscioli said.

Day 4 was not Halladay's only day to study—he typically went through three hitters a day—but this was his final opportunity to review. He kept notes in his notebooks on every hitter. He constantly rewrote them. Camiscioli eventually digitized them. If Chris Carpenter faced the same team recently, Halladay watched that video because they were so similar. Halladay watched other right-handers too, along with his most recent plate appearances against each hitter. Hitters change. If they adjusted, Halladay found out.

"For me, I wanted to see—when in doubt—where can I throw my fastball to this guy?" Halladay said. "It's either usually in or away. If I have to throw a fastball in a 3-2 count, where can I throw it and not get killed? And then I wanted to know if he was better hitting a curveball or a changeup. It was very simple. I would do that, but I wouldn't cheat myself. I made sure I got every guy on the roster."

The notes were remarkably detailed. Here is what Halladay had for Braves slugger Freddie Freeman and Brian McCann before a game on July 8, 2011, at Citizens Bank Park. Freeman was a rookie then.

FREEMAN (L)

FB—cutt deep up in quick down in on plate, sink in edge must be in for freeze. Sink away down and expand will chase off, he's good sink away up on plate. Back door cutt edge ok.
CB—cb very good early and often. Back door down middle down bounce and back foot big bounce.
CH—CH very good work down all across will wrist flip up middle and away

"He's saying he can cut balls in and away, early-count curveballs away, changeup's down and away," Freeman said. "That's spot on. That's why he's in the Hall of Fame. He did this. He could have easily said, 'Oh, he's a rookie. I'll just go with what I want.' He still took time to write down what he thought. That's the thing. If I start doing something he can go in and change his notes."

Freeman batted .500 (8 for 16) with three home runs, nine RBIs, three walks, and two strikeouts in his career against Halladay. He homered off Halladay in the first pitch he ever saw against him (a cutter) in a pinch-hit at-bat on September 21, 2010. It was the first homer of Freeman's career.

"I got him in the Cy Young Award era for a couple years, but I wish I could have faced him all the way through his career," Freeman said. "I think it would have been a great battle. Those were the games I was just trying to get a broken-bat hit. You're really just grinding for a walk. What made him tough is that every pitch was competitive. When you throw 110 pitches, most of the guys now are throwers. You're throwing 80 pitches that are competitive and the other 30 are balls right out of the hand. It's nothing. It's just like a pointless pitch. If he throws sinker in, it's almost enough to make you swing at it. If it's a changeup away, it's on the right plane where you like, 'Is that going to stay up?' No, it's gone. Now you're 0-1 because you swung at it. Curveballs were always in the strike zone or below. Every pitch was competitive. That's what separates guys from good to great."

McCANN (L)
Timing hitter.
FB— Quick belt in, cutt in above at hands or back foot get deep. sink away OK down, down is key will expand off. Back door cutt edge ok. Sink in edge only after cutt.
CB— CB very good all along bottom big expand chases, CB early and often, OK on back door hangers work down.
CH— CH down away must be to expand, very good FB counts.

"Bulldog," McCann said. "He tried to get you out within the first couple pitches. He came right at you. He made you hit his pitch. When you're that good you've got to pick a side of the plate. You can't cover both sides with No. 1's. Pick a side, wherever you think he's going to go and try to guess along with him."

Halladay studied on the plane too. The Phillies flew to Miami from New York on May 27. Most teammates watched movies, played cards, or slept. Halladay had two iPads and his notebooks spread across the tray tables in front of him. The iPad on the left had each hitter's last 20 plate appearances against right-handed pitchers. The iPad on the right had Halladay's last 10 plate appearances against each hitter. The dueling screens allowed him to study how each hitter approached right-handers most recently and how he attacked them most recently. If a hitter moved closer to the plate since the last time he faced him, he knew it and he adjusted.

"He's playing boureé, it just happens to be baseball and scouting," Chad Durbin said.

Halladay and Durbin had similar arsenals, although Durbin did not have the same stuff. But because they shared something in common he often sat behind Halladay on the plane and peeked over his shoulder.

"I felt guilty," Durbin said. "I'd be like, 'These are the guys in the lineup that I'll probably face.' We had the same arsenal so we'd talk. I loved doing that. I'd pick his brain and stand next to him in the outfield. In those moments you just saw how he forgot where he was, what he was doing. He just wanted to talk baseball. So we'd talk about what shape we want that cutter to be to Daniel Murphy vs. someone who might drop down and get it. It was never just, 'I think we need to throw a cutter.' It was two balls above his belt, in the top of the zone, or miss off. Or, 'I want my sinker to be flat against this guy, not depth.' And he could make the ball do that stuff. He was just better at it than anyone. But knowing that stuff made all of us better. I'd watch him pitch from the bullpen and I'd know how to attack hitters and I'd have no questions about his convictions because I knew how hard he worked at it. I'd be like, 'How do you get this guy out right now? I haven't seen his last 10 at-bats.' And he'd go, 'I just looked at them.' And he's dead-on."

Halladay spent the week preparing physically and mentally for the Marlins. He was ready.

| 16 |

Perfection

HALLADAY NEVER EXPECTED to become the 20th pitcher in baseball history to throw a perfect game. If he expected to throw one May 29 in Miami, he would have told his family to fly in from Tampa to watch.

He told everybody to stay home instead.

"There's no point," he told Brandy. "It's a crappy stadium. There's nobody there. There's nothing for the kids to do."

He wasn't wrong, so Brandy and the boys spent the weekend at home. Halladay got to Sun Life Stadium early that afternoon with a chip on his shoulder. He pitched poorly in his last start against the Red Sox. He got questioned about being overworked and needing rest. It fueled him. He wanted to set the tone and attack the strike zone from the very first pitch. His teammates assumed his personality.

"You were a different person on the day he pitched because of how much it meant to him and how serious it was to him," Jayson

Werth said. "Cliff Lee was out there blowing bubbles or whatever, so you were really loose. He's throwing wads of paper into the trash can for $100, 20 minutes before the game. You're like, 'Oh, Cliff's pitching today. Oh, so it is his day.' But with Doc, you ran into him in the clubhouse, it was like, 'Wow. We're not fucking around today.' So you knew early in the day where you were at. It made those games a bit more—not tight or tense—but it made them different. You knew from early on what was going on. And it was really awesome to play under those circumstances with a guy who it meant so much to. He puts his whole heart and soul into what he does. And you play all these games all these days and sometimes you just go through the motions. But when you have a guy like that, it puts you on your heels a little bit like, 'Hey, motherfucker. This is my day.' It's cool."

Halladay studied his iPad and notes one final time. He met with Rich Dubee and Carlos Ruiz to discuss the game plan. He got into the weight room around 5:00 PM to begin his prep work. Dong Lien stretched him at 6:00. He met Dubee and Ruiz in the dugout for the walk to the bullpen at 6:30.

Then it started.

He struck out Chris Coghlan looking on a 3-2 cutter for the first out in the first inning. Coghlan flung his bat toward the Marlins' dugout. He thought the pitch missed the plate and he walked. Gaby Sánchez struck out swinging on a 2-2 curveball and Hanley Ramírez grounded out to end the inning. Ramírez, like Coghlan, thought he walked, when a 3-1 cutter hit the outside corner.

Halladay struck Jorge Cantú swinging on a 3-2 sinker and Dan Uggla swinging on a 2-2 curveball for the first two outs in the second. Cody Ross grounded out to third baseman Juan Castro to end the inning. Cole Hamels and Jamie Moyer sat together on the far right side of the visitors' dugout. They thought Doc did not look sharp, throwing 31 pitches and getting into three three-ball counts in two innings. Halladay had trouble gripping the ball. It was 85 and humid. He wiped his hand on his pants after every pitch.

"He was dripping wet," Chase Utley said.

The Phillies took a 1–0 lead in the third when Utley poked a line drive to center field. Marlins center fielder Cameron Maybin misjudged it. He took a few steps in, only to realize Utley got more of the ball than he thought. He jumped, but the ball tipped out of his glove and rolled to the warning track. Wilson Valdez scored from first. Utley cruised into third. Halladay needed nine pitches to finish the third and 12 pitches to finish both the fourth and fifth innings. He found his groove. He threw his sinker, cutter, curveball, and changeup for strikes.

Phillies general manager Rubén Amaro Jr. joined his half-brother and a friend behind home plate early in the game. They chatted for four innings, but when Amaro looked at the scoreboard in the fifth to see zeros next to the Marlins' line score it hit him.

"I don't know if they've had any base runners," he said.

Amaro and his brother said nothing the rest of the night. The pitchers in the Phillies' bullpen said nothing, either.

"We didn't even stretch," Chad Durbin said.

Marlins catcher Brett Hayes struck out swinging on a 0-2 changeup to start the sixth. Maybin chopped a ball to Valdez, who fired a strong throw to first to get the speedy runner by a half step.

"When I hit a ball like that I always smell a base hit," Maybin said. "He made a great play, great throw."

Josh Johnson flew out to Raúl Ibañez in left field to end the inning.

"We were in the sixth inning and I just sat there and I thought to myself, 'Man, the game's moving kind of quick,'" Phillies first baseman Ryan Howard said. "And then all of a sudden it was, 'Hmm, I don't think there's been any hits.' And then I was like, 'Matter of fact, I don't know if there's been anyone on base.' I turned around and looked and saw zeros all across the board and I was like, 'Oh, I probably shouldn't have done that.' Not that you're not in it before, but you get into that heightened state of like—boom—you try to get that extra adrenaline to try and go and make an extra play."

"In the sixth inning like, 'Oh, shit,' someone mentioned it," Utley said. "I was locked-in before, but now I'm ultra locked-in."

Halladay struck out Coghlan looking on a 2-2 cutter to start the seventh. He did not like that call, either. He complained to home plate umpire Mike DiMuro. Sánchez flied out to Ibañez and Ramírez struck out looking on a 3-2 cutter on the inside corner to end the inning. Ramírez stood at home plate in disbelief. He thought he walked again.

"In the third inning, I was aware that I hadn't allowed a baserunner," Halladay said. "Earlier than you'd think, right? But it wasn't until the seventh that I started to think something special could happen, and it wasn't until two outs in the ninth that I didn't feel there was still a long way to go."

The Phillies knew they had something special brewing too.

"Oh my God," Ruiz said.

"You knew what was on the line," Werth said. "They say you don't talk about perfect games, you don't talk about no-hitters. By the third, fourth, fifth inning, if you have a pulse you know what's going on. And you don't want to be the guy who blows it."

Phillies clubhouse manager Phil Sheridan was down the third-base line in the stands with his kids, watching the game as a fan. He got into the ballpark late, so he asked the person in front of him in the third or fourth inning if anybody reached base. It was Plácido Polanco's cousin. He told Sheridan that somebody reached in the first, but got picked off. In the seventh, Sheridan texted Phillies media relations manager Kevin Gregg in the press box.

"Is this perfect or a no-no?"

"Perfect," Gregg replied. "Leave me alone."

Cantú ripped a 2-1 sinker that one-hopped to Castro to start the eighth. It was the hardest hit ball of the night. Castro dropped to the dirt as he fielded the ball and threw to first for the first out.

"I dove, I threw to first and we threw the ball around and I was the last to receive it and I gave it to Doc and he kind of acknowledged me," Castro said. "He wasn't very verbal, but he kind of looked at me."

Atta boy, atta boy.

Castro puffed out his chest a little bit. Phillies manager Charlie Manuel started Castro at third because Polanco had a sore right elbow and Greg Dobbs let an inning-ending double play roll between his legs in Halladay's last start. Manuel said that Dobbs' error was on his mind when he made the lineup that night. He wanted Halladay to have the best defense possible. Still, it was

Castro's first start at third base that season and only his third start there since 2007.

Uggla struck out looking on a 2-2 sinker on the outside corner for the second out. It was Halladay's 10th strikeout. Ross popped up to Valdez to end the inning. Halladay had thrown 103 pitches.

"I was at a horse show," Brandy said. "Our kids were actually with my brother, who lived around the corner. We went to a friend's house to barbeque. We were just kind of sitting there, grilling and watching the game. The game was on, but I was kind of checking in and whatever and kind of watching. And then after a while it's like, 'Okay, okay.' Still watching. After a while I'm like, 'Okay, okay, okay.' By the sixth inning I thought if I sat down and really watch I'm going to ruin this so I'm trying to do other things. I'm like pacing around. I didn't want to sit down and hyperfocus on it because I thought I was going to mess it up or something."

Halladay stood in the on-deck circle in the top of the ninth, ready to hit if Ruiz reached base. He did not. Halladay returned to the dugout, removed his batting gloves and helmet, and put his bat back in the bat rack. He grabbed his glove and cap and emerged to cheers. The Marlins had more than 35,000 fans at the ballpark, but only because they had a postgame concert. They still knew what was happening.

The Marlins sent three pinch-hitters to the plate in the ninth because they had to try something—give Halladay a different look, make him think a little bit, maybe get lucky. Mike Lamb pinch-hit for Hayes. He ripped a 2-1 cutter to the warning track in center field, but Shane Victorino settled underneath it and caught it.

"I was hoping for some wind," Lamb said.

One out.

"I was nervous on every single play," Victorino said. "But on the flip side, I wanted the ball hit to me on every single play too. I was like, hit it out here, please. I want to make every out. But yeah, of course you're nervous because anything can happen. In a perfect game everything has to go right."

Wes Helms pinch-hit for Maybin. He struck out looking on a 1-2 cutter. It was Halladay's 11th and final strikeout.

Two outs.

"I think once you think it's possible, it's probably two outs in the ninth," Halladay said. "Up to that point you're aware of it, but it's never something you think is possible. But really, once I got the two outs, I felt like I had a chance."

Ronny Paulino pinch-hit for Leo Núñez. The Phillies had Paulino in spring training in 2009 before trading him to the Giants for left-hander Jack Taschner. Amaro could not help but think about Paulino ruining Halladay's bid for perfection.

"If this guy breaks up... I will... what an idiot," Amaro said.

Castro removed his glove as Paulino walked to the plate. He looked at the scoreboard and saw zeros.

"My hands started sweating," he said. "That's about the only time I was a little nervous playing defense. But I remember—I have to change my mentality, I have to change my mind. So I remember I grabbed some dirt, put my glove back on, and said, 'Hit it over here.'"

Paulino fouled off a first-pitch sinker and took a changeup for a ball to even the count at 1-1. He fouled off a second changeup for strike two. Halladay got the sign from Chooch. He wanted a curveball. Halladay started his windup for his 115th pitch of the night. He threw it. Paulino swung and hit the ball toward the hole between shortstop and third. Castro broke to his left.

"I knew it wasn't going to be easy," he said. "My first reaction is I've got to get to the ball, I've got to catch it, I've got to catch it first."

He caught it. Now he needed to make a strong throw. As his momentum carried him toward second base, he knew he could make a strong throw if he spun.

"You learn how to catch a ball there and turn," he said. "As you get older and become a professional you start learning with your coaches that the easiest way—depending on the situation and the ground ball—is going that way to my left and throwing that way. It's kind of hard to stop and put my feet in the right position. So it's easier for me to turn around because it was a ball in the hole. If it was close I could have set my feet, but because I had to stretch for the ball I could control my body more, spin, and throw to first rather than try to go the opposite way."

Halladay turned his body and followed the play. He spent the past nine years following Harvey Dorfman's mantra that a pitcher only controls the ball until the moment it leaves his hand. After that, anything can happen. The ball left Castro's hand. Halladay's eyes followed it the entire way. It hit Howard's glove. He squeezed it.

Game over.

Perfection.

Halladay punched his right hand into his glove. He smiled, opened his arms, and embraced Ruiz, who sprinted to meet him. Howard and Castro joined. Everybody else did too.

Ibañez ran into the scrum from left field.

"I remember running—not running alongside Victorino because he was too fast—but running toward the pile and feeling like I was 10 years old," he said. "Just running toward the mound feeling like I was 10 years old for a game in May. And I remember just feeling like we won the World Series because it happened for him and he deserved it. Because of the intensity, the focus, the preparation, the execution. He was everything that was right about the game of baseball."

"As I saw Howard catch the ball, I felt like something left my body," Castro said. "*Yeah!* A lot of people ask me what I was feeling. Sometimes you've got to be there to feel it. But for me it was a big accomplishment and I was happy to be able to contribute to something. After the third out, it was that relief like, 'Yes, I helped! Yes, he did it! Yes, we did it!' I felt like a kid afterward. I have people send me that video a lot. It'll be there forever. It's good, you know why? At some point I'm not going to be on this Earth and maybe the sons of my sons will be watching that and say, 'That's my grandpa.'"

Brandy and the boys celebrated back home.

"I can't believe I just saw this," she said. "It was the 20th time in history you've seen that. That was the 20th time. It was the first one I'd seen. It was so cool. I didn't really even understand how amazing it was until after. You don't really think about, 'Hey, I really want to throw a perfect game someday.' That's no humans goal ever. Nobody. Fewer people have thrown perfect games than have been in the Hall of Fame, and we know how rare that is. It really was special and exciting."

Howard tapped Halladay's chest a few times to get his attention. He had the ball in his glove and he wanted him to have it. Halladay did not notice. He was lost in the moment. Imagine that. Halladay finally turned to Howard, who stuck the ball in his glove. They smiled and embraced again.

Amaro bawled and hugged his brother in the stands. He made his way into the visitors' clubhouse. He saw Ruiz.

"¡Que clase de caballo!" Chooch shouted. "¡Que clase de caballo! ¡Este de verdad es un caballo!"

What a horse! What a horse! This is really a horse!

Phillies' broadcaster Gary Matthews interviewed Halladay on the field. The ballpark's lights turned off. Fireworks shot into the air. The concert started. Halladay returned to the clubhouse.

"Speech! Speech!" a few players yelled.

Halladay walked over to Ruiz and pointed.

"Chooch is the man," Halladay said, still smiling.

"He smiled!" Victorino yelled.

Everybody laughed and cheered.

"I followed him the whole time," Halladay said, talking over the laughter and applause. "I swear to God, so…"

He threw up his arms.

"I don't know what else to say," he said.

He pointed again at Chooch, mumbled something, and walked away.

Halladay began his post-start arm care. He held a press conference after that.

"Like clockwork, bro," Victorino said. "Typical Doc. Postwork was him being the best him."

"If he didn't do that stuff, days like that wouldn't happen," Brandy said. "That's why they happened. Because he was so diligent in his workouts. You don't do that so you can win. You do that so you're prepared for whatever happens. He wasn't going to be prepared for that if he hadn't done that work the day before or the day before that or the day before that. So that side of him never changed, that workout. They say he was maniacal about it. You did your job and that's what you did."

The Marlins dug up the pitcher's rubber so Halladay could have it. Vice president Joe Biden called to congratulate him. Eventually, Halladay spoke to Brandy, Braden, and Ryan on the phone.

"You're the 20th pitcher ever to throw a perfect game!" Braden screamed.

Halladay cracked up.

"He obviously was paying attention to what they said on TV," he said.

Dubee asked Doc later why he threw Paulino back-to-back changeups. It was his fourth-best pitch and he threw it *twice* in the final at-bat to lock down a perfect game.

"I'm a big believer that if you're going to get beat, you get beat with your best stuff," Dubee said. "He said, 'Listen, I really felt like at that time it was the best pitch for me to throw to him. I knew if I executed it the way I can, he was out.' And that was the commitment he had to every pitch he threw."

Halladay boarded the bus back to the team's hotel at 10:45 PM He returned to the ballpark at 8:45 AM the next day. He had work to do.

"I had two or three [games] where I had gotten in the eighth or ninth inning with no-hitters," Halladay said. "I'd finally gotten to the mentality of, 'It's not going to happen so quit worrying about it.' And I couldn't care less if I threw one or not. I figured it wasn't going to happen anyway. So, once it did, it was like, 'Huh, that's interesting.' And I tell everybody, it's kind of funny that you have this perfect game and you celebrate on the field, you go in the clubhouse, and then it's like, 'Now what?' Because it's so fun being on the field and competing that there's nothing else that can compare to that. After the game, it was almost like, not a letdown, but the climax and the excitement was during the game. After the game was over, it was gone. It was gone. So, it was easy for me to move on from that, but that was a strange experience for me because I thought this would be something that would stick with you and it really, after that game was over, was like, 'I just want to go home and sleep.'"

| 17 |

It's Only Going to Get Funner

HALLADAY WANTED TO COMMEMORATE the perfect game with something special. He wanted to buy everybody watches.

"Define everybody," Frank Coppenbarger said.

"Well, the manager, the coaches, the players," Halladay said.

"Anybody else?" Coppenbarger said.

"You, the clubhouse guys, the training and strength and conditioning staff."

"Kevin Camiscioli?" Coppenbarger said.

"Of course."

"What about Marc [Sigismondo], who helps Kevin?" Coppenbarger said.

"Yeah."

"What about Rubén and David?" Coppenbarger said, asking about general manager Rubén Amaro Jr. and president David Montgomery.

"Yeah, I want them to have one."

"What about the bat boy?" Coppenbarger said.

"Sure."

Halladay added Brandy, Braden, Ryan, Harvey Dorfman, the late Bus Campbell, his dad, Greg Landry, financial manager and friend Steve Trax, and Brandy's brothers, pushing the number to 67. Coppenbarger had an eye for these things. He served on the committee that designed the Phillies' 2008 World Series championship ring. He knew somebody that helped David Cone buy watches following his perfect game with the Yankees in 1999. Halladay settled on a watch from Baume & Mercier, a Swiss watchmaker founded in 1830. Each one cost somewhere between $3,000 to $4,000, but Halladay paid about $2,800 each. Still, he dropped nearly $200,000 on watches. They were silver with a black case and white face. The backs had engravings of the recipient's name, the line score from the game, "Perfect Game," and "5/29/10." It came inside a cherry-wood box. The top of the box had a glass window with "Perfect Game" and "May 29, 2010" etched onto it. The watch rested on a red velvet pillow. The front of the box had a gold plate with an inscription: "We did it together. Thanks, Roy Halladay."

Coppenbarger talked Halladay into the inscription on the front. He assured him that it would be a nice touch to an unforgettable gift.

"Thirty or 40 years from now they're going to pull this down off the shelf and show some grandchild and say, 'Hey, the great Roy Halladay gave me this watch after he pitched a perfect game,'" he said.

"Do you really think that?" Halladay said.

"I'm 100 percent certain," he said.

Halladay enjoyed doing these things for people, but the attention made him uncomfortable. The watches arrived in late August. Phil Sheridan asked him how he wanted to distribute them. Did he want to hand them out as players came off the field following batting practice? "God no," Halladay said. He asked Sheridan if he could just put them on everybody's chairs in front of their lockers. Batting practice ended. The players came off the field, they found the watches on their chairs and their eyes lit up. Halladay was nowhere to be found. He went into a back room to avoid the fuss.

"They're like, 'Wow, look at this thing!'" Sheridan said. "It's like the box we got with our World Series rings!"

Everybody thanked him. He downplayed it.

"Like he gave them an autographed baseball," Sheridan said.

THE PHILLIES WERE STRUGGLING when Halladay faced the Yankees at Yankee Stadium on June 15. They'd lost 14 of their last 20 games. They needed him to stop the bleeding. He was 18–6 with a 2.84 ERA in 35 career starts against the Yankees, including an 8–4 record with a 3.18 ERA in 18 starts in the Bronx. But Doc lost his focus that night. He allowed eight hits and six runs in six innings in an 8–3 loss. He allowed three home runs, trying a career high. He shouted as he walked off the mound in the sixth.

"You try and hold things in as long as you can while you're out there sometimes," he said. "There's certain points where you let it go."

Rich Dubee waited until the next afternoon to talk to him. He preferred to look at the game film first. Sometimes he found something amiss in his delivery. But sometimes it was just mental. He suspected that was the case this time. He believed Halladay felt pressure to carry the load.

"Did you talk to him?" Dubee said.

"Yeah, I called him last night after the game," Halladay said.

He called Harvey Dorfman. Halladay wasn't happy because he gave up two runs in the second inning. Knowing that the team was struggling, he walked to the mound in the third and tried to take those runs off the board. He gave up three more runs instead, which made him even more upset. Dorfman set him straight.

"Harvey wasn't a sugar coater," Dubee said. "He dealt with behavior. If he felt like a guy wasn't behaving in the right manner he'd tell you about it."

Halladay walked into Charlie Manuel's office and apologized. He explained everything. He told him that he did not behave properly against the Yankees.

"Get the hell out of here," Manuel said. "We'll take you any day, even if you don't behave well."

Halladay behaved better when he faced the Blue Jays for the first time at Citizens Bank Park on June 25. The series had been scheduled for Toronto, but the G-20 Summit forced the series to Philly. It created for odd sights, like the Blue Jays wearing home uniforms and hitting last, while the Phillies wore road grays and hit first. They used the DH. Halladay pitched seven scoreless innings in a 9–0 victory. He struck out six.

He was unfazed facing his former team.

"You stick to the plan," he said. "And avoid eye contact."

Halladay went 2–4 with a 3.27 ERA in six starts in June, ending the month with a 13-hit, complete-game loss in Cincinnati on June 30. He was the first pitcher since 2006 to allow 13 or more hits in a complete game. He emerged from a back room 50 minutes afterward to meet with reporters. He was still upset about the two runs he allowed in the eighth inning to lose the lead. A reporter wondered if Halladay's aggressiveness sometimes hurt him because hitters knew they would get a pitch to hit in the strike zone. Halladay could have killed the reporter with his look.

He went 3–1 with a 1.54 ERA in five starts in July. He made the National League All-Star team. He pitched eight scoreless innings in a win against the Rockies on July 23, which started a remarkable run. Halladay went 11–2 with a 2.51 ERA in his final 13 starts, helping the Phillies overcome a seven-game deficit to the Braves. Halladay was loving life. Jayson Werth's two-run, walk-off home run to beat the Nationals on September 19 maintained the Phillies' three-game lead over the Braves.

"I've never seen a team so excited in the clubhouse; players and coaches were literally screaming," Halladay said. "At one point I had to sit down and close my eyes because I was starting to get dizzy. It started to die down before Jayson was done giving his postgame interviews on the field, but then he entered the clubhouse and everything erupted again. He's an excitable guy too. He pretty much lost it. It was awesome, incredible, and definitely something I'll never forget."

Halladay won his 20th game two days later in a 5–3 victory over Atlanta at Citizens Bank Park, which extended the Phillies' lead to five with 10 to play. Halladay allowed three runs in seven innings. He waited for his teammates after the game, standing at the top of the steps that lead to the Phillies' clubhouse. Ryan Madson, who pitched a scoreless eighth, stood behind him. Shane Victorino, Raúl Ibañez, and Chase Utley greeted Halladay, shaking his hand as they passed.

"Congratulations," said Jamie Moyer, who won 20 games in '01 when he was 38, and 21 games in '03 when he was 40.

Brad Lidge, who pitched a scoreless ninth to earn the save, followed.

"Congrats, bro," Plácido Polanco said.

"Twenty games!" Jimmy Rollins said.

"Atta, baby!" Charlie Manuel said. "Congratulations!"

Coppenbarger had a bottle of champagne chilling on ice in front of Halladay's locker. It rested on a silver tray with eight champagne flutes. The label featured a photo of Halladay with "Halladay, 20 wins, 2010" below it. He bent over and examined it. He smiled.

"I don't want to open it," he said to Kyle Kendrick and Brian Schneider, who were sitting nearby.

Halladay's teammates slowly gathered around his locker. He smiled again.

"I'm not speaking," he said.

"Chooch, you got it," Lidge said.

"I've got to do it in Español and English," Ruiz joked.

The room quieted.

"Listen, I want to say congratulations and… 20-20," Ruiz said. "It was a big win for us."

Ruiz and Halladay shook hands and embraced. Their teammates applauded.

"Now can we get that in English, please?" Victorino joked.

Everybody laughed, but nobody moved. They wanted Halladay to talk. They would not leave until he did.

"Me?" Halladay said. "Uh, man, I've got nothing. Other than, I love playing with you guys. That's all I've got. I mean, it's, uh, this stuff has been secondary for me. It's been a dream come true to get to this point in the season and to be able to get a chance to finish it. So thank you guys for everything. I appreciate it."

They applauded again. It was a big moment, but it wasn't why Halladay came to Philadelphia. He came for his next start on September 27 against the Nationals in Washington. If the Phillies won they clinched their fourth consecutive National League East title. Halladay pitched a two-hit shutout in an 8–0 victory. He struck out six, including Danny Espinosa swinging on a 1-2 changeup to end the game. Ruiz removed his mask, pointed it at Halladay a couple times, and hugged him in front of the mound. Their teammates joined them, making a point to hug Halladay and slap him on the back.

The Phillies poured into the clubhouse to celebrate. There were containers full of champagne and beer. There were goggles on standby because champagne burns. But before Halladay joined his teammates he joined Phillies broadcaster Gary Matthews for a live interview on TV. Doc finished his season 21–10 with a 2.44 ERA in 33 starts. He struck out 219 and walked 30 in 250⅔ innings. Thirty walks in just 33 starts. He did it again.

"How good was it, Roy?" Matthews said.

"It was fun, but it's only going to get funner," Halladay said, beaming.

Funner!

Halladay got to the clubhouse. He expected to see champagne dripping from the ceiling tiles and soaking into the carpet, but he noticed everybody waiting for him. Halladay, Schneider, and Mike Sweeney played a combined 40 big league seasons without a trip to the playoffs. Their teammates wanted them to pop the first corks.

"The gesture meant a lot to all three of us, and we talked about it for weeks afterward," Halladay said.

"I remember Jimmy [Rollins] telling me, 'Go around, go around,'" Schneider said. "Sweeney was already standing there and Jimmy said, 'You guys are popping it first, but we've got to wait for Doc.' I remember putting the goggles on and Doc coming around. It was kind of surreal just thinking about it. This team was coming off two World Series, winning one, high-profile guys, and they would wait for three guys who have been in the league for a while but never had a chance to make the playoffs. That separated that group of guys from a lot of guys because I don't know if a lot of teams would do that."

Halladay put on a pair of goggles.

Pop! Pop! Pop!

"We all wanted to see Roy's first time popping champagne," Werth said. "Let's see this guy let loose. It was an opportunity for all of us to share a special moment with him. We've all done this, we've been here, we've reached the highest level. Let's enjoy this moment with Doc. We loved and cherished this guy for all the hard work and all the time he puts in. We wanted to share that moment with him because it's a special thing and not everyone gets to do it. And for as good as he was for as long as he was and this was his first time to do it, I wanted to be here for that."

Halladay, robotic at times, ran around the clubhouse like a three-year-old with a fully-loaded squirt gun. He doused teammates with champagne and beer. He smiled. He laughed. He loved it. At one point he surveyed the scene with a Bud Light in his left hand and a cigar in his right.

"He probably wants to get done and go work out," Victorino joked.

Halladay heard Victorino. He looked at him.

"You heard what I said," Victorino yelled.

Halladay nodded and smiled. He was right. In fact, Halladay told reporters he hoped to work out before the left. He smiled again.

"This is the coolest thing I've been a part of," he said. "And this is just the start."

NOT LONG AFTER HALLADAY told his teammates, "No speech, let's win two more," following his Game 1 no-hitter against the Reds, Sheridan asked Halladay which items from the game he wanted authenticated. The memorabilia business is big business, and these days everybody wants to know the jersey that Halladay wore in Game 1 of the NLDS really is the jersey he wore in Game 1 of the NLDS. Major League Baseball has off-duty law enforcement officers work as independent contractors to authenticate autographs and game-used memorabilia. The items receive a tamper-proof hologram to identify authenticity.

"I've got a guy back there who will do whatever you want so you can save it," Sheridan said.

"Nah, I really don't want any of it," Halladay said. "I just want to wear it next time."

Halladay undressed and headed to the back of the clubhouse to begin his post-start workout. Sheridan quickly scooped up everything: jersey, shoes, glove, cap, etc., took it into the Phillies' laundry room and had everything authenticated. Sheridan placed everything back in Doc's locker. Halladay never knew because the items were marked with invisible ink.

The next afternoon, Halladay said, "Hey, my wife said I should have gotten that stuff authenticated."

"Don't worry, I did it," Sheridan said.

Halladay felt that way about his things because he never considered himself a big deal. He had an endorsement deal with Nike and before the season started the company wanted to make him spikes with "Roy" stitched onto them. Halladay declined. He thought they were too flashy.

"He was totally fine wearing stock shoes, like the ones you'd go buy at Dick's," Sheridan said.

Halladay finally agreed to let Nike put "34" on them.

"He thought even that was a little much, you know?" Sheridan said.

At the end of the season, Halladay had about 10 pairs of game-used spikes in his locker. He asked Sheridan if anybody could use them in the minor leagues.

"If you don't mind, would you sign them and I'll give a pair to each guy on the staff," Sheridan said.

"Do you really think they'd want them?" Halladay said.

"Yeah," Sheridan said. "I'm pretty sure."

THE PHILLIES SWEPT THE Reds, setting up a National League Championship Series against San Francisco. Halladay pitched Game 1 in a highly anticipated matchup against Giants ace Tim Lincecum.

Doc vs. The Freak.

It drew comparisons to Game 7 of the 1991 World Series, when Minnesota's Jack Morris outdueled Atlanta's John Smoltz. Morris pitched 10 scoreless innings in a 1–0 victory in one of the greatest pitching performances in baseball history. Even Morris bought into the hype of Halladay vs. Lincecum. After all, Halladay was expected to win the NL Cy Young, while Lincecum won the previous two.

"I'm going to say something real bold here," Morris said. "It would not shock me if [Halladay] joined the likes of Johnny Vander Meer and went back-to-back in the postseason with no-hitters. That's the kind of stuff that he possesses. I know it's a far-fetched idea, but every time he takes the mound, he has that ability."

Halladay allowed a pair of solo home runs to Cody Ross in the third and fifth innings in Game 1 to hand the Giants a 2–1 lead.

Ross started the season with the Marlins, going 0-for-3 against Halladay in the perfect game in Miami and 3-for-16 against him in his career. Halladay had a runner on first with two outs in the sixth, when former Phillies left fielder Pat Burrell stepped to the plate. Burrell fell behind 0-2, but home plate umpire Derryl Cousins called a third-pitch cutter down and in a ball. The pitch was in the zone. It should have been strike three. Instead, Burrell survived and ripped a double off the glove of Ibañez to score a run. Halladay stalked off the mound and shouted at Cousins. Halladay needed to refocus. He needed to let it go and make his next pitch. Juan Uribe followed with a single to score Burrell to make it 4–1.

"It's part of the game," Halladay said about Cousins' call. "You have to be able to make a pitch on the next one."

Doc lost. The Phillies found themselves behind in the best-of-seven series.

"It's obviously not what you prepare for," he said, "but it's part of it. You find out what you're made of."

The Phillies were on the brink of elimination five days later on October 21, when Halladay faced Lincecum again in Game 5 in San Francisco. The Giants needed one more victory to advance to the World Series. Halladay called Dorfman for some last-minute advice.

"You got anything for me?" he said.

"Two things," Dorfman said. "When you're scared, be aggressive. When you're worried, be aggressive. When you're confident, be aggressive. When you think it's over, be aggressive. The other thing is your behavior is the litmus test for you today. How you behave, how you handle yourself, regardless of the results, good or bad, how your handle yourself will make you a winner or loser today."

Dorfman was telling Halladay to keep fighting, even if shit hit the fan.

Game 5 did not start well. Halladay walked Andrés Torres and allowed a single to Freddy Sanchez to put runners at the corners with no outs in the first inning. Dubee walked to the mound to settle his ace.

"I don't feel comfortable," Halladay said.

He did not elaborate. Halladay allowed one run, but worked out of the jam when he struck out Burrell looking on four pitches. Halladay stared at Burrell, who argued with home-plate umpire Jeff Nelson. Burrell noticed and shouted a few obscenities at Halladay. Doc kept his cool, but in the dugout he looked pissed. He pitched a scoreless second, but pulled his right groin throwing a cutter to Ross in the first at-bat of the inning. Dubee knew something was wrong. He knew because in between innings Halladay always sat wherever he put his towel, whether it was on the bench or in the tunnel leading into the clubhouse. Dubee saw Halladay's towel on the bench. Halladay was in the tunnel near the indoor batting cage.

"I pulled my groin," he said.

"How bad is it?" Dubee said.

"Well, it's okay," he said.

"Let me get somebody going," Dubee said.

"No, you won't," he said. "I'm going back out there."

Dubee informed Manuel that his ace pulled his groin in the second inning of an elimination game on the road, but that he wanted to pitch. They prepared for the worst. Cole Hamels started to throw in the batting cage.

"That was the biggest adrenaline rush I've ever had, not just because I might go into the game from the bullpen, but because I was going to go in for Roy and I didn't want to disappoint him and let the game get away," Hamels said. "I wanted to win it for him, but he was Roy and he would never give in that easily and just grinned and went back to taking care of business no matter how bad he felt. One of the most mentally tough personalities."

Halladay retired Lincecum to start the third. Torres singled on a ground ball that deflected off first baseman Ryan Howard's glove. Halladay moved toward first for a potential throw. He dragged his leg.

"Charlie," Dubee said. "That might have done him in. That didn't look very good. I think that probably put the injury over the top."

Halladay retired the next two batters to end the inning. His cutter averaged 89 mph in the third. It averaged 92 mph during the regular season. He threw one sinker. It was 89.2 mph. It averaged 93.3 mph during the regular season. Dubee approached Halladay, who pedaled a stationary bike in the tunnel to keep his legs warm.

"Are you done?" Dubee said. "Did that put you over the hump?"

"No, I'm going back out there," Halladay said. "I can do this. I just can't do certain things."

He could throw his cutter and sinker to his arm side. He could throw his curveball and changeup. He could not throw his sinker or cutter to his glove side without bothering his leg.

"Okay, avoid that," Dubee said. "Cut it out there and just sink to your arm side where you're comfortable and see how far you can go. If it bothers you, just look over at me so I can get somebody going and we can maybe come out and give you some time or whatever."

"Okay," Halladay said.

Halladay allowed back-to-back doubles to Burrell and Ross in the fourth to cut the Phillies' lead to 3–2. He stranded runners at the corners in the fifth and runners on first and second in the sixth. Halladay threw 108 pitches in six innings. It was enough. José Contreras, J.C. Romero, Madson, and Lidge pitched three scoreless innings in relief to hold the lead, win the game, and send the series back to Philadelphia for Game 6.

"It wasn't ideal," Halladay said. "We had the same game plan, but I had to find another way to get it there."

"That was probably the most gutty, grittiest performance I've ever seen," Dubee said.

The Phillies returned to Philadelphia. They had a mandatory workout before Game 6. Halladay missed it. He spent the afternoon at the doctor. He received at least one injection into his groin to numb the pain. He got to the ballpark later and told Dubee about it.

"The doctor said I did some pretty good damage to my groin," he said. "But I'll tell you right now, we need to win the next two games because I'm pitching Game 1 of the World Series. No matter what I'll be out there."

The Phillies lost Game 6, 3–2. Uribe's game-winning homer in the eighth inning against Madson ended Halladay's shot at a World Series. Halladay won the Cy Young Award in November, but it wasn't what he wanted.

"Moving forward, there are parts of the season you are going to enjoy, parts you are going to remember," he said. "But I think the one thing that's gonna stick out there is you still want to try to win. I think that—more than anything—is going to be the overwhelming thing for me this winter. If we would have won it, I would have retired."

He was joking. Maybe.

| 18 |

The Rotation

HALLADAY KNEW THAT Harvey Dorfman was sick, although they never really talked about it. But he knew something was wrong because their conversations changed. In the past, they talked about the previous game, the next game, a way to improve Halladay's mental approach. But now Dorfman reviewed the things he taught Halladay. He talked about the future.

Remember this.

Don't forget that.

Dorfman asked Halladay for help.

"I've got this kid I'm working with," he said. "I'd love to have him talk to you. Would you call him and talk to him for me?"

"Why are you sending people to me?" Halladay said. "This is your thing."

Halladay sensed that Dorfman was changing the nature of their relationship. It was no longer teacher-student. It was teacher-teacher. Halladay worried as spring training opened in 2011.

Dorfman died two weeks later on February 28. He was 75. Halladay, who never missed a day of work, flew to North Carolina to attend the funeral.

Dorfman worked with several players inside the Phillies' clubhouse, including Halladay, Raúl Ibañez, Brad Lidge, and Kyle Kendrick. The following morning, Halladay broke the news to Kendrick, who was eating breakfast at a table in the middle of the Phillies' clubhouse. Kendrick fought back tears.

"He could tell I was getting emotional and just walked away," Kendrick said. "I knew how much he meant to Roy. I felt horrible about it, but I could tell Roy was really hurt about it. Harvey was probably his second dad. Like, no joke. He called him every day, I think. He talked to him all the time. He said the good thing is I have everything saved, talking to him. I wrote down everything."

A while back, Halladay started to save every email from Dorfman, who sent one to his clients on the days they pitched. They were simple, effective reminders.

Go kick ass today.

Be aggressive.

Strike one.

The hitters aren't as good as you think they are.

Fuck everybody.

"He was big on that," Kendrick said. "Because you worry about stuff when you're out there. What is the media going to say? What are the fans going to do? What are my teammates going to do? I wish I could go back. So many guys have said that that I've played with. I wish I could just go back, knowing what I know

now and do it on the mound. You just worry. You want to stay, you don't want to get sent down. You don't want the fans to boo you, you don't want the media to write shit about you. You want the coaches to like you and trust you."

Halladay stood in front of his locker the morning after Dorfman died and tried to put his life and legacy into words.

"I struggled over the years, trying to find ways to thank him for it," Halladay said. "I don't know where I'd be. I'm certain I never would have had the success I've had if it weren't for the time I spent with him. It really helped me turn the corner professionally, personally. It really made all the difference. He was quick to call your bluff on a lot of stuff. He made you be accountable to yourself and accountable to him. I don't think you ever got the feeling that he was a psychologist. It wasn't warm and fuzzy, you know? It was, 'Let's figure this out.' You didn't feel like you went in and told him all your problems and he gave you a solution. He teaches you to do it yourself."

Phillies' camp opened on Valentine's Day on a much different note. The front office shocked the baseball world in December, resigning Cliff Lee to form one of the most talented and accomplished rotations in baseball history. Halladay, Lee, Roy Oswalt, and Cole Hamels had a combined three Cy Young Awards, 10 top-five Cy Young Award finishes, six 20-win seasons, 13 All-Star appearances, one World Series MVP, and one National League Championship Series MVP. Lee signed a five-year, $120 million contract, which was noteworthy because 12 months earlier the Phillies refused to offer Halladay more than a three-year extension, citing organizational policy, while CAA fought hard to get him $20 million per season. Phillies general manager Rubén Amaro Jr. called Halladay during the final days of negotiations with Lee.

"I know I told you I wasn't going over three years," he said, "but I've got a chance to get Cliff back and it's going to take me five."

Halladay put Amaro's mind at ease. He said he did not care about the numbers in Lee's deal. He encouraged him to sign him. Amaro hung up the phone more determined than ever to close the deal.

"That was the beauty of Doc," Amaro said. "That kind of epitomized what he was all about. He just wanted to put the ring on his finger."

Phillies fans called Halladay, Lee, Hamels, and Oswalt the "Four Aces." Others called them "The Rotation." They were the biggest story in baseball. Fans wanted to see them, reporters wanted to interview them and photographers wanted to shoot them. It was impossible to accommodate everybody, so the Phillies' media relations department considered its options. Phillies' director of baseball communications Greg Casterioto thought about the 1971 Orioles, whose rotation included 20-game winners Jim Palmer, Mike Cueller, Pat Dobson, and Dave McNally. Casterioto thought it would have been cool to see them together at a press conference. He envisioned the same thing with the Phillies' four aces, wearing their red Phillies jerseys, talking about their chances to make history and win a World Series. It would be a PR dream, an unforgettable visual that captured a historic moment for a franchise beginning its 129th season.

Casterioto just needed the four aces to agree. On his drive home one evening in January, he called Halladay. He knew if Doc said yes everybody else would say yes.

Who says no to John Wayne, remember?

Halladay answered the phone and Casterioto explained the idea. He told Doc it would allow everybody to answer every big-picture question in one shot. The Phillies would make the transcript available, so reporters could refer to it throughout the spring.

"We'll have the four of you guys up there," Casterioto said.

"What do you mean the four of us?" Halladay said.

"You, Cliff, Roy, and Cole," Casterioto said.

"No," Halladay said. "There's five of us."

Oh, yeah, Joe. Joe Blanton was the fifth member of The Rotation. He went 27–14 with a 4.38 ERA in 78 starts with the Phillies from 2008 to 2010, including the postseason. He helped the Phillies win the 2008 World Series, smashing a home run in a blowout victory over Tampa Bay in Game 4. Blanton was a middle-of-the-rotation starter at his best, but teams needed pitchers like that. Teams won with pitchers like that. But with Halladay, Lee, Oswalt, and Hamels, Blanton was an afterthought. He was the fifth Beatle. Casterioto assured Halladay that Blanton would be there.

"Okay," Halladay said.

Everybody else said okay too.

More than 70 media members packed the press conference at Bright House Field. Lee sat in the middle. Halladay and Blanton sat to his right. Oswalt and Hamels sat to his left. The Rotation answered questions about its chances to make history and lead the Phillies to their third World Series title.

"A big part of it for me is not having the best pitching staff in history, but having the best chance to get to the postseason and the best chance to win a World Series," Halladay said. "To be on a team that has that chance is what every player wants. I remember five, six years ago wanting to go to Oakland to pitch with [Mark] Mulder, [Barry] Zito, and [Tim] Hudson. I think that's something every pitcher wants to be a part of. You want to be a part of a good group like that. It's why you come to places like this, to be around the best players. This is definitely a great group. But I think the ultimate is if it gives you the best chance to get to the postseason and win a World Series. That's why I still want to play this game. I want to be part of a world championship team. That is the biggest thing for me, and, yeah, it would be tough if we got close again and didn't win it."

National media continued to roll through Clearwater, long after the press conference ended. *The New York Times* put the four aces on its Sunday magazine cover. *Sports Illustrated*'s Gary Smith spent a week with the team for a 5,000-word story that ran in the magazine's baseball preview issue. *SI* put The Rotation on the cover with a shot that renowned photographer Walter Iooss modeled after a 2007 *Rolling Stone* cover with Maroon 5. Lee sat front and center for the shoot. *SI* chose him for the center spot over Halladay, not because he was the better pitcher, but because his return sparked the hysteria.

Camp eventually settled and the four aces prepared for the season. It would be the most highly anticipated season in Phillies' history, although some old-timers said Pete Rose's first year with the Phillies in 1979 might have matched it.

"When I look at the Phillies' rotation from a distance I am in awe of what they could possibly accomplish," Hall of Fame pitcher Don Sutton said. "I know the book isn't written yet, all we have is an outline, and I don't think we'll be able to evaluate until we look back on it. But looking forward to it, I think it should be the envy of every major league ball club. If you don't want those four guys running out there for you, there's something wrong with you. It has the potential to be the best rotation in all of baseball and one of the best in history."

HALLADAY WENT 10-3 WITH a 2.40 ERA in 17 starts through June. He finished the month with a complete-game win over the A's. It was his fifth complete game of the season, 14th with the Phillies, and 63rd of his career. The Phillies opened a series in Toronto on July 1, Halladay's first time in Canada since the Blue Jays traded him. George Poulis received an envelope from the Phillies upon their arrival. He thought it might be Halladay's medical records or something. He opened the package to find a pack of Reese's Peanut Butter Cups. It came with a note.

"Dear George, I hope you found the rat. Love, Roy Halladay."

A few years earlier, Halladay, Poulis, and Donovan Santas made a pact to eat organic. Everybody committed to it, but eating healthy during the baseball season is hard. During one particularly long game, Poulis left the bench and walked into the clubhouse to find a snack. A three-pack of Reese's called his name. He tore open the package, grabbed two peanut butter cups, and snuck into the x-ray room to eat them.

"I wasn't hiding, but it was a great hiding spot really if you ever needed one," Poulis said.

He started to eat them when… oh, shit, *Roy*. Poulis shoved the first cup into his mouth and stuffed the other one into his pocket. He chewed like hell.

"Hey, George, what are you doing?" Halladay said.

"Just checking this x-ray," Poulis said. "We had to take a film of somebody."

"Really? What's in your mouth?"

"A banana."

"Really, you just ate a banana?"

"Yeah, I did."

"Where's the peel?"

"I'm actually offended you're asking me that right now because I have no idea what you're talking about."

"Well, I'm just standing here looking at an open Reese's package. There's one in here and I'm just wondering if you're eating Reese's cups? We agreed to each other that we're going holistic."

"Doc, I'm eating a banana, but I do know there's a rat issue in here. It chewed open a few of the packages and I think that may have happened. It's the rat."

Halladay said okay and left. Poulis pulled the other Reese's cup from his pocket and ate it before he returned to the dugout. He sat within earshot of Halladay and Santas.

"Hey, Dono, guess what I just saw?" Halladay said.

"What?" Santas said.

"I think George is lying to me," Halladay said. "I just went into the food room and saw George chewing on something. He said he was eating a banana, but there was no banana peel. I didn't see one. But I see this Reese's cups package open and he tells me it was the rats back there. That they chewed open the package."

"George, are you lying?" Santas said.

"Dono, I am not lying," Poulis said. "I did not eat a Reese's cup."

"Doc, George is a man of his word," Santas said. "If he says he didn't eat it, I believe him."

"You're exactly right," Halladay said. "I believe George. I would trust him with my own family."

A few minutes passed. Poulis confessed. There was no banana. There was no peanut butter cup–loving rat. He ate the cups. Halladay and Santas cracked up. Santas told Poulis he should have stuck with his story because they believed him.

It was good to be back in Toronto. The Blue Jays thought so too. They wanted to honor Doc on Canada Day, but they knew an elaborate ceremony was out of the question because he pitched the next day. They asked the Phillies if he might take the lineup card to home plate before first pitch. Fans could acknowledge him while the Blue Jays played a highlight video. Halladay agreed. The crowd stood and cheered as Halladay twice tipped his cap to the crowd.

Halladay pitched on July 2, coincidentally, the 10-year anniversary of his return from Dunedin.

"It went fast," he said. "Those first few years feel like so long ago until you're back here, and you start thinking about where it all began, everything you went through and things you came back from. You don't realize how long it's been and sometimes how hard it was. It was a good reminder."

Halladay got an ovation while he warmed up in the first inning. He thought about tipping his cap, but he thought it might disrespect the Blue Jays. A bedsheet hung over a railing in center field.

"Welcome back, Doc. Please be gentle."

Halladay pitched his second-consecutive complete game in a 5–3 victory.

"Something I'll never forget," he said.

Halladay was 11–3 with a 2.45 ERA in 19 starts at the All-Star break. He not only made the All-Star team with Lee, Hamels, Shane Victorino, and Plácido Polanco, but he started the game. The Phillies were 57–34 (.626) at the break. They had the best record in baseball. They were playing well, but they had issues. Oswalt had a back problem that continued to flare up. Injuries depleted the bullpen. The offense struggled. Utley missed the first two months of the season with a chronic knee condition. He did not look the same since he returned in May. The team missed right fielder Jayson Werth, who signed in December with the Nationals.

The Phillies needed help. Halladay lobbied Amaro to find some.

"Knowing that I'm only here for a certain amount of time, yeah, I'd sell the farm," he said.

Halladay opened his second half against the Cubs at Wrigley Field on July 18. It was 91 degrees at first pitch, but the humidity pushed the heat index over 100. Halladay often struggled with the heat. The Phillies' clubhouse staff always had two jerseys and a few red-sleeved undershirts ready for him every time he pitched. He switched into a dry jersey and undershirt every other inning.

"He had to change a lot," Phil Sheridan said. "He would come inside and cool off, especially when it was warmer. It's funny, he had one certain Nike t-shirt that they stopped making so he pretty much had every one we had left. He tore through them. I never saw a guy wear so many clothes. Even his cleats would be soaking wet after a game. He sweated a ton."

But Halladay's body reacted differently this night at Wrigley. His face was bright red from the first pitch. He kept raising his arms over his head, trying to peel the sweat-drenched undershirt from his body. He grinded through the first two innings. He threw 31 pitches in the third. Twice, he hunched over at the waist, trying to collect himself. Utley saw that his teammate needed help. He whistled to the umpire. He called timeout.

Utley pretended to tie his shoes. Halladay crouched as Utley tied and re-tied them.

"It was so hot," Utley said. "I was uncomfortable not moving so I can't imagine what he was going through. You just see how hard he works and I know he puts the preparation in before each start to be successful in those moments. But as a teammate, you want him to be successful and you also want to help him. So I always thought if you could give a guy a bit of a breather, they had a better chance of being successful."

Halladay changed his jersey and undershirt after the third inning. A trainer cooled his body with frozen towels. Rich Dubee asked Halladay if he wanted to stop. He said no. He survived the fourth. He threw one pitch in the fifth, an 87 mph cutter. (His cutter averaged 91.8 mph during the season, according to Brooks Baseball.) He backed off the mound and summoned Carlos Ruiz. Dubee and head athletic trainer Scott Sheridan joined them. Halladay felt lightheaded. He could not see the signs from Chooch. He left the game.

Two doctors treated Halladay. They said he suffered from heat exhaustion and dehydration. He seemed fine the next day.

"I thought I could get through it, but that last inning I felt like I was about to get wheeled off the mound," Halladay said. "Between innings I couldn't get away from the heat. I couldn't escape it. It got to the point where I kept getting hotter and hotter and I couldn't stop it."

Halladay pitched seven scoreless innings in a 10–3 victory over Pittsburgh on July 29. In the middle of the game, Casterioto left the press box at Citizens Bank Park to write a press release. The Phillies got Hunter Pence in a trade with the Astros. Amaro sent prospects Jonathan Singleton, Jarred Cosart, Josh Zeid, and a player to be named later (Domingo Santana) to Houston. It was a steep price, but the Phillies needed to take their shot to win another World Series.

"We're a better team," Halladay said. "I'm sure the guys they gave up have a chance to be great major league players, but that's why guys want to be here, because of the sacrifices the organization is willing to make. I know as a player it's greatly appreciated. It's a good feeling to know that even when you're five or six games up, management is still trying to make you a better team. New York and Boston did it. That's one of the big reasons I was adamant about coming here."

The Phillies clinched their fifth consecutive National League East title on September 17. They celebrated, but the party was subdued. They set their sights on a much bigger prize.

"This is just one piece," Charlie Manuel said.

The Phillies won a franchise-record 102 games. The Rotation went a combined 76–42 with a 2.86 ERA. Its 27.0 WAR is the best in baseball since 1871, according to FanGraphs. Its ERA is the lowest in baseball since 1985. Its 1,064⅔ innings is ninth since 1989. Its 4.22 strikeout-to-walk ratio is fourth since 1900. Its 1.11 WHIP is fifth since 1975. Its 2.94 Fielding Independent Pitching is third since 1972. The Phillies did not have a 20-game winner, but it did not mean they were not better than the '71 Orioles.

"They might be better," said Davey Johnson, who played second base for Baltimore in '71. "We had Cueller and McNally and they were very good, but I don't know that they were better than Hamels and Lee. And Halladay is as dominant a pitcher as Palmer, if not more. Oswalt and Dobson? It was more of a special year for Dobson, where Oswalt's been special for a long time. The Phillies staff is awful good."

Halladay finished 19–6 with a 2.35 ERA. He struck out 220 and walked 35 in 233⅔ innings in 32 starts. He threw eight complete games, the fifth consecutive season he led his league in complete games. He finished second to Dodgers left-hander Clayton Kershaw for NL Cy Young. Kershaw went 21–5 with a 2.28 ERA. He was worthy, but once again Halladay's dominance was underappreciated. He posted an 8.8 WAR, according to Baseball Reference. Kershaw had a 6.7.

Lee finished third in Cy Young voting. He went 17–8 with a 2.40 ERA and an 8.5 WAR. Hamels finished fifth. He went 14–9 with a 2.79 ERA and a 6.4 WAR. Oswalt went 9–10 with a 3.69 ERA in 23 starts, but he seemed healthy as he entered the postseason. Rookie Vance Worley (11–3, 3.01 ERA) and Kendrick (8–6, 3.22 ERA) pitched well when they filled in for Oswalt and Blanton, who made only eight starts because of an elbow injury.

HALLADAY STARTED GAME 1 of the National League Division Series against the Cardinals. Phillies fans were nervous. The Cardinals went 6–3 against the Phillies in the regular season. They went 16–5 down the stretch to win the Wild Card. The Phillies, meanwhile, finished 4–8.

Halladay was not scared.

"I came here to bury Caesar, not praise him," he said, quoting Shakespeare before Game 1. "I think it's true. We're all well aware of how good the team is. We obviously have a respect for what they've done and how they've played, but you have to be confident going in that you're going to be able to beat them. You have to be confident the guys around you feel the same way. It is important. I think we all don't take them lightly. But at the same time, I feel like, without an arrogant tone to it, we believe we have a team that can go out and get the job done."

Halladay allowed a three-run home run to Lance Berkman in the first inning in Game 1. Phillies fans were stunned.

"I couldn't think of a worse start, really," Halladay said.

Doc channeled Dorfman: Forget what happened. Stick to the plan. Execute the next pitch.

"It took a long time for me to be able to learn that," Halladay said. "You can't get it back. And I think that's something you learn as a pitcher: being able to put things behind you and continue to move on, and really as a player, pitcher, hitter, you can't lose hope. You can't lose the aggressiveness and the feeling that you have a chance to win."

The Phillies stormed back to win 11–6. Halladay pitched eight innings. He did not allow another run.

The Phillies had a 4–0 lead entering the fourth inning in Game 2, but Lee blew it and they lost 5–4. The Phillies won Game 3, but lost Game 4 to send the series back to Philadelphia. The Phillies and their fans could not have been wound tighter. They were supposed to cruise to the World Series. Instead, it would be Halladay vs. Chris Carpenter in a decisive Game 5.

Halladay and Carpenter talked in St. Louis about a potential Game 5, but once the teams arrived in Philadelphia they put their friendship on hold. No phone calls, no text messages, no dinners.

"That's the only way you can be successful," Carpenter said. "He was just as strong mentally as I was. I knew the pressure, the size of the stage, all the other stuff that was going on was not going to affect him one bit. I had to work just as hard to make sure it didn't affect me one bit, either."

"We've talked about this scenario," Halladay said. "We haven't had a chance to pitch against each other, and if you're going to do it for the first time, it might as well be now."

Rafael Furcal opened Game 5 with a triple, smacking a sinker to the wall in right-center field. Victorino's throw missed the cutoff man, ending a shot to throw out Furcal at third. Skip Shumaker finished a 10-pitch at-bat by ripping a two-strike curveball to right field for a double. Furcal scored. Halladay finished the inning without further damage, but the Cardinals had a 1–0 lead.

Then... *snap!*

Halladay felt a hard pop in his lower back as he threw one of his pitches in the second inning. He didn't know what it was. He continued to pitch while the adrenaline flowed through his body. He threw seven more scoreless innings. He allowed only four more hits. He walked one and struck out seven. He did his job, but Carpenter was better.

"I knew he wasn't going to give up any more runs," Carpenter said. "So for me in the dugout, once I got back there, it was constant—one inning at a time, one pitch at a time. That was our mindset. We learned that from Harvey."

The Phillies mustered only three hits against Carpenter. They had runners at the corners with two outs in the fourth inning when Ibañez sent a 3-2 cutter high toward the right-field wall. Berkman caught it, just a couple feet short of the fence. Utley crushed a first-pitch sinker toward the Phillies' bullpen in center field to start the ninth. Cardinals center fielder Jon Jay caught it, his momentum carrying him into fence for the first out.

"I hit it pretty well and I know the wind was blowing in and it was cold," Utley said. "I thought it had a chance to sneak out."

Pence grounded out for the second out in the ninth. Ryan Howard stepped into the batter's box with the season on the line. He hit so many big home runs for the Phillies over the years. Maybe he could hit one more. But Howard grounded a 2-2 curveball toward second baseman Nick Punto. Howard moved out of the box, but he ruptured his left Achilles tendon and collapsed. Punto tossed the ball to Albert Pujols at first base to end the game.

The Cardinals won. They poured onto the field to celebrate. Phillies fans watched in stunned silence. Howard got carried off the field.

The Phillies had The Rotation. They made a big trade in July. They won a franchise-record 102 games. They had Doc on the mound in Game 5. They still lost. They slowly made their way into the clubhouse. Utley walked past Halladay, who sat alone on the floor in a back hallway.

"He was just sitting there just thinking," Utley said. "Not like sad, not happy, just thinking. And that vision, for some reason, is just embedded in my head because I just felt terrible personally because he pitched just unbelievably and we weren't able to score any runs for him. He didn't want the season to end."

Halladay got up. He took a seat and stared into the back of his locker for the next 25 minutes. He finally removed his uniform, threw on some shorts and a t-shirt, and met with reporters in the middle of the clubhouse.

This was not the interview he imagined.

"This is tough," he said. "The hard part is you think about all the work you put in over the year, you think about the game today and how big it was going to be, and then all of a sudden that just kind of dissipates. It's hard to have it end like this. You always want to finish happy."

Carpenter boarded the Cardinals' bus. He texted Halladay. He felt joy whenever he watched his friend pitch because he knew the man, how much he struggled early in his career and how hard he fought to get back. He also knew how badly he wanted to win a World Series. He told Halladay that he was proud of him and that it was a great game. It was. It might be one of the best-pitched games in postseason history, considering the stakes, the two pitchers, and their history together.

"Even though I won, I was just thankful that I had an opportunity to do this with him, go through this journey, go through that experience with him," Carpenter said. "Because we know where we came from."

Halladay received the text at his locker. He replied. He congratulated his friend. He said he was grateful for the opportunity too. He said if he had to lose to anybody, he was thankful he lost to him.

"It goes back to the human being that he is," Carpenter said. "It was our relationship that we knew exactly what we were bringing to the field every single day, but we also knew deep down inside—without the hugs and kisses—that we cared for one another a lot. And, although it matters—this game matters, those results matter, and all that other stuff in our world—when you come down to your family and your really good friends, it really doesn't."

Halladay eventually showered, changed, and left.

"That game," Brandy said, "that's literally when our whole world changed. That was it. That was the start of the end."

| 19 |

He's Human

HALLADAY AND CARPENTER sat on the top deck of a four-floor houseboat somewhere along the Amazon River in December, just a few weeks after they faced each other in Game 5. A while back, Halladay planned a fishing trip to catch peacock bass in central Brazil. He invited Carpenter to come along.

The group included professional angler Skeet Reese and former Blue Jays closer B.J. Ryan. The fishing was not great. Rainstorms raised the river and scattered the bass into the jungle. Halladay had a big one on the line on the final day of the trip, but it broke free. They returned home with stories anyway. Carpenter and Ryan shot a couple caiman, while Halladay, Reese, and others rescued a native that had been attacked by an anaconda. They found the man naked and alone, sitting on a tree on the shoreline. He escaped the anaconda uninjured, other than the bite mark on his ass, but the snake ripped the motor from the man's canoe and dragged it into the river. Halladay and Reese helped the man, who was catching exotic fish to sell to aquariums. They flipped his canoe, gathered his belongings and towed him home.

They recapped stories like these every night on the houseboat's patio. Everybody wanted to talk about baseball the first night, especially after the Cardinals beat the Rangers in a thrilling World Series. Carpenter pitched on short rest in Game 7. He allowed two runs in six innings in a 6–2 win. But Halladay and Carpenter had no interest in Game 5 or the World Series. They flew to Brazil to get away. They came to fish.

Still, Carpenter could not help himself.

"Doc, I'm not going to allow you to get away without me talking about the knock I got off you," Carpenter said.

Carpenter singled to center field in the eighth inning in Game 5. He fouled a 1-0 cutter over the Phillies' dugout, which stung his hands. He shook his hands outside the box, perhaps convincing Halladay that he had no plans to swing again. He took a 1-1 cutter for a strike. Halladay then threw a 1-2 cookie over the plate. Carpenter swung and lined the ball to center field for a hit. He got to first base and turned to look at Halladay, who spiked the rosin bag to the ground.

"I'll remember that forever," Carpenter told Halladay.

Halladay uttered a few expletives. He told him to shut up. Everybody laughed. Halladay got the last laugh on the trip, however, when he told Carpenter they should jump into the Amazon for a swim.

"You're freaking nuts," Carpenter said.

"I know," Halladay said. "Come on, Carp. It's wicked hot, I'm sweating like crazy, and we can say that we swam in the Amazon River. Who do we know that can ever say that?"

He made a good point, but was it a good idea? Their guides spoke Portuguese and very little English, while Halladay and Carpenter spoke no Portuguese at all. But Halladay wanted to swim, so he mixed English, some basic Spanish, and a few hand gestures to assess the absurdity of jumping into a river that anacondas, caiman, and piranhas called home. Imagine the Phillies and Cardinals announcing in spring training that their aces would open the season on the DL because of a piranha attack.

"We wanted to make sure that there's nothing in there that's going to eat us when we jump in," Carpenter said.

As the boat moved from fishing spot to fishing spot, Halladay and Carpenter kept asking the guide.

"Swim?"

"No swim," the guide replied each time.

Sometime after lunch, they found another fishing spot.

"Swim," the guide said.

Halladay belly flopped into the river almost immediately. He backstroked as Carpenter contemplated his next move. Does he trust the guide's knowledge of the river and jump into water that was as "clear as a cup of coffee?"

"Dude, get back in the boat," Carpenter told Halladay. "You're going to get eaten by something."

"Come on, get in," he said.

Carpenter jumped in. They swam for a few moments, returned to the boat, cracked open a couple beers and toasted their bucket-list moment in the Amazon.

"That's when you get to see the real Doc," Carpenter said. "You get to see the real Roy that is just laughing and joking and just playing. Those are the times that I'll remember the most: fishing, golfing, things where we're away from the game, where we can just sit back and not have those high expectations, that high pressure."

"I WAS NOT WRESTLING snakes," Halladay said. "I was nowhere near snakes."

The story about the anaconda and the naked man on the tree spread in the weeks and months following the trip. Reese's blog post about the encounter got the ball rolling. A photo of the man squatting on the shoreline soon surfaced. Phillies fans, who considered Halladay a real-life superhero, took good-natured leaps and decided that Halladay not only rescued the man, but he jumped into the river and beat the shit out of the anaconda, if not killed it.

The brilliantly funny Halladay-tribute blog I Want to Go to the Zoo with Roy Halladay captured the moment best: "Roy Halladay, Phillies ace, tireless humanitarian, workout warrior and [blog] muse is **BATTLING GIANT DEADLY ANACONDAS IN THE AMAZON DURING THE OFF-SEASON.** I can now never quit this [blog]. You know that, right? Also, local natives are now left to ponder the circumstance that led to a puzzling face-less anaconda in their waters." (Zoo With Roy started, by the way, because the anonymous blogger wanted to go to the zoo with Halladay. They went together in August 2014.)

Still, Halladay felt compelled to set the record straight as he addressed reporters for the first time in spring 2012. He talked about the upcoming season too. The Phillies fell short of a World Series championship in his first two years with them, but it returned most of the roster that won 102 games in 2011. Roy Oswalt, Raúl Ibañez, and Ryan Madson moved on and nobody knew when Ryan Howard would return from left Achilles surgery, but they added Jonathan Papelbon and believed top prospect Domonic Brown could take the reins in left field. They signed Jim Thome to provide Hall-of-Fame power off the bench.

"I realize that I'm not getting younger," Halladay said. "I'm probably going to play less going forward than I've played already, so I understand that. But you know, the greatest thing that's ever happened to me was coming here. So to this point, I have no regrets. If I go the rest of my career and never get another shot, I'll have no regrets."

Halladay made no mention of the pop he felt in his back in Game 5 or the pain it caused. He believed in the Navy SEALs' motto: "Suffer in Silence." Halladay often watched SEALs videos on flights when he wasn't studying. In Toronto, he once made visors with "Suffer in Silence" written on the front. He mandated that only the hardest workers in the Blue Jays' weight room get them.

"It would just drive him crazy to see people whine and complain," George Poulis said.

But Doc's back was not a sore hamstring, sprained ankle, or broken arm. It was a serious and chronic back condition. He had pars fractures in the spine, which caused a 25-percent slippage of one vertebrae on top of another. If you looked at him from behind, you could see the spot in the back where it moved forward. He had degenerative discs in at least a couple different levels, including the disc between the L4 and L5 vertebrae. A healthy disc is like a stuffed cream-filled doughnut, making it an excellent shock absorber. The cream dissolves and hardens in degenerative discs, causing pain that ranges from nagging to disabling. Brandy said because a few of Halladay's discs eroded and compressed, he lost an inch or two in height. Halladay told the *The New York Times*' Tyler Kepner that his back problems were "due more to running. I had done so much running over my career, so much lifting and squats."

"He remembers being a kid and feeling something pop in his back," Brandy said. "Later, going to back specialists, we were told those pars fractures were from when he was a kid. They hardened before they had a chance to heal. Vertebrae are soft as a kid, so when you do get them they heal if you rest them and take care of your body. As he went through his career, the torque, the pressure—the worst things you can do for a back like that is run, jump, pressure. Low impact things like biking and swimming were good for him, but he couldn't get what he needed to be prepared to pitch. He could run between three and six miles or he could bike for 30 miles. It would take him three times as long to get the same result. It just wasn't working."

Scouts noticed almost immediately in the spring that something was wrong. Two of them talked to Ken Rosenthal. He wrote a story for FoxSports.com that said Doc's velocity was down, he threw from a lower arm slot and his secondary pitches lacked bite. The story implied that Halladay might be injured. Halladay blasted the report, even though his velocity was down, even though he altered his mechanics, even though his secondary pitches lacked bite, even though he was hurt. Halladay never wanted to look vulnerable. He walked off the mound in Texas in July 2005 to prove a point, despite a shattered leg.

"You know, the older you get, the more you throw, the longer it takes to get yourself going," Halladay explained. "When I came up, I threw 98. Last year, I was throwing 92–93. So, you know, it's not unusual. But when you get older, it takes longer. The more innings you throw, the more time it takes to get yourself going again."

The injuries "just didn't really allow him to transfer the load in his legs to his upper body really well, to get that extension over and over," Scott Sheridan said. "I just don't think he could do that anymore without being uncomfortable. Every time he went to do that, it would kind of grab him. I don't think when we got him that we knew he had that slippage. Then he started having back pain and we did x-rays somewhere along the line and like, holy shit, that thing is a lot more forward than we would have expected."

Halladay had a 5.73 ERA in 22 innings that spring, although he struck out 27 and walked three. Did it mean anything? Maybe. Maybe not. Some springs are better than others. Halladay had a 0.42 ERA in 21⅔ innings in spring 2011, but a 4.00 ERA in 18 innings in spring 2010. Maybe Halladay was right. Maybe he only needed more time.

He allowed two hits in eight scoreless innings in a 1–0 victory over Pittsburgh on Opening Day. He had a 1.95 ERA in his first five starts, which had everybody feeling better. He was 4–3 with a 3.22 ERA in nine starts through May 17. It was not great, but not even Halladay at his best threw shutouts all the time.

His velocity, however, never returned. His sinker averaged 91.6 mph through May. It averaged 93.0 mph in '11 and 93.3 mph in '10. It was a notable drop, but he seemed to be working with it. After all, he was not a power pitcher. He relied on movement, command, and aggression. But then he allowed five runs in six innings against Washington on May 22 and left his start in St. Louis on May 27 after just two innings because of soreness in the back of his right shoulder.

"It's been lingering," Rich Dubee said. "Some days it's better than others. He hasn't looked right and he didn't look right today. I knew he wasn't going to come out of the game. I basically said that was enough."

Halladay had shoulder problems in 2004, which limited him to 21 starts. He insisted this was nothing like that.

"I felt it every single start from the beginning of the season on [in 2004]," he said. "That's not the case right now. I'm hoping it's something we can calm down quickly and get back out there. That's obviously my hope. It's not to a point where I'm in agony throwing pitches. The two years before [2004] I threw 500-plus innings and threw a lot of bullpens in the winter and wore myself out. I didn't know what I was doing. I'm smarter now. I'm going to make sure we address it and move on."

The Phillies placed Halladay on the DL with what they called a strained right lat. He returned on July 17 and allowed two runs in five innings against the Dodgers. He had a 3.74 ERA in 10 starts following his DL stint. He struck out 53 and walked 11 in 65 innings. It seemed to be going okay, but then Halladay allowed 19 runs in 19 innings in his final four starts of the season. He allowed seven runs and lasted just 1⅔ innings against the Braves on September 22. It was his shortest start since September 11, 2006, when he lasted just two-thirds of an inning after a line drive struck him on the elbow in Anaheim. Halladay blamed spasms in the back of his shoulder.

"I don't think it's a major concern," he said. "My only concern is that I keep having things like this. I've got to come up with some programs—whether it's less throwing or different arm things or whatever it may be—where I can avoid these types of things. When you're young, you never have them. I need to find a way to adjust to that."

Halladay finished the season 11–8 with a 4.49 ERA, his highest ERA since 2000. He hinted for the first time that his back bothered him when he said he needed to strengthen his core in the off-season.

"Getting older you have to do things different," he said. "The running has to change a little bit. The throwing program has to change. Flexibility has to improve."

The Phillies finished 81–81. They missed the postseason for the first time since 2006. They finished without a winning record for the first time since 2002. But the Phillies believed 2013 would be better. Halladay did too.

"There's no doubt for me," he said.

HALLADAY AND CARPENTER TRAVELED to Argentina for another December fishing trip. It had been more than a year since Game 5 and much had changed. Halladay struggled with his back and shoulder. Carpenter made only three regular-season and three postseason starts in '12 because of surgery to repair a nerve issue in his right shoulder. Both hoped to rebound in '13.

Halladay called Carpenter before they left. He wanted to know what he planned to bring. They talked rods, reels, and lures. They talked baseball too. Halladay planned to bring his glove and some TRX bands, which are used in suspension training. He asked Carpenter to bring his glove and a couple five-pound cuff weights. Halladay hung the TRX bands from a tree in the front of the farm where they stayed. They did full-body workouts every day. They ran. They played catch. This was not unusual. Halladay brought cuff weights, bands, and a glove with him whenever he traveled with Brandy and the boys. Brandy would be getting ready to go out and she would look over and see her husband on the ground in the hotel room doing arm exercises.

Halladay told Carpenter that he could not skip his workouts because he did not want to fall behind.

"This is a guy that just could not *not* do his work," Carpenter said. "It drove me. It just shows his commitment to what he wanted to accomplish."

Halladay finally acknowledged his back problems as camp opened in '13. He said the back, not the shoulder, caused him the most problems the previous year. But he had a new workout routine, which he hoped would help. It was a long shot.

"The damage was irreversible," Brandy said.

Halladay had a 6.06 ERA in six spring starts. He struck out 16 and walked nine in 16⅓ innings, which alarmed everybody because he never walked anybody. Another reason for concern: his sinker sat anywhere from 85 to 89 mph.

Blue Jays minor leaguers crushed Halladay in a start at Carpenter Complex in Clearwater in late March. He retired only seven of the 18 batters faced. He threw 81 pitches, getting only three swings and misses. He fiddled with his cutter grip—the one Mariano Rivera showed him in 2008—in the middle of the game. He spoke afterward of "evolving with his body" and said, "It's not a boxing match. It's not strength vs. strength. It's a chess match. It's competition of the mind and execution and being smarter and being more prepared." He sounded like an old boxer, trying to fight a younger, faster, stronger, better competitor, then explaining how the beating he took wasn't as bad as it seemed.

Halladay allowed five runs in just 3⅓ innings in his first start of the regular season on April 3 in Atlanta. He faced 19 batters. He struck out nine, but nine reached base. He walked three and allowed two home runs.

"I'm going to fix it," he insisted. "I'm going to fix it. It will be fixed. And the results will be better."

Halladay allowed seven runs in four innings in a loss to the Mets on April 8. He had a 14.73 ERA after two starts. Braden texted him afterward.

"You are my hero."

"The more you want it, the harder it is," Halladay said. "It is a job. It is a game. You're doing it for fun. You're doing it because you love it. As much as you want it, you have to enjoy it as well.

If you don't enjoy what you're doing, it makes it awfully hard to be successful. I need to get back to that."

He relayed advice from Harvey Dorfman, who once told him that if you're trying to catch a bird, you flail when you first attempt to grab it.

"You have to hold your hands out and let it land in your hands," Halladay said. "It's the same way with pitching."

Halladay missed Dorfman. He knew he would have something helpful to say. Before his next start on April 14 in Miami, Halladay searched for emails that Dorfman sent him before the 2010 postseason. He found a few. They pertained to big games and big situations. A mid-April game against the Marlins is not comparable to Game 1 of the 2010 NLDS against the Reds or Game 5 of the 2011 NLDS against the Cardinals, but following an injury-plagued 2012 and two terrible starts to begin 2013, it felt like it.

"My focus was on trying to prove something that necessarily didn't need to be proven," he said. "I just tried to readjust and get back to having my focus on singular pitches and working counts and simplifying. That has always been my bread and butter, and for some reason, I got away from that. I think just coming off the injuries that I had [in 2012], obviously, being under a microscope and a lot of questions being asked, I let that kind of divert my attention. Just getting back to really simplifying is what I always tried to do."

He allowed one run in eight innings in a 2–1 victory over the Marlins to earn the 200th win of his career. He smiled. It had been a while since he smiled. He walked into the visitors' clubhouse afterward and Jimmy Rollins picked up a huge bottle of champagne that rested on a table in the middle of the room. Teammates gathered around them.

"For all that didn't know, that was Doc's 200th win," Rollins said. "He had to grind it out today. Congratulations. Finally got it out of the way. Let's get the wins rolling. You know, you have everybody thinking you're hurt or something. There's a lot of pressure getting to 200. So congratulations. And I'm sure the other white guy wants to say something."

"I think I can speak for everybody here," Chase Utley said. "Very well deserved."

"I appreciate it," Halladay said.

He took the champagne from Rollins. He studied it. The label on the bottle recognized his 200th win.

"I want one with the World Series on it," he said.

Halladay had two pretty good starts after that, but he needed help. He was in pain, and the pain changed the way he threw. The pain coupled with the poor performances made him desperate and depressed. Desperate because he needed to find a way to be Doc again. Depressed because he felt like he was letting everybody down. Halladay found a doctor on the side that prescribed him painkillers, perhaps as early as 2012.

By 2013, he was hooked on them. The medications became part of his routine, like a run along Lake Ontario or flinging an Aerobie.

"He was so desperate to finish on his terms and to be good and to be liked and to be successful," Brandy said. "He was doing everything he could to do his job. It's not like he was depressed so he was out there looking for a medication to numb the pain so he didn't have to deal with reality. That was never Roy. He wasn't that guy. He was out there trying to find a way to manage the pain so that he could do his job. He was just trying to do what he had always done and he didn't know how to do it. And the problem was he couldn't do it. He wasn't supposed to be doing it.

"He was embarrassed that he wasn't doing well. He just wanted to come back, be great, and then be done. He wanted to honor his contract. He didn't want to take money if he didn't earn it. What I couldn't get him to understand was that he was already not honoring his contract by doing the things that he was doing in order to play. I'm like, 'How do you justify this action because it's giving you what you think you want? But you're going to ignore this action because you don't like the way it feels?' He didn't want to hear it. All he cared about was what it looked like and what people thought of him. I struggled with that because it was like, well, what about what we think of you?"

Halladay and Brandy talked about it. She wanted him to quit. She wanted him to quit last season, but nobody can tell Halladay not to pitch. Not her. Not the Phillies. Not doctors. Not anybody. Halladay felt an obligation to his teammates, the organization and the fans. He felt a responsibility to live up to his contract.

"We had enough money," Brandy said. "We had enough money 10 years before that. We had enough money if he never played baseball a day in his life. We were always going to be fine. My issue with those two years is he shouldn't have been playing. He should not have been on that field. That's where I was hurt. That's what I couldn't understand. I didn't understand why baseball was bigger than the man playing it. Why is the game more important than the man or family behind it? Everybody else is getting the hero and we're getting whatever is left over. He would come home at night and he would be in so much pain. He couldn't go outside and play with our kids. We couldn't travel anymore because he couldn't sit on a plane or drive in a car. He'd be uncomfortable if he had to sit in a car for more than 30 minutes. He was in so much pain. But instead of stopping the problem he was trying to Band-Aid the symptoms."

Halladay lost weight over the course of the season. He told people it related to a genetic illness, but it was a cover story for the medications. His speech slowed at times. He said things out of character, like when he criticized Charlie Manuel after the Phillies replaced him with Ryne Sandberg in August. The drugs did not help him pitch better. He could not replicate his old pitching mechanics. The change in his mechanics strained his right shoulder, which caused a partially torn rotator cuff and frayed labrum from a bone spur. He visited Dr. Neal ElAttrache in Los Angeles in May. ElAttrache recommended arthroscopic surgery. Halladay sounded optimistic about it.

"I don't feel as lost as before," he said. "I feel like there's some answers there, some things that we see that can be done and I'm optimistic that we'll get it fixed and I'll be able to come back and pitch. The doctor seemed pretty optimistic that if what they saw is correct, I could come back and be a lot more effective and have a chance to pitch this year and turn back the clock. He said he thought they could turn back the clock two or three years for me."

Folks inside the Phillies cringed when they heard that. No surgery turns back the clock, other than maybe plastic surgery, and a quick glance around Hollywood proves even that is debatable. A few days before surgery in Los Angeles, Halladay called the Phillies' beat writers together for a few minutes at Chase Field in Phoenix. Some fans were upset that Halladay tried to pitch through the pain. They could not understand why. Of course, those fans did not understand the mind and competitiveness of a world-class athlete. They clearly did not understand what drove Halladay.

"It's tough," he said. "You feel an obligation to the organization, to your teammates, to the fans to try to go out and pitch. Especially on a competitive team that sells out. For me, that was a big factor. If I'm playing for a last-place team, and there's things going on, you maybe speak up. But we have a chance to go win a World Series and we have sellouts and fans have expectations. You want to do everything you can to try to make it work. Really, that was a lot of the reason I tried to keep going. I just wanted to reach out to the fans, thank them for their support, and apologize to the ones who pay the money and show up in the second inning and it's 9–0. I apologize to the fans that I won't be out there for three months. I understand that some people are upset, and that's fine, that's a part of it. I'm not trying to sway their opinion. If they don't like me, they don't like me. That's fine. I think they mean a lot to the organization; they mean a lot to Philadelphia. We couldn't do what we do here without them spending their money to come see games. I think that sometimes gets overlooked in sports. They're a big part of the team success."

Halladay spent the next few months recovering from shoulder surgery before he got back on the mound. He rejoined the rotation on August 25, allowing two runs in six innings in a 9–5 win over Arizona. He pitched okay, but the numbers in his first five starts following surgery told the story. He had a 4.28 ERA, but walked an eye-popping 17 and struck out only 16 in 27⅓ innings.

Halladay continued to search for solutions that did not exist. Mark Connor was his pitching coach with the Blue Jays in 2001 and part of 2002. His cell phone rang one afternoon. It was Doc. They had not talked in a couple years. Halladay did not say hello when he answered.

"Talk to me about my cutter," Halladay said.

"What?" Connor said.

"Talk to me about my cutter. I've lost my cutter," he said.

Connor offered a few suggestions. The conversation lasted only a few minutes.

"That makes sense," Halladay said. "Thanks."

But the last month felt like the end. Everybody could see it, even while Doc continued to fight.

"Hard to watch," Dong Lien said. "He pushed his body to the limit, both physically and mentally. It was difficult to see that because you want them to shine forever. Greatness like that doesn't come around that often. So when you're a part of it and you understand what you're involved in you just want that to continue forever. He's Superman. Superman's not supposed to break down.

You give him that label of Superman, but he's human. And he's still an amazing human being."

THEN IT WAS OVER.

Halladay threw the final pitch of his storied career at 7:25 PM on September 23 at Marlins Park in Miami. He was beet red as he walked off the field. He was drenched in sweat. He looked gaunt. It was 77 degrees inside the climate-controlled ballpark, but Halladay looked like he was back at Wrigley Field in July 2011.

He threw only 16 pitches. Only five were strikes. Not a single pitch cracked 83 mph. Halladay walked leadoff hitter Donovan Solano on four pitches. The fourth pitch hit the backstop. He got Ed Lucas to a full count before he popped out in foul territory to Utley. Halladay walked Christian Yelich on five pitches. Ball four traveled at 76 mph.

"You could tell he was hurting," Yelich said.

"We didn't know what those pitches were," Sandberg said. "Changeups? We didn't know."

Dubee jogged to the mound. Carlos Ruiz followed. Dubee and Halladay exchanged a few words. Halladay shook his head a couple times. Dubee said, "Okay," and turned and looked into the Phillies' dugout. Sandberg and assistant athletic trainer Shawn Fcasni emerged. Utley, Jimmy Rollins, Cody Asche, and Darin Ruf gathered around them. Halladay bowed his head as they talked.

"There's just nothing coming out," he said.

Two minutes after Dubee arrived, Halladay walked off the field and disappeared into the clubhouse. Halladay wanted to leave the game on a positive note. He had given so much to baseball and impacted so many people in so many ways. The ending seemed cruel.

"It was just tough to watch, just knowing who he was and how proud he was," Sheridan said. "You could just tell that was kind of it. 'I don't have any bullets left in the gun.' I don't remember him coming into the trainer's room for anything that day. It was kind of like, 'I'm done.'"

"Anytime you see greatness in somebody then all of a sudden injuries take that away, it's hard to watch," Dubee said. "Probably more so in Doc because the game meant so much to him and his accountability was off the charts. I mean, every player is accountable to a certain degree. Everybody wants to be as good as they can be to a certain degree. But this guy took it to the nth degree. He was the most accountable, most determined guy I had ever been around."

Halladay said afterward that he did not know what the future held for him. He would be a free agent after the season. He said he hoped to pitch again and he hoped to finish his career with the Phillies.

"In his heart, he knew," Brandy said. "He was talking himself into everything being okay. He was looking for something short term to get him through the end of his career and feel okay. All he ever talked to me about was getting his tenure and coming home. 'I just want to be normal. I want to be out of the limelight. I want to be out of the public eye. I just want to be Roy.' And then when he came down to the opportunity to come home, he couldn't let go. It wasn't on his terms."

| 20 |

How You Fit In

Halladay left Marlins Park that night knowing he could not continue. His body was broken. It could not be fixed. But he hardwired his brain long ago to push himself, regardless of the odds or circumstances.

It was not easy to cut that wire.

"What can I do now?" he wondered. "What is the next step to make this better?"

He returned home following the Phillies' 73–89 finish and imagined two futures. In the first, he pitched. In the second, he retired. Halladay had back pain in both futures, but he could make things worse if he pitched. He might need his spine fused. He was 36. Did he really want to risk that? He worried about crippling himself. He worried about spending his life in a wheelchair. For what? One more season in the big leagues?

Doctors told Halladay that if he took the stress off his body, they could address the pain with injections and physical therapy.

267

Most important, they could help him better manage the pain, so he was not dependent on painkillers to get through the day. Eventually, he might live a more normal life.

"There wasn't a decision to make. It was just, can we accept it?" Brandy said. "It was hard for him to admit that he was done, to grasp the fact that he would never step on the field as a pitcher again. That was hard for him. He couldn't let go. The answer was really clear. It was very clear, but I just don't think he could grasp what his world would look like without that."

Halladay announced his retirement on December 9 at baseball's winter meetings in Lake Buena Vista, Florida. He spent the previous day in Tampa as the pitching coach for the Dunedin Panthers, a team of 13-year-old boys, including his oldest son, Braden. Braden won the final game of a double-elimination tournament when he slapped a game-winning single over a drawn-in infield in extra innings. He tossed his helmet into the air as he reached first base. His dad picked him up by his legs, flipped him over, and held him by his ankles. Braden howled. Halladay rarely smiled on the field when he played, but he showed unbridled joy as a coach and proud dad.

"They're starting to strive for their dreams, and that's something I want to be a part of," he said.

Halladay got emotional as he spoke at his press conference. He choked up a bit, but he found moments to laugh too. Brandy, Braden, and Ryan sat in the front row. Current and former Blue Jays and Phillies general managers Gord Ash, J.P. Ricciardi, Alex Anthopoulos, and Rubén Amaro Jr. attended at his request. Halladay, who signed a one-day contract to officially retire as a member of the Blue Jays, sat on the dais with a microphone in front of him, a Blue Jays cap to his right, and a Phillies cap to his left. He placed the caps of his sons' baseball teams next to them, a nod toward his new life.

"I'm helping out coaching," he said. "I'm trying not to ruin them."

He talked and answered questions for 30 minutes. He talked about his family, thanking Brandy, Braden, Ryan, his parents, and his sisters. He talked about his time in Toronto and Philadelphia and his pursuit of a World Series championship. He reiterated that his back—not his shoulder—pushed him into retirement earlier than he anticipated.

"It's just something we couldn't overcome," he said. "I want to be active. I want to continue to do things I enjoy doing. Spend time with my family. The best way for me to do that is to retire and not continue to put the strain on my body and get myself in a situation where they have to help me stand up to throw batting practice."

He said not to worry about him.

"There is a lot for me to look forward to," he said. "As much as baseball has been a part of my life, there are other things that I want to accomplish, and it became time to start going after those things. I'm looking forward to it. My family's looking forward to it. I had to stop my wife from cracking the champagne this morning. We're definitely excited. We've been very blessed, very fortunate. Baseball has given us a lot. It was a tremendous run, tremendous experience, something I'll never forget."

Halladay finished his career 203–105 with a 3.38 ERA. He won two Cy Young Awards, joining Gaylord Perry, Pedro Martínez,

Randy Johnson, and Rogers Clemens (and later Max Scherzer) as the only pitchers to win the award in both leagues. He finished in the top five in Cy Young voting five other times. He made eight All-Star teams. He won 20 games three times. He threw a perfect game and a postseason no-hitter. He led the league in complete games seven times, strikeout-to-walk ratio five times, and innings and shutouts four times. He had a 65.5 WAR from 2001 to 2011, according to Baseball Reference. It was the best mark in baseball in that span. Roy Oswalt (51.2) finished a distant second.

Halladay threw 2,787⅓ innings in his career, including the postseason. He fired 41,141 pitches. How many miles did he run? How many hours did he work out? How many hours did he spend in the video room and on a plane studying? Nobody knew. A lot.

"There is going to be a point where it comes to an end," he said. "I feel fortunate that I tried to absorb every bit of it that I could and poured myself into it. I really don't have any regrets, and I think that is the biggest thing. There are going to be parts I miss, but I have no regrets."

The press conference ended. The Halladays posed for pictures. Braden and Ryan happily waved at the cameras.

"I feel like the baseball world got the best of him," Brandy said that day. "But I feel like there is enough of him left for us too."

HALLADAY SPENT THE FIRST couple weeks of retirement asking Brandy every morning what she was doing and what she needed him to do. She finally told him to stop asking. He could plan his own day. If she needed help, she would ask.

This was a strange new world.

"It's different when you go from one lifestyle to another and trying to find out how you fit in, how you're going to do things," he said.

Halladay had some ideas. He thought about his final conversations with Harvey Dorfman. Maybe because of that, or maybe because he just needed something to do, he found himself in spring training with the Phillies in 2014 as a guest instructor.

"I learned so much from Harvey," he said. "That's something that I think baseball needs. I feel like that's where I can help the most. Mental fortitude, an awareness, that extra edge. That's what Harvey taught that was so valuable, and really I feel more of a responsibility to share what I learned from him than anything. Because he is unable to do it and there is nobody out there teaching the way he taught or the principles he taught. It's so basic. It is a weapon. It is absolutely a weapon."

Halladay introduced himself to everybody that spring as "Roy Halladay, stay-at-home dad." He worked with some of the Phillies' young pitchers, including top prospect Jesse Biddle. The Phillies selected Biddle in the first round of the 2010 draft. He went 5–14 with a 3.64 ERA in 27 starts with Double-A Reading in 2013. He walked 82 batters in 138⅓ innings. Halladay remembered being a self-doubting young man in the Blue Jays' system. He could have used a hand back then.

"I've been trying to help them think about the mental parts and preparing themselves and getting themselves ready to start," he said. "Really brainwashing themselves into thinking that's something they can do consistently. That's really what it takes. It's kind of fake it until you make it. I had to do that with myself.

That was something Harvey was very good at. He used to tell me to keep acting the part until I actually became it. That's something I really had to try to do. I really had to try to repeat these mental phrases, try and exude confidence, all that stuff until it became part of me."

Biddle threw live batting practice one morning to Chase Utley, Ryan Howard, and Bobby Abreu. Carlos Ruiz caught. The trio hit nonstop rockets into the outfield. Fastballs, curveballs, they crushed everything.

"Hey, you threw the ball really well," Halladay told Biddle afterward.

"What are you talking about?" he said.

"You threw the ball great."

"Did you see that? I just got rocked."

"Oh, Chooch was telling them what was coming."

Ohhhhhh!

"But at the moment he said, 'Yeah, you really threw the ball well. I really like watching you throw. You have great stuff,'" Biddle said. "I needed to hear that because I was kind of coming off a rough last couple months from the season before."

Halladay gave Biddle a copy of *The Mental ABC's of Pitching*. They chatted on the phone a few times. Biddle, like many pitchers, knew Halladay's story. It made his personal struggles not feel so insurmountable.

HALLADAY EMAILED THE PSYCHOLOGY department at the University of South Florida in April 2015. He hoped to audit classes there.

"I am comfortable in sports psychology with the 10 years I spent under Harvey Dorfman," he wrote. "I would however like to take some general psychology courses because I feel the root of many athletes struggles is a warped or underdeveloped self worth and identity."

Halladay could not commit to the classes or the work. He lined up a job with the Mets at one point because of his connection with Ricciardi, who joined New York's front office in 2010. Halladay met with Mets general manager Sandy Alderson, who gave Dorfman his first job in baseball with the A's in 1983. But Halladay backed away at the last minute. He told Ricciardi that he had a personal services contract with the Blue Jays, which prevented him from taking a paycheck from another team. Doc planned to start a volunteer job as a mental skills coach with the Phillies in 2016, but he again backed away at the last minute. Halladay was struggling at home. The back pain consumed him, but he also battled depression. He medicated for that too. He tried to stop taking painkillers and anti-inflammatories. He wanted to get off everything, including the anti-anxiety drug lorazepam. He knew aches, pains, and problems would follow, but he had to try.

"I think that there was just a bad mixture of him not knowing what to do when he retired, his back just wanting to be so sore, him not wanting to go and do surgery on his back for whatever reason, then all of the outside issues that he also had," his sister Heather said. "I think it was a bad mix. Had it just been one of those things at a time, I think he would have been able to handle it."

Halladay sought help for his back, but doctors told him that he was not a candidate for disc replacement surgery. It was a helpless and hopeless feeling. He had been the model of peak physicality for more than a decade in baseball. Now more than anything he just wanted to sit in a chair and feel comfortable. It seemed out of reach.

"They were crooked and broken and fractured and bulged," Brandy said. "It was a lot to be dealing with. That's when he realized how truly hurt and crippled his body was. When you stop taking the medications that you're used to taking to take the edge off, all of a sudden it hits you full blown like a Mack truck."

He tried to quit cold turkey at one point, but the withdrawal from the painkillers made him sick. He could not exercise because of the pain. He lost interest in eating healthy. He gained weight. He needed Zolpidem (sold under the brand name Ambien) to sleep. Halladay always had trouble sleeping on the nights before he pitched because of anxiety. Now he had trouble sleeping because of the pain.

Things snowballed.

"There is the forest through the trees, but Roy never saw the trees," Brandy said. "It was the forest. It's all he ever saw. He couldn't ever just stop and appreciate where he was and what he had. Roy, his whole life was about work, so when he wasn't working he was lost. He was so lost. Then the depression came."

Halladay felt a void in his post-baseball life. He was not the first former professional athlete to feel that way. Pro sports is a crazy, awesome world. There is fame, money, and adulation. There is world-class travel on chartered jets and room service in five-star hotels. There is camaraderie with other elite athletes and once-in-a-lifetime opportunities around every corner. It provides structure. It provides purpose. It is easy to lose balance between home and work because the work becomes so important. It was important to Halladay. Sometimes it felt like it was everything.

Then—*poof*—it's gone.

Halladay hated the fact that he left baseball like he did. He went 4–5 with a 6.82 ERA in 13 starts in 2013. It was his highest ERA since 2000. He could not shake the feeling that he did not have the career he should have had, even though he was the best pitcher in baseball for 11 years. It gnawed at him.

"He would get so overwhelmed with what wasn't good enough that I don't think he ever truly appreciated what was good," Brandy said. "He was always looking for something that could fill that, but he had it all along. What he wanted was family. What he wanted was home and peace and sanctuary. He couldn't stop long enough to realize he already had it.

"He was trying to find a place. He wanted to run the boys' baseball teams. I'm like, 'You don't have to do everything. Just do it a little bit. Meet in the middle.' But he couldn't do it. It was all or nothing."

Halladay coached the boys. He got his pilot's license. He threw out ceremonial first pitches in Toronto and Philadelphia. He got inducted into the Colorado Sports Hall of Fame (joining his mentor Bus Campbell), and the Canadian Baseball Hall of Fame. The family took bucket-list vacations to Italy, Australia, and Alaska. They talked about opening dog rescues, restaurants, and other businesses. He thought about enrolling at Embry-Riddle

Aeronautical University so he could work on planes. Of course, he wanted to take psychology classes at the University of South Florida and continue Dorfman's work. He wanted to be involved in baseball.

"It was endless, the things we wanted to do," Brandy said. "And then he would hurt. And all of a sudden he's spending all of his time trying to make himself feel better."

Halladay entered rehab twice. The first time he lasted only a few weeks because somebody recognized him there. The person had a phone and Halladay worried about a picture leaking onto the Internet. He panicked and left. He got home and promised to work on things on an outpatient basis. He did. He went to physical therapy. He changed his diet and tried herbal medications. He introduced massage therapy. He eventually returned to the medications.

"It broke my heart to see him like that," Brandy said. "You know, an addict isn't somebody on the street shooting up with dirty needles just trying to get high. That's not what addiction always is. That's not what rehab is. It's about someone who has a chemical dependency for whatever reason. He realized that after taking them for so long to do what he was doing, his body stopped making dopamine for itself. His body got dependent on doing what the medication does."

He entered rehab a second time. It was a place for celebrities, CEOs, and other high-functioning professionals. He stayed there for three months, although he tried to leave a few times. He hated it there. Each time Brandy convinced him to stay for himself and his family. It helped him learn how to handle his symptoms in a healthier way. He started a journal, which helped him express his feelings and work through his past.

Things were not perfect when he returned home, but they improved. He seemed to be finding his footing. He found doctors that helped him manage the pain, but also were mindful that he wanted to be healthier in the long term. He did not know if he could ever stop taking medications completely, but his goal was to no longer rely upon addictive substances. He wanted to be in control again, just like he was when he pitched.

"He fought to live a healthy, functional life," Brandy said. "But it wasn't easy."

| 21 |

Second Callings

HALLADAY FOUGHT TO MAKE HIMSELF whole again, but while he fought, he felt a pull to help. He accepted the Phillies' invitation to speak at their annual prospect seminar at Citizens Bank Park in January 2016. He scribbled a few notes onto a legal pad, but referred to them only sparingly as he spoke for nearly an hour. He knew his material well. He looked comfortable speaking to Nick Williams, Andrew Knapp, Edubray Ramos, Mark Appel, and other Phillies prospects.

It was easy to see him making this his second career.

"I don't know if it's my calling, but I think it's unique because I had a chance to go through almost everything," he said. "You know, from growing up, at times being pushed, struggling, not just a little bit, but a lot, and then starting to understand what's going on, starting to understand what Harvey's talking about, and really just trying to morph myself into what I was hearing, and I became that. So it's unique to be able to go through all

279

of those experiences and come out on the other end with that knowledge."

Halladay discussed the things that he thought could help: dos and don'ts as rookies, dos and don'ts as teammates.

"If you are not pitching that day," he said, "we need you in the dugout, watching the game. It's becoming an epidemic in baseball, and a bad one."

He opened to questions. They asked about his early-career struggles. They wanted to know how he overcame them.

"I had no belief system," he said. "My belief system was what my dad thought, what the coaches thought, what the pitching coach thought, what my GM thought, what the assistant GM thought. That was my belief system. If they thought that I had thrown the ball pretty good or if they said hello to me that day walking down the hall, then I had a lot of confidence. I got up [to the majors] and started struggling and I would go down the hall and the manager would see me and turn around and go the other way. My self-worth went there with it. I wasn't doing it for me. They sent me all the way back to A-ball. That's a long way back. I decided two things: that I was going to do it for me; I was going to do everything I could, the best that I could, and if it didn't work out, it didn't work out. But I knew I could walk away giving everything I had and be happy, but I could not walk away if I knew I had so much more left in me and I never found out. So I committed myself to doing everything I possibly could from that point forward."

He told them about how he talked about jumping from his apartment window in Dunedin. He told them how Brandy stumbled upon Dorfman's book and changed everything.

"Which is why I feel like I need to share so much of what I learned," he said.

He hammered home his next-pitch-only philosophy and his belief in preparation and routine.

"Any one of you guys in here, if you were asked to go out there and throw one pitch at the major league level to [Giancarlo] Stanton, throw one pitch, could you do it? Hell, yeah," he said. "But you think about going down and pitching against the Marlins for seven innings and giving up less than three runs, then it gets a bit overwhelming.

"I guarantee you Lance Armstrong [prepared] way better than me, but I was doing it to the best of my ability. Therefore, when I took the mound I felt like I had prepared better than anybody on that team. And it's tough to feel like a team is going to beat you when you feel like you are overprepared to beat them. That's where my confidence came from. And I promise you guys, if you do it for the right reasons, if you do it for yourself, you'll feel the same thing. It's extra work, it's extra dedication, but I love the saying, 'Men don't differ in their desire to win, they differ in the price they are willing to pay in order to have a chance to win.' Just a chance. So what's the price you guys are willing to pay to have a chance to be in the big leagues, to win at the big-league level, to be an All-Star, to have a long career?"

Halladay could have written a book. He talked about writing one.

"He wanted to change lives," Chris Carpenter said. "He knew that he had something to give. He wanted to give back."

HALLADAY CREATED A TWITTER account in March 2014 because he wanted to raise money for an event in Clearwater that benefited pediatric cancer. He enjoyed interacting with fans, so the tweets continued. He tweeted mostly about flying, fishing, family, dad jokes, dog rescues, and coaching Braden and Ryan.

He loved coaching. It kept him close to his boys and baseball.

"He loved the game," Brandy said. "He missed the team camaraderie—that energy in the clubhouse is infectious. You want to be part of something bigger and amazing. That was hard for him when he left, but that's why he was a big part of youth baseball. I think that was a big part of him learning how to be home and figuring out what he was going to do."

He had other motivations too.

"Just seeing what a mess youth baseball was, was an eye-opener," he said.

He hoped to change that. He worked with Florida Burn, a traveling squad of elite youth baseball players, and coached at Calvary Christian High School in Clearwater, where Braden attended. He took an interest in Positive Coaching Alliance, a national nonprofit that worked on "creating a positive, character-building youth sports environment;" the City of Clearwater parks and recreation department, speaking at banquets and Little League opening ceremonies; and Clearwater for Youth, which helped children participate in sports regardless of their financial situation.

Parents often approached Halladay. They asked what they should do to make their son the next big thing. Did he have any training tips? Throwing tips? He saw some of those parents in the stands yelling and pushing. "Daddy Ball," parents called it. It bothered him. He told them to teach their children to love the game first. If they loved the game, they will want to excel at it.

He made a point to teach Braden and Ryan that way. He told them after every game at least one thing they did well and at least one thing they could improve. He wanted them to celebrate their accomplishments, while continuing to strive for more.

"That's where Roy really started changing in his last few years as he kind of accepted who he was and started teaching his kids," Brandy said. "Just wanted them to always work harder, always want it, but you've got to love it at the same time. You've got to enjoy that process."

It explained why Halladay not only set standards and expectations for his Florida Burn players, but for his players' parents. He had both players and parents sign contracts, where he laid out policies and rules. He asked everybody to do things the right way, on the field and in the stands. If parents did not, they would not be allowed to watch their child play. Or their child would not play.

They were not raising baseball players. They were raising young men that happened to play baseball.

"It was all about family and playing for each other," said Mike Lockwood, who works with the City of Clearwater's parks and recreation department and whose son played with Halladay's son Ryan on Florida Burn. "Roy sometimes would bring a box of doughnuts on a Sunday morning. It's dark out, it's cold. It was something that we were all going to be around, that we could all share. He was trying to create a culture of positive experiences, even from the smallest things like breaking bread with a box of doughnuts. He was so deep. Nothing was done just willy-nilly. Everything was done systematically."

Halladay's players described their coach with words like "leader," "caring," "humble," "motivated," "generous," and "gentle giant." It might have surprised him to know that his players felt that way about him, but they did.

"It's crazy," Calvary Christian pitcher Jonny Bunner said. "I would go home and play MLB The Show and throw with him. This man is teaching me how to pitch! He is teaching me my walk through life."

Halladay joined Calvary as an assistant coach in fall 2016. The team went undefeated and won a state championship in 2017.

"I think he enjoyed that more than anything he ever did in his own career," Brandy said. "By far. By far. It was so intense and so exciting. It was him helping bring them to something bigger and he saw the result of all that hard work. It was really cool."

HALLADAY'S LIFE STARTED TO turn for the better in 2017. He had a long way to go, but he made gains. He accepted a job with the Phillies in March. He moved into an office on the second floor at Carpenter Complex in April. The placard on the door read: "Roy Halladay, mental skills coach." He posted his cellphone number below it.

He purchased his own furniture, equipment, and supplies. He bought a four-figure zero-gravity massage chair to make his office more inviting to players. He posted two sheets of paper on the clubhouse bulletin board. On one sheet players scheduled one-on-one meetings. On the second sheet they scheduled time in the massage chair. He prepared diligently for his one-one-one sessions. He experimented with note-taking formats and templates on his iPad. He kept stacks of copies of Dorfman's books and empty notebooks in his office. He gave them to players. Players read Dorfman's books as homework. They jotted down notes in their notebooks. They reviewed everything later.

He planned to fly his own plane to the Phillies' affiliates in Pennsylvania, New Jersey, and New York. Told that the Phillies would not reimburse him for the fuel, he said he did not care.

"This wasn't just, 'I don't know what to do with my life and I think this would be cool,'" Phillies mental skills coach Geoff Miller said. "It was, 'I really benefited from this. Harvey left this lasting impression on me and I want to be able to help others the way he helped me and what do I need to learn so I can do it better?' He had so much potential in the role. He didn't have any formal training, and yet from the moment I sat down with him, I thought his instincts and insights were on a very high level. He had these natural gifts of insight and empathy and humility that I think would have made him a big star in this field."

Miller told Halladay one day that they needed to hire somebody fluent in Spanish before next season.

"Well, what if I show up for spring training next year and I'm fully bilingual?" Halladay said.

He was serious.

"Just the idea of that and the willingness to try and do that," Miller said. "That was just how he attacked every problem. He was going to work on it until he had it."

Halladay cultivated relationships with his players. He texted, emailed, or called before and after games. He drove to the ballpark one night while right-hander Jacob Waguespack charted pitches behind home plate. They were unable to connect a few times, so Halladay showed up to talk to him for a few innings. Waguespack, who signed as an amateur free agent in 2015, made his big-league debut with the Blue Jays in '19. Halladay showed up one afternoon in a limousine loaded with pizzas to take a few players to a Rays game at Tropicana Field. He took players fishing. He took them to the airport and showed them the airplanes he loved. He often just grabbed a sandwich, sat at a table in the middle of the lunch room at Carpenter Complex, and waited for somebody to approach him.

"I don't know if he was just bored over there or just trying to make it seem like he was pretty approachable by being available," said right-hander Luke Leftwich, a seventh-round selection in 2015. "Like, 'Here I am. I'm sitting at the table in your locker room. I am *this* available right now.'"

Halladay and Leftwich met a few times. They talked about pressure. He told Leftwich about the pressure he felt to please his father. It helped.

"A big change for him was when he gave himself an internal look," Leftwich said. "'Why am I doing this? I'm doing this because I love it. I'm not doing this just for them. I want to do this because I love it and this is what I want to do with my life.' We talked a lot about getting rid of external pressures and concentrating on what I can do internally to make myself better."

Halladay talked with Phillies right-hander Jerad Eickhoff in the spring about his struggles to throw a changeup. Eickhoff looked forward to future talks. Halladay watched Phillies right-hander Zach Eflin throw a couple live batting practice sessions while he recovered from an injury. They talked about being aggressive and trying to stay in the game as long as possible. He handed him a copy of *The Mental ABC's*.

Halladay highlighted the names of a few of his favorite chapters: Adversity, Anxiety, Belief, Confidence, Emotions, Joy, Relentlessness, and Warrior. He highlighted the numbers of a few other chapters: Perspective, Pressure, and Umpires.

"He talked about being a bulldog on the mound, not showing emotion, not showing anybody what you're thinking," Eflin said.

"For all the greatness of him, the mental aspect of it was just out of this world," CAA agent Jeff Berry said. "It was a passion of his to share it. It wasn't to share it so guys could be good major leaguers. It wasn't to share it so guys could make a lot of money. He would do it with a kid that's on the back of the bench on the JV team with the same approach he would do it with a top Phillies' prospect. He would treat them equally, the same. It didn't matter what it was. And I think that's the essence of what his passion was. It wasn't, this can help you be as good as you can be. It was more personal development for the individual."

Halladay gave a group lecture November 6 in a conference room at Carpenter Complex. He spoke to players from the Phillies' strength and conditioning camp. He put together a PowerPoint presentation, but he spoke mostly from memory.

"I could see him light up when he was working with players and when he knew he had just done something well," Miller said. "It's funny because it was probably the only place he was different as a pitcher. You never knew what he was thinking as a pitcher. There was never a change in expression. But he couldn't help but be proud of himself and he couldn't help but be excited for the people that he was talking to. You could just see it on his face that he really truly enjoyed what he was doing and he really truly cared for everyone he came in contact with."

Brandy wondered if the players helped Roy as much as he helped them.

"He was trying to fill a void to feel valuable and important and that he was still contributing to baseball in some way, shape, or form," she said. "I hope there are guys out there that did benefit from talking to him. Everybody has a right to struggle. Even though you're a big professional athlete you still have a right to struggle, no matter what people think. I think it was good for people to maybe talk to him. It was probably therapeutic for him to open up a little bit more about what was hard and what he didn't manage and how he needed help because people are like, 'Oh, God, well, if Roy Halladay went through that I guess I'm not so off.' That was a bigger part of it than anything, showing the normal side of himself too.

"We were finally there. That last year we were working through things. It was a lot better. I really feel like he was doing a lot better. We finally found good doctors that could help him try to manage the pain. We finally found some good support. They were coming up with plans to help manage the pain that it wasn't going to affect him physically and emotionally. Antidepressants on top of pain medication, they all counterbalance each other. Every positive effect there's also two negative effects. So you have to find the right recipe for pain management. We finally were in a place where I feel like it was manageable."

| 22 |

I Love You Too

HALLADAY LOVED FLYING SINCE CHILDHOOD. He would have been a pilot, if he was not a baseball player. But because he played baseball he flew for fun and he flew for peace of mind. If he ever felt lost, he hopped into a plane, took off, and found himself.

"When Roy would get depressed, when he would be struggling with something, he would fly," Brandy said. "It would help him clear his head. It's kind of an Enya moment. Go up, clear his head. Go through whatever he wanted to do and come back. It was kind of a mental timeout for him. I understand that. He needs that. I ride horses. Sometimes it's relaxing to just shut your brain off and do what you love to do. And when he flew, he flew. He loved that feeling. He loved that same feeling of being on the field. The adrenaline. The excitement. The challenge of doing something like that. That's why he loved it. And I got it. I understood that."

But Brandy never felt completely comfortable flying in a plane with Roy. Not because she felt unsafe. She felt safe. But she knew accidents happened. She could not help but think about Braden and Ryan when she flew with Roy. If something happened to them, the boys would be alone. It was not an unusual thought. Parents worry. But Roy never really thought that way. He grew up around airplanes. Heck, he grew up in airplanes. He read magazines and newspaper stories about plane crashes and air safety all the time. He discussed them with teammates and staff members. The stories never fazed him. He knew the odds were in his favor.

"You ride horses," Roy told Brandy. "More people get hurt riding horses."

It might be true, but she reminded Roy that while there are automobile accidents and horse-riding accidents, there are no plane accidents. There are plane crashes. Very few people survive plane crashes. He told her that she did not understand. He suggested that she take flying lessons to learn more.

"We would talk about this all the time," she said. "It is an unnecessary risk. When I was a kid I'd get on a motorcycle and I wouldn't think twice. Now you couldn't pay me to get on a motorcycle. I don't enjoy flying, but I'm not scared of flying. I'm still not scared of flying. I'm just really happy when I land."

But following her husband's retirement, Brandy had another reason to want to keep Roy on the ground. She thought it was best while he battled his demons.

"He just needed to get everything else under control and focus on some other things," she said. "It was the last thing we needed to do was spend more money and have more hobbies. We can't do what we've already got to do. Until I knew he was okay, I just didn't want him doing it."

But Halladay heard about the ICON A5 late in 2015. The A5 is a 23-foot-long amphibious light-sport aircraft. It looks like a flying sports car. It's sold that way too. "It turns flying from a mode of transportation to a sport—what flying was meant to be," the company says on its site. The cockpit is sleek. Its control stick is inspired by military aircraft. It takes off and lands in water. The side windows can be removed, so the pilot and passenger in the two-seater feel like they're flying a convertible. Once on the water, they can climb onto the wings and relax or jump in.

Halladay wanted one, but he was told if he ordered one of the $389,000 planes it would not be delivered until 2018. He didn't want to wait that long, so he sought help on Twitter. The company tweeted at him the next day: "Let's talk, Roy." Halladay got an email from the company's CEO Kirk Hawkins.

The plane arrived at his home on October 10, 2017.

Halladay kept it either on the lake behind the house or at a nearby airport. Halladay and Brandy enjoyed it. They packed lunches, flew to Three-Rooker Bar, a crescent-shaped island on the Gulf of Mexico, just north of Clearwater. They looked for fish and sharks as they flew across the sea. They landed on the water, pulled onto the beach, ate lunch, and flew home in time to pick up the boys from school.

"It was like having a vacation in the middle of the day," Brandy said. "It was amazing. Of course, we got stuck out there in the sand a couple times. You can't call AAA when you're on a beach, so we were just stuck. We were like, 'Well, guess we've got to wait for high tide again.' We had some funny stories and some amazing pictures."

THE HALLADAYS WOKE UP on Tuesday, November 7, 2017, like any other school day. The boys got ready and Roy drove them to school. Roy and Brandy would return to Ryan's school in the afternoon to see him play at a band recital. Brandy needed to run errands beforehand with her mother. She asked Roy if he wanted to join. They could get lunch and make a day of it. But Roy said he had other things he needed to do. He declined. He still had his good days and bad days. He seemed sad this morning.

"He struggled a lot with depression," Brandy said. "He struggled a lot with anxiety. Social anxiety. He never felt like he was good enough or funny enough or liked. He was a sad spirit. But I don't want that to overshadow all the great times."

Brandy took a car and left. Roy texted her while she drove. He said he planned to fly the plane from the lake to the airport. He would take the Jeep they kept there and drive to the recital.

He texted her again about an hour later. He had not left the house.

"I'm so sorry," he said. "I feel like you're upset with me. I should've just gone with you."

"I'm not mad at you," Brandy replied. "I'm just disappointed that you couldn't just go with me."

Roy got into the plane. He took off at 11:47 AM. He logged 703.9 flight hours to that point, including 51.8 hours in the ICON A5 and 14.5 hours in his own ICON. He climbed to a little more than 1,900 feet. He flew north for about four miles before turning west, flying 10 miles toward the Gulf of Mexico. He texted Brandy from the air. He did not have enough time to get to the airport, which was a 40-minute drive north of the house, then drive south and get to Ryan's school by 1:00 PM. He said he would just fly home and drive from there.

"I love you. Just get here," Brandy said.

"I love you too. I'm sorry. I should've just gone with you. Another wasted day."

Halladay crossed U.S. Route 19, a highway that runs along the Gulf Coast, at about 600 feet. He descended to 36 feet as he flew over the water. He turned south. He flew past Green Key Beach at 11 feet. He made a 360 degree turn to the right as he climbed to 100 feet. He continued to fly south. He came with 75 feet of some homes, which was in violation of FAA rules. The last airplane data had Halladay at 200 feet and flying at 87 knots (100 mph). Video footage showed the plane descending left at a 45-degree banked turn then steadying about 10 feet above the water. The plane made another climb between 300 to 500 feet. It made another 45-degree nose-down maneuver.

The plane crashed into the water at 12:04 PM.

Brandy got to Ryan's school. She texted Roy. She told tell him where they were sitting. They saved him a seat. It got closer to one o'clock. She texted him again.

"Where are you? The show is starting in five minutes. You're supposed to be here."

The concert started. She sent another text.

"Where are you?"

A girlfriend texted Brandy about 30 minutes into the concert.

"Please tell me you're not flying today," she said. "A small plane crashed behind the house."

"Roy was flying earlier, but he's not now," Brandy replied. "What kind of plane was it?"

Her friend didn't know. It landed upside down in the water, but she thought it was a bigger plane—not the smaller ICON A5. "It was not Roy," Brandy told herself. He landed a while ago. He was probably parking the car and walking through the door at any moment. She texted Roy again.

"Oh my God, I heard there was a plane crash. Where are you?"

She started to worry, but she remained calm because she knew it wasn't him. There was no way. The concert ended. Roy never showed. Brandy started to panic, but she also knew how forgetful he could be. He misplaced his phone all the time. She bet that he left his phone in the plane, got in the Jeep, and drove away. He was in a hurry. He didn't have time to go back and get it.

Roy was going to show up. She just knew it.

Brandy's brother called. He was at the house.

"There's a sheriff here," he said, crying. "He needs to talk to you."

Brandy screamed. She knew.

"Fuck!"

She got home and called the boys' schools and left word that they needed to come home immediately; there was a family emergency. Nobody confirmed yet that it was Halladay's plane, but word started to spread. He was a celebrity. It would not take long. Brandy confirmed the tail number to the sheriff, which began a race against time. A local TV station showed up in front of the house before Braden and Ryan got there. She asked the crew to leave. The reporter coldly replied, "Ma'am, I'm sorry for your loss, but I have a job to do."

Brandy needed to be the first person to tell her boys that their father died. One of Braden's friends shot him a text.

"I just saw a tweet that your dad died in a plane crash. Is it true?"

The boys got home. They knew the worst had happened.

"I literally can't even talk to my kids to tell them on my terms or in my words, you know?" she said.

A stream of family and friends arrived at the Halladay home to lend their support. Brandy tried to collect her thoughts, but she struggled. Braden had friends at the house. Ryan preferred to be alone. Brandy wanted to be with both of them, but she had a houseful of people. She didn't know what to do.

"You're stuck between a rock and a rock," she said.

CHRIS CARPENTER WAS IN a coffee and ice cream shop at home in New Hampshire when George Poulis texted him. Poulis said people thought Roy's plane might have crashed, but nobody knew for sure. Carpenter texted a friend that worked for the New Hampshire state police department, but now worked security in Tampa Bay. He told him that he needed to find out. The friend texted back within 15 minutes. Nothing had been confirmed or announced, but he told him that it was Halladay's plane. Carpenter went home, turned on the TV, and watched. He felt numb for days.

"Just sadness," Carpenter said. "Where do you go now? What are you even supposed to do?"

Carlos Ruiz woke up that morning in Panama to a dark sky. "It's a sad day," he told his brother. He took a nap in the afternoon. He awoke to a phone call from his agent, Marc Kligman. Chooch could tell something was wrong. Kligman told him that he had bad news. Was he ready for it? Chooch said yes. Kligman told him.

"Right there I felt something in my body," Ruiz said. "I never expected something like that."

Big Roy got a call from his daughter Heather, who heard from Brandy. He could not believe it. He wondered if there was a mistake.

Juan Castro recorded the final out of Halladay's perfect game in 2011. He was in his backyard in Phoenix when a reporter from Mexico called for comment. Castro had not heard. He cried.

Jesse Biddle got advice from Halladay in the spring of 2014. They talked on the phone a few times, but lost touch over the years. He got a notification on his phone. *Is this real?* he wondered. He felt like he was in a movie. He picked up the phone and called his parents in Philadelphia.

Halladay considered Pat Hentgen one of the most important mentors of his career. Every fall Hentgen hosted a two-week hunting camp at his cabin in Ontario. He was in a deer stand when former Blue Jays teammate Paul Spoljaric texted him that Halladay died. Hentgen pulled out his phone and scrolled through Twitter. Everybody from former Blue Jays president Paul Beeston to former general manager Alex Anthopoulos called. Hentgen never got more texts and calls in a single day before or since.

"Everybody was in disbelief," he said.

Ken Huckaby caught Halladay 30 times with the Blue Jays. He cherished every moment. He was in the dugout in the Arizona Fall League. He got a text from Clay Bellinger, the former big leaguer and father of Dodgers star Cody Bellinger.

"Did you hear about Doc?"

Huckaby had a bad feeling as soon as he read the text. He called Bellinger, who told him. Huckaby went home. His wife was crying over the news.

Few people spent more time with Halladay during his career than Donovan Santas. He was driving when his wife called. She asked if he talked to Doc lately. He said he got a text from him a few days earlier. He wanted to know if he could speak to the kids at Braden's high school and offer some training tips. Halladay thought the kids could be something special. Santas' wife said she would call him back. She did. She said there was a report that Halladay's plane crashed, but nobody knew if he was in the plane or if somebody else was flying it. Santas' heart sank.

"I knew there was no one flying that plane other than him," he said. "There was no, 'Hey, do you want to take my plane up?' It didn't matter who it was. Like, there was no way there was anyone else in that plane but him. I was devastated. I didn't need the news to be confirmed to know. I couldn't believe it."

Jimmy Rollins got the news in a text from Ryan Howard, but it didn't hit him until later that night when he crawled into bed and his wife, Johari, kicked him to his side.

"It hit me that Brandy doesn't have this anymore," he said. "She doesn't say, move over or give me the pillow. Their sons don't have their dad coming through the door and hearing his voice. That's when it really got heavy."

Rich Dubee got a call from his wife on the golf course. He spent the rest of the night watching the news at home on TV.

J.P. Ricciardi was on a flight with his wife. The plane landed, he turned on his phone, and text messages poured in.

Dong Lien, Santas' counterpart with the Phillies, got a text from a former Phillies employee.

"Devastation," Lien said. "Not Doc. He's Superman."

Rubén Amaro Jr. saw the news on TV. He sent Halladay a couple texts.

"I was freaked out, I was in shock," he said. "I couldn't have been any more shattered. Just like it's hard to describe winning the World Series and that feeling, it's equally difficult to describe how horrified I was. Even today."

Chase Utley and his wife, Jen, were coming out of a yoga class when he got a text from former teammate Brian Schneider. Utley hoped there was a mistake. He immediately thought about Brandy, Braden, and Ryan.

Jayson Werth saw the news on TV. He texted Kyle Kendrick, who remained close with Halladay and lived nearby in Florida. Werth could feel the shakiness in Kendrick's response.

"You don't ever want to lose any of your teammates or friends or anyone like that, but the fact that it was Roy..." Werth said. "We all have so much to live for. You play this game, you put all your time into it and once you retire, it's like you finally have time to do things you want to do. And to even think that that's something that happened was unthinkable. It was just tough, man.

And even right now, there's times when you're like, 'Oh, I want to call Doc and ask him about that.' And you're like, 'I can't.' And it's crazy to think about that."

Nobody other than Ruiz caught Halladay more than Gregg Zaun. Like Hentgen, he was hunting. He turned on his phone as he left his deer blind. The phone started to fill up with text messages and voicemails. He was a puddle by the time he reached camp.

"It changed things for me," he said. "It changed the way I deal with my other friends. You know how guys are. We're low maintenance. We don't speak for six months and then all of a sudden it's, 'Hey, buddy. I'm coming to town. Let's go out.' Guys do that. I hadn't talked to Roy in eight months to a year and I felt really shitty that I hadn't. Now I have regular times during the week where I check in with people just to say hello, just to say I'm still a part of your life, I'm still here. I still care about you."

Everybody gathered a week later for Halladay's "Celebration of Life" service at Spectrum Field in Clearwater. An estimated 2,000 people attended the 90-minute service, including many of Halladay's former teammates with the Phillies and Blue Jays. There was a highlight video and words from Phillies owner John Middleton, Charlie Manuel, Utley, Cole Hamels, Ricciardi, Carpenter, and Poulis.

Big Roy shared his favorite memories of Little Roy. Brandy shared hers.

"We miss him," she said, looking at Braden, 17, and Ryan, 13. "But we still have so much of him. We still have a million phone cords and iPads. We have enough cigars to open our own store.

We have a garage full of model airplanes. We still have his not-so-secret stash of hidden ice cream sandwiches. And best of all, I still get to see him every day because I look at you. And if this is what it took for me to have you boys then it's worth it."

NOBODY TRULY KNOWS WHY Halladay's plane crashed that afternoon. Everybody has theories and opinions following the National Transportation Safety Board's investigation and the Pinellas-Pasco Medical Examiner's Office's autopsy. Halladay flew the ICON A5 erratically before it crashed into the Gulf of Mexico and landed upside down in four-and-a-half feet of water. The medical examiner said he died from blunt force trauma with drowning a contributing factor. He had morphine, amphetamine, and zolpidem (Ambien) in his system. He had traces of hydromorphone, a narcotic better known as Dilaudid; fluoxetine, an antidepressant better known as Prozac; and alcohol. The FAA prohibits pilots from flying under the influence of most of these medications. Pilots can be prosecuted for it.

Halladay's medications were prescribed, but the family knows how it looks.

"The autopsy report says that prescribed medications were not a factor in this accident," Brandy said. "In my mind, that says that he didn't have excessive amounts in his system. But they were in his system. Of course, they were in his system. The issue and the sad part to me is because of that everybody is always going to wonder. That's what breaks my heart for him and for my kids. Because people will always have that little shadow of a doubt, you know? Well, he was taking this, how do we know? We don't. We never will. And sadly he's not here to tell us, you know?"

Brandy knows that besides the autopsy report, people have questions about Roy's final moments in the plane. What was he doing? She does not know, but she said that he sometimes performed touch-and-go landings when he flew. It is a practice maneuver. The pilot lands on the runway, then immediately takes off. She said they made one once because the runway was too short and they didn't have time to stop. She said she flew with him when he practiced them. She wonders if he might have been doing something like that.

"Was he being reckless with it?" she said. "It certainly sounds like he might have been. But I don't think that he was being reckless for the sake of being reckless. He just wasn't that person. He was never a reckless person. He liked the feeling of going up and down, that feeling of flying. But he would never just go up and down, up and down. It's hard to know. I can see how it would look like he was being reckless if he was going up and down and up and down. But I also know when Roy had that time to himself he worked on things like that. So I wonder if maybe he was doing touch and goes. If he went down too quickly and the nose tipped, if a wave came by and it just went up over the nose of the plane, that could have... if he came down too steep and wasn't level enough. There's a million different things that could have contributed to it."

Big Roy is a pilot. He taught his son to fly. Their love of flying connected them. He tried to figure out what happened that day.

He talked to people. Lots of people. He finally stopped searching for answers because he knows the true answer will never come.

"The only thing that I would know is by what he told me; and he didn't tell me anything about it," he said. "He's gone."

Brandy is certain about one thing, however. Very certain.

"Do I think it was suicide?" she said. "One hundred and fifty percent no. Anybody who would assume that clearly did not know Roy. Anybody who knows Roy, if they truly know him, he would never do that. He would never leave his children that way. He would never take his own life. At that point in time things were pretty good. We were working through a lot of issues, but we were in a pretty good place. He had his job with the Phillies that he truly loved. He was developing friendships and working with the kids. Our team had just won the state baseball tournament. There were all of these things going on. It was not the time that that would even occur to me would be an issue. It just wouldn't."

In time, Brandy has accepted the fact that people will think what they think. The plane crashed. She cannot change that. She cannot change anything. She just knows that her family loved Roy, he loved them and they miss him terribly.

"It didn't feel like he was gone," she said. "It's not like he was sick. It's not like we were in a car crash together and he was in the hospital and finally passed away. We went to school and he's just not coming home. That was the hardest part. There was no finality to it. It's just like you're there then you're not. It was tough because we were so used to him not being there that it didn't feel abnormal. It just felt like he was on a road trip for a long time. It was probably three or four weeks I think before it really hit me like he's really not coming home. And I still every now and then have these dreams where I'll be somewhere in my dream and I'll look over and I'll see Roy. I'll be like, 'How is that possible? It actually wasn't you. You've been alive this whole time.' We'll have conversations or something because it doesn't seem like he should be gone."

| 23 |

The Legacy

BRANDY AND THE BOYS expected a phone call on January 22, 2019, the day the Baseball Writers' Association of America announced its latest induction class into the National Baseball Hall of Fame. Halladay needed to appear on 75 percent of the ballots cast for enshrinement, but everybody expected him to make it. Even if Brandy never saw Ryan Thibodaux's closely monitored Hall-of-Fame tracker on Twitter, friends and family offered updates.

"Everyone is posting on Facebook," she said. "'Mom, stop! Knock it off!' So you know it's coming."

Still, she worried. What would people say if he made it? Halladay had the credentials to be a first-ballot Hall of Famer, but in a hot-take world, people could be cruel, particularly on social media. Would Twitter trolls say terrible things? Would somebody in the media say or write something stupid or hurtful? Brandy worried about Braden and Ryan.

"I didn't want people to think that he made it because he had passed away," Brandy said. "I wanted him to be there because he deserved to be there. Not because of the story or the drama. So that was my only concern. It's very easy to say flippant, blank, heartless things when nobody is in front of your face that you have to be accountable to. Granted, 99.9 percent of the media has been very positive, but there have been a couple things that have happened that were really hurtful. So for me, I was nervous. Anytime you make yourself visible, you open yourself up to scrutiny or judgements in some way shape or form. I just didn't want to open that back up and have to relive it."

Brandy did that countless times over the previous 14 months. She could not escape it.

"It's hard to move forward when you're constantly looking back," she said. "Not that you don't want to remember, but I want to remember the funny stories and the conversations. Not, 'How are you doing? Are your boys okay?' 'Yes, we're fine. Yes, we're fine.' Everybody assumes how you're going to feel. 'Well, I know this is a tough time of year for you.' Why would it be? I know what I'm missing. You don't have to keep reminding me of that—so that was my concern with the Hall of Fame. What's the take going to be? Is it going to be a celebratory thing? Or is this going to be a we're-so-sad-he's-not-here thing? It's a combination of both. But I've made it very clear that anything I do, it has to be on the positive side. Because I can't keep dragging my kids through sadness. I can't."

BBWAA secretary Jack O'Connell calls every player that the organization elects to the Hall of Fame. He calls every player that wins MVP, Cy Young, Rookie of the Year, and Manager of the Year Awards too. He called Halladay when he won the AL Cy Young in 2003 and the NL Cy Young in 2010. He called Brandy on the 22nd to tell her that Doc made it. He appeared on 363 of 425 ballots cast (85.4 percent).

"I was very apprehensive," O'Connell said about the call. "My presentation is very brief, unless I know the person very well on the other end. It's just to say, 'Congratulations. The baseball writers select you to the Hall of Fame.' And I decided to do the same thing when she picked up the phone. And, to tell you the truth, she was exuberant. She was very happy, she was excited. You could hear—I think she had her kids around her—you could hear cheering in the background. I talked to Doc twice when he won the Cy Young award and I told her that. And I think I said something along the lines of, 'And I think you'd agree, Brandy, I wish I was speaking to him right now.' And she said, 'Yes. Me too.' But her whole attitude was really joyful."

Halladay would join Mariano Rivera, Edgar Martinez, and Mike Mussina, whom the BBWAA elected; and Lee Smith and Harold Baines, whom the veterans committee elected; for enshrinement in July in Cooperstown, New York.

Brandy, Braden, and Ryan asked themselves afterward if Halladay would have a Blue Jays or Phillies cap on his Hall of Fame plaque. It was an important question. Greg Maddux and Tony La Russa were the only two people in the Hall of Fame without a team's logo on their plaques. Maddux could not choose between the Braves and Cubs. La Russa could not choose between the Cardinals and A's. The Hall said okay. Sometimes the Hall

309

says no. It believes in historical accuracy. It does not want teams campaigning or enticing players to choose one team over another.

Gary Carter felt a strong connection to the Mets because he won a World Series with them in 1986, but the Hall told him that he needed an Expos logo on his cap because he played 12 of 19 seasons in Montreal. Andre Dawson wanted a Cubs logo, but the Hall said he needed a Montreal logo because he spent the first 11 of his 21 seasons there. Dawson called the decision "gut-wrenching." On the flip side, Reggie Jackson spent 10 of 21 seasons with the A's, but entered as a member of the Yankees because he earned his "Mr. October" nickname in New York.

Then there is Nolan Ryan. He did not make his first start with the Rangers until he was 42, but he has a Texas "T" on his cap.

Halladay spent 12 seasons with the Blue Jays and four with the Phillies.

"I'd go as a Blue Jay," Halladay told reporters at Rogers Centre in August 2016. "I wanted to retire here too, just because I felt like this is the bulk of my career."

But Brandy and the boys decided there would be no logo on his cap. It upset a few Blue Jays fans, who remembered Halladay's comments in 2016. Brandy knew the interview well, but the family interpreted his comments differently.

"Retiring as a Blue Jay is the right thing to do," Brandy said. "And I truly think that's what he meant. He wanted to be a Blue Jay to go into the Hall of Fame. I don't think that's a question of, if you had to choose between one or the other for your hat, which would you pick? Of course, then everybody wants to pop in like they have the right to an opinion or whatever, which is fine. But I know he would have never chosen. He wouldn't, if he knew that was an option. I didn't even know that was an option. It took me half a second to make the decision. They're like, are you sure? Do you want to think about it? I said, 'Well, I'll talk to the boys, but I'm pretty confident in that one.' So I talked to the boys and they absolutely said, no, no logo."

Phillies owner John Middleton sent his private jet to Florida to fly Brandy and the boys to New York for a press conference for the BBWAA electees the next afternoon. The family took an elevator up to the press conference with Rivera. He told the boys to enjoy the moment.

Brandy did not sit on the podium alongside Rivera, Martinez, and Mussina, but afterward reporters spoke with her. They asked what she thought about everything, and what she thought Halladay would have thought about everything.

Halladay spoke publicly about the Hall of Fame in March 2017 in Clearwater. He said, "It would obviously be a tremendous honor. I don't try to think about it, honestly. You see guys get in that are deserving and you see guys that are possibly deserving that don't get in. Boy, it's a tough thing to figure out. But absolutely, I would love to be there. I think every player who ever played the game would love to be there. It would be a tremendous honor. I just hope for the best." His sister Heather asked him a couple times about it. He never wanted to say if he thought he would make it. She thought he didn't want to jinx himself, but she said, "When it came down to it he was really hoping that he would. I think he would have been thrilled."

"I think to be inducted into the Hall of Fame is beyond... I mean everybody wants that, but you don't expect that to happen and when it does it is very surreal," Brandy said. "I know with our family it was always the work every day, so this is the result of the hard work we watched him do year after year after year. To me, the greatest part is seeing this end result.

"Those who know Roy, he was never focused on what he wanted in the end. He was focused on every step and that was a big part of his career. When he went down to the minors it was all about slowing things down to one pitch at a time. He never thought that far ahead. When baseball was over and he was ending his career, there was never a thought of 'Do you think I'll make it?' It was, 'Do you think I did enough?' He always wondered if he did and this is the answer: 'Yes you did.' It's amazing. I think he'd be relieved."

JULY CAME. BRANDY FOUND herself backstage with 53 returning Hall of Famers and the five men that joined her husband in the 2019 class at the induction ceremony at Clark Sports Center in Cooperstown. MLB Network's Brian Kenny introduced them all, including Hank Aaron, Sandy Koufax, Steve Carlton, Johnny Bench, Ken Griffey Jr., and Cal Ripken Jr. He introduced the incoming class, starting with Mussina and Baines before introducing Brandy.

Fans applauded every Hall of Famer that afternoon, but they stood and applauded a little longer for Aaron, who made his way on stage with the help of a cane and slugging first baseman Jim

Thome; Rivera, who drew tens of thousands of Yankees fans to the ceremony; and Brandy. She sat on stage next to Frank Thomas, who played with Halladay in Toronto in 2007–08. Halladay and Thomas became friends, and Thomas provided a familiar face and support before Brandy delivered her speech in front of an estimated 55,000 people.

Mussina spoke first. Brandy followed. Hall of Fame chairman Jane Forbes Clark stepped to the podium and asked everybody to turn their attention to the video board to watch a Halladay tribute. Chris Carpenter narrated his friend's career.

"He was the best pitcher in the game, for his time period, in that era," he said as highlights from Halladay's career played.

Carpenter retold Halladay's baseball story one more time, from his second big-league start at SkyDome to the demotion to Dunedin to the storied work ethic to his emergence as one of the greatest pitchers in baseball history.

"It's about celebrating one of the greatest pitchers who have ever played this game," he said. "It's about recognizing how much he brought to the game, how much joy he brought to people when he competed, how much joy he brought to the people around him, how many people he touched. A great teammate, friend, dad, husband, son, you put all those things together and he turned not into just a Hall of Fame pitcher, but a Hall of Fame man.

"It's just real life that he's not there speaking for himself, but we all know he's going to hear it and he knows it. And the great thing too is that his kids and his grandkids and everybody else is going to get to see what Roy Halladay was to the game of baseball."

313

MLB commissioner Rob Manfred read the words on Halladay's plaque:

HARRY LEROY HALLADAY III
"DOC" "ROY"
TORONTO, A.L. 1998–2009; PHILADELPHIA, N.L. 2010–2013

Top-of-rotation workhorse blended a blistering, sinking fastball with pinpoint control, earning Cy Young Awards in both the A.L. and the N.L. Eight-time All-Star delivered a .659 winning percentage, 203 career victories, and three 20-win seasons. Led his league in strikeout-to-walk five times and innings pitched four times. League leader in complete games seven times, most of any pitcher whose career began after World War II. Threw two no-hit games, both in 2010, a perfect game in the regular season, and the second-ever postseason no-hitter in Game 1 of the NLDS.

"I knew I was going to cry at some point," Brandy said at the podium. "I never know what it is that's going to get me. That video, I couldn't watch it. If somebody would send me a copy of that, I'd appreciate it."

Roberto Clemente was the last player posthumously inducted into the Hall of Fame by the BBWAA. He died in a plane crash in 1972, attempting to deliver aid from Puerto Rico to earthquake-ravaged Nicaragua. His wife, Vera Clemente, addressed the crowd that summer. She spoke less than a minute. Most of it was thanking the people involved in inducting her husband.

"This is Roberto's last triumph," she said, her voice cracking. "If he were here, he would dedicate this to our people of Puerto Rico, our people in Pittsburgh, and to all his fans throughout the United States. Thank you."

Brandy had been thinking about her speech for months, trying to remember random thoughts that entered her mind in the shower, the car, or wherever she happened to be. A lot of people asked her what she thought her husband might have said, if he could be on stage. Nobody knew, but she tried her best in a speech that lasted nearly seven minutes. She thanked the people that made Halladay's induction possible. She thanked the Hall of Famers behind her. She thanked the Blue Jays and Phillies for coming together to help her family celebrate her husband.

"This is not my speech to give," she told the crowd. "The thank yous could and should go on for days when you consider the impact so many people have had on Roy's career.... To the scouts, the coaches, the mentors, general managers, teammates, our families, and our friends, the fans, there are not enough words to thank you for your friendship, your support, your tutelage. Roy's natural talent was obviously a huge part of this. Without the unconditional and continued support from every one of you, he never could have dedicated himself to being the best ballplayer he could be. I say it a lot, but it takes a village, and we truly have a great one.

"I think Roy would rather be remembered by who he was, not what he did on the ball field. He was a very private person, often quiet and introverted, but he was also very generous and caring. The kind of man who made outrageous bets, would lose on purpose to help out a friend, the kind of brother who left cash in his pockets when he asked a sister to help with laundry, telling her she could keep whatever she found. I did the same thing. I kept what I found too. He was a great coach, a nervous husband and father only because he desperately wanted to be as great and successful at home as he was in baseball."

Brandy knew that better than anybody.

"I think that Roy would want everyone to know that people are not perfect," she said. "We are all imperfect and flawed in one way or another. We all struggle, but with hard work, humility, and dedication, imperfect people still can have perfect moments. Roy was blessed in his life and career to have some perfect moments. But I believe that they were only possible because of the man he strived to be, the teammate that he was, and the people he was so blessed to be on the field with. I am so humbled to say congratulations to this year's Hall of Fame inductees, to say thank you to all of you on Roy's behalf."

She left the podium and returned to her seat. Afterward, she was asked what she meant when she mentioned that people are not perfect. It was obvious what she meant and what she was referring to, but she never previously spoke about Halladay's death and the reports and stories that followed.

It could have been an uncomfortable moment. It was not.

"I've said this as long as I can remember," she said, "Roy was a very normal person with a very exceptionally amazing job. So these men who were up here that are doing these outstanding things, they're still real people, they still have feelings, they still have families, they still struggle.

"And so many of the guys that I've known in my life through baseball, they work so hard to hide that. I know Roy did, and Roy struggled a lot. Sometimes it's hard to present the image that you know everybody wants to see. It's also hard to be judged by the image people expect of you. It's a perception and an idea, and I think it's important that we don't sensationalize or idealize what a baseball player is but really look at the man and the human that's doing such an amazing thing. That's all I wanted to say there—real people doing really great things."

Braden smiled afterward.

"My mom, she's a rock," he said.

COOPERSTOWN WAS THE FINAL big moment of Halladay's big baseball life, but real life continued for Brandy, Braden, and Ryan. Braden returned to Penn State University, where he enrolled to play baseball. Brandy and Ryan returned home to Florida.

"I've made a very, very conscious effort to change the way that I look at things and the way that I allow things to make me feel," Brandy said. "I think obviously it's a sudden and tragic thing that you never want to happen. But I also look at this as another… this is a sad moment, but it's a great moment. Not great as in, it was an awesome thing, but a grandiose-type moment. Nothing Roy ever did was tiny and had no impact. Everything Roy did was big, it was strong, it was bold, it was impactful. I see this as another impactful moment. And trying to steer my thoughts and my feelings away from loss and pain and grief and regret and remorse. Because you could live there and be miserable. I don't have that luxury of laying in bed and crying. I have children that

I love more than this world that deserve a mom, that deserve a life, that deserve to find happiness too. Instead of focusing on the negative things, which we did. We took that time and got some help. Believe me, I've done my share of sad. But I self-talk myself every single day. This is what's good. This is what comes."

So what comes next? Halladay planned to spend his post-playing career trying to help people. Brandy wants to continue those efforts in whatever way she can.

"Something good has to come out of this or what's the point?" she said. "People don't just leave your life and nothing happens. Nothing does not happen. Something always happens. So what are we going to do? Are we going to be ugly and talk about the ugly things and the regrets? Are we going to talk about the horrible things? Or are we going to use this platform and turn it into something positive for someone in some way? This cannot just be a senseless loss of my husband and my kids' father."

Brandy still has 501(c)(3) tax exempt status for The Halladay Family Foundation. She hopes to raise money for the Positive Coaching Alliance and other charities. She joined the board of directors for Clearwater for Youth. Youth sports is one way to carry on Halladay's legacy.

"He didn't want a kid to feel scared," she said. "He didn't want a kid to feel yelled at from the stands, to be nervous. He told the parents, 'Listen, I'm the coach, if you want to talk to me, you can talk to me, but do not yell at your kid on the field.' It was really important to him to make a positive impact on youth sports. We're raising citizens, not athletes. And that's important. That's really important to both of us. He wanted to help people grow self-esteem, be confident. It's okay to fail, it's okay to struggle. But it's how you overcome those struggles that decide what kind of man you are, that show what kind of person you are."

Halladay's former managers, coaches, and teammates still light up when they talk about him. They loved their time together. He touched them.

"To this day, speaking about Roy and the impact he had on me and baseball will always be one of the hardest things I've had to do," Cole Hamels said. "It's the people we come in contact with and the relationships we make that define our character. It will always be a work in progress to honor him."

"I've caught some amazing pitchers—[Clayton] Kershaw, Curt Schilling, those guys—but whenever I can bring his name up, whenever I'm asked about a pitcher who was elite control, command, secondary pitches, I default straight to Roy," Rod Barajas said.

"He wanted no glory," Raúl Ibañez said. "Even the watches that he gave out after the perfect game, I was moved by it because at that point I was 38 years old, I had been playing for a long time, and I had never been on the field for a perfect game. And when he gave us the watches, I got emotional. I was deeply moved by the gesture because I thought we should have been giving something to him, you know? But that's who he was. He was constantly professional, ultimate teammate, ultimate warrior on the baseball field, and everything about him was just—he represented everything that was good in the game."

"Things work mysteriously," Rich Dubee said. "I mean, the things that happen in life and you try to put the map to them. Brandy finding the Harvey Dorfman book, Roy talking to Mariano about the cutter, two of the best buddies pitching against each other in Game 5, the no-hitter in his first playoff performance. The stuff that happens that makes you say oh my goodness gracious."

"By no means are you trying to replicate another Roy Halladay, but if any of our younger athletes can take a small tidbit of how he went about his work or how he treated people, it would help a lot of people," Dong Lien said.

"When you're in a video game and you're building a pitcher in a video game, all of his qualities—mental toughness, determination—he is the prototypical guy you'd build for me," Chase Utley said. "Listen, his arm was great and he had good stuff, but there was much more to it for him to have that amount of success."

"There's no better mold of somebody that fits into the Hall of Fame than him," Donovan Santas said. "He lived and breathed the game. He never took it for granted. What he went through from the peak of success to the minor leagues and back up. Just reinventing himself. He wasn't doing it to be the best. He was doing it not to leave any stone unturned. It was about the team. He just wanted to make sure he was the most prepared he could possibly be to compete."

"I use his name a lot," George Poulis said. "I'll stretch pitchers now and I still do it to this day. I stretch pitchers and I tell them, 'Have a good one.' But I'll tell some of them, I'm doing the exact routine that I did with Roy Halladay. They love it. That carries a lot of weight for him. So just being able to say that, I just want Roy's name to live on as long as possible."

It will carry on, and Brandy hopes that even her husband's final few years can offer hope and help.

"Everybody does struggle," she said. "People aren't perfect. We're all trying to do the best we can. And if you're humble and you're kind—Roy was working every single day to get better. Was he better? Did he have bad days? Sure, so did I. He's a real person. But to put these guys on pedestals and expect superhuman things isn't fair. It's not realistic. You're always going to be disappointed if you don't look at the human side of the person that you're talking about. You're always going to be disappointed.

"You're never going to learn how to not struggle. You're always going to struggle. But how do you struggle better? How do you struggle in a more functional way, in a healthier way? Everybody struggles, no matter what their office is, no matter what their stature is, no matter what their situation is. What you struggle with is not what I struggle with. And things that are easy for me to handle are not easy for you. So everybody has a right. How are you going to handle it?"

She hopes to share that message over time.

"That's maybe the silver lining on a rain cloud," she said. "Something good has to come from this."

Acknowledgments

THE NIGHT I EMAILED the final chapters of this book to my editor at Triumph Books, my wife, Ryan, and I celebrated like parents of a three-year-old and six-month-old (or at least how I want to believe most parents of a three-year-old and six-month-old might celebrate): we opened a mini-bottle of champagne and watched *The Mandalorian* on Disney+.

I could not have written this book without Ryan's love and support. When I started to work on *Doc* in February 2019, I was covering Phillies' spring training in Clearwater, Florida, while she was back in Philadelphia, working and raising our son, Henri. She had our daughter, Margot, in May, and soon after I was back on the road covering the Phillies. Even then she let me escape on weekends to write at a nearby library or coffee shop. How did she do it? I don't know. I love her and I am lucky she married me.

Of course, I must thank Brandy Halladay for her participation. She showed a tremendous amount of trust in me and I never took that trust for granted. She not only provided insight on Roy, she provided remarkable perspective on life. I wanted to write this book because it always struck me how Halladay not only overcame his demotion to Dunedin in 2001, but how he wanted to help people in retirement. He knew there were other people out there struggling. I hope I captured the essence of that.

The New York Times' Tyler Kepner and MLB Productions' Danny Field contributed in major ways. Tyler is one of the best baseball writers in the country. He also is one of the nicest. I mentioned to him in spring training that I was writing a Halladay book. He told me that he had a long interview with Roy in March 2017. He sent me the transcript. Field is another one of the nicest people in baseball. He had a long interview with Chris Carpenter at Citizens Bank Park in May 2019. Afterward, he let me watch it. During the interview, Field casually told Carpenter that he interviewed Halladay for 90 minutes a few years ago. I almost fell out of my chair. I immediately texted Danny and asked if I could see that interview too. He sent me the entire thing. Most of the quotes in this book about Halladay's perfect game, no-hitter, and thoughts and philosophies learning and throwing pitches came from interviews from Kepner and Field.

The Phillies' "Video" Dan Stephenson provided similar help. I asked if he had any behind-the-scenes moments of Halladay. He said yes, including the nearly 60-minute talk that he gave to Phillies' prospects in January 2016.

I started to panic early in the season because I spent most of my time transcribing interviews instead of writing. My good friend John DiCarlo works at Temple University, where he advises and teaches journalism students. I asked if he knew anybody that could help me transcribe. He recommended Graham Foley, who saved my life with hours of excellent transcriptions. He was enthusiastic and incredibly hard working. The person that gives Graham his first full-time job will be lucky to have him.

Bonnie Clark from the Phillies introduced me to Brandy. Greg Casterioto from the Phillies set up numerous interviews with Halladay's former teammates. Thanks to them.

I interviewed more than 100 people for this book. Many folks helped me find those people. Others simply went above and beyond with their time to help me tell Halladay's story. The list includes Jerry Crasnick, Donovan Santas, George Poulis, Dong Lien, Scott Sheridan, Kevin Camiscioli, Frank Coppenbarger, Roy Halladay II, Heather Basile, Zach Eflin, Pat Gillick, Buck Martinez, Ed Price, Rubén Amaro Jr., Scott Proefrock, Ronny Reyes, Tim Wilken, Ed Hayes, Chris Ware, Kenny Ayres, Jim Hogan, Jordan Bastian, Adam McCalvy, Anthony DiComo, Bryan Hoch, Richard Griffin, Jason Latimer, Joe Vieira, Kyle Brostowitz, Mike Vassallo, Rob Butcher, Dave Haller, Jon Kerber, Jim Capra, Cassidy Lent, and John Labombarda.

Jim Salisbury, Matt Gelb, Matt Breen, Meghan Montemurro, and Bob Brookover cover baseball in Philadelphia. They offered advice and support along the way.

Jesse Jordan is my editor at Triumph. We talked throughout the course of this project. He was always incredibly helpful, offering encouragement and honest feedback.

Matthew Leach is my editor at MLB.com. Thanks for giving me the okay to do this.

I've got to thank my family for their love and support. My parents, Steve and Sue. My brother, Mark; sister-in-law, Maryam;

and niece and nephew, Arthur and Bebe. My sister, Betsy; brother-in-law, Dan; and my nieces, Evelyn and Nora; and nephew, George. My mother-in-law, Joanne Hayes, who stopped by to help my wife while I ran off to write. (I'm certain my late father-in-law, Jim Hayes, would have gotten a kick out of this whole process and enjoyed the book.) Thanks everybody for checking in. And thanks for knowing me well enough to know to sometimes check in with Ryan instead!

I am lucky to have a smart, kind, caring, and beautiful wife. I am lucky to have two sweet children in Henri and Margot. I love them very much. This job takes me away from home a lot, but they are always on my mind. It was tremendously rewarding to write this book, but the best part about finishing is that I get to spend more time with them.

Sources

Chapter 1: Doctober

Hall of Fame announcement segment on MLB Network on January 21, 2019

Halladay throws no-hitter as Phils win playoff opener, by Matt Gelb, *The Philadelphia Inquirer (Oct. 7, 2010)*

Reds have to hand it to Halladay, by Ray Parillo, *The Philadelphia Inquirer (Oct. 7, 2010)*

"We did it together," by Roy Halladay, *The Sporting News (Dec. 20, 2010).*

Doc and the Freak, by Phil Sheridan, *The Philadelphia Inquirer (Oct. 16, 2010)*

Roy Halladay interview in Lutz, Florida, by Danny Field, MLB Productions *(2014)*

Chapter 2: The Basement

Halladay had plenty of help fulfilling his dream, by Bob Elliott, *Toronto Sun (May 20, 2006)*

Roy Halladay interview, DiscoverBoating.com

From Arvada to all-star, Halladay, 25, still improving, by Mike Klis, *Denver Post (July 20, 2002)*

What Made Roy Fly, by Stephanie Apstein, *Sports Illustrated (July 17, 2019)*

Chapter 3: Bus
Colorado legend Campbell dies at 87, by Joshua Lindenstein, *Daily Camera (Feb. 14, 2008)*
"Bus" helped area pitchers in a major way, by Irv Moss, *The Denver Post (Feb. 14, 2008)*
In Colorado, Moyer gets quick refresher course, by Paul Hagen, *Philadelphia Daily News (Oct. 6, 2007)*

Chapter 4: Arvada West
Halladay, A-West gain final, by Neil H. Devlin, *The Denver Post (May 20, 1994)*
Remembering Roy Halladay, a hometown all-star, by Shanna Fortier, *Arvada Press (Nov. 13, 2017).*
Creek adds to title glut, by Neil H. Devlin, *The Denver Post (May 22, 1995)*
Blue Jays declare Roy Halladay, Arvada West pitcher, is No. 1 in Toronto, by Neil H. Devlin, *Denver Post (June 2, 1995)*
Halladay's talent was obvious early on, by Paul Willis, *Rocky Mountain News (July 3, 2007)*
Gillick's drive may help Orioles fly, by Mark Maske, *The Washington Post (Feb. 4, 1996)*
Braves' Bourjos has deep connections to Blue Jays, by Bob Elliott, CBC News *(June 21, 2018)*
Blue Jays declare Roy Halladay, Arvada West pitcher, is No. 1 in Toronto, by Neil H. Devlin, *Denver Post (June 2, 1995)*
Roy Halladay interview, by Danny Field, MLB Productions *(2014)*

Chapter 5: Doc and Carp
Blue Jays notes, by Tom Maloney, *The Spectator (Feb. 19, 1997)*
Jay hurler impresses with poise, by Richard Griffin, *Toronto Star (March 9, 1997)*
Chris Carpenter interview, MLB Productions *(May 2019)*

Jays' hot prospect hopes he can measure up, *Toronto Star (Feb. 15, 1998)*

Just what Jays ordered, *Toronto Star (Sept. 12, 2003)*

Former A-West star gets his shot today, by Neil H. Devlin, *Denver Post (Sept. 20, 1998)*

Roy Halladay nearly no-hit Detroit Tigers in 2nd MLB start, by Gene Guidi, *Detroit Free Press (Sept. 28, 1998)*

Halladay fashions near-perfect finish, by Geoff Baker, *Toronto Star (Sept. 28, 1998)*

Jays callup misses no-hitter by one out, by Tom Maloney, *The Ottawa Citizen (Sept. 28, 1998)*

High-country heat Arvada West's Doc Halladay has gun, and he will fire for the Toronto Blue Jays, by John Henderson, *Denver Post (April 1, 1999)*

Reds rips the Jays twice, by Allan Ryan, *Toronto Star (March 8, 1999)*

Jays fire Johnson for Vietnam lies, by Ben Walker, Associated Press *(March 17, 1999)*

Fregosi lashes out at critics of trades, by Geoff Baker, *Toronto Star (Nov. 18, 1999)*

Fregosi flexes his muscles, by Tom Maloney, *National Post (Nov. 15, 1999)*

Chapter 6: 10.64

In Dunedin, it's babes with arms, *Toronto Star (March 24, 2000)*

Halladay accepts stint in bullpen, by Larry Millson, *The Globe and Mail (May 8, 2000)*

Jays option struggling Halladay to Syracuse, call up Munro, by Larry Millson, *The Globe and Mail (May 17, 2000)*

Kids get steady targer, by Bob Putnam, *St. Petersburg Times (March 3, 2000)*

Halladay hammer, by Mark Zwolinski, *Toronto Star (July 1, 2000)*

Canadian jinx ends for O's, by Jeff Blair, *Globe and Mail (July 22, 2000)*

Fregosi left out of pitching coach decision, by Ross Newhan, *The Los Angeles Times (July 30, 2000)*

Roy Halladay interview in Lutz, Florida, by Danny Field, MLB Productions *(2014)*

Chapter 7: Mel Queen

The Big 50: Toronto Blue Jays by Shi Davidi, Triumph Books

Roy Halladay adopts fresh mental approach to the game, by Jack Etkin, *Baseball Digest (March 1, 2003)*

To hell and back, by Geoff Baker, *The Toronto Star (Sept. 27, 2003)*

Halladay back on the ball, by Skip Wood, *USA Today (June 30, 2005)*

The Doctor's Cure, by Jeremy Sandler, *The National Post (June 27, 2003)*

Inside Major League Baseball, by Larry Millson, *The Globe and Mail (July 2, 2001)*

Lost and Found, by Buster Olney and Jim Callis, ESPN.com *(July 10, 2003)*

Roy Halladay interview in Lutz, Florida, by Danny Field, MLB Productions *(2014)*

Second to One, by Michael Farber, *Sports Illustrated (April 16, 2007)*

Mozart of the Mound, by Marty York, *Maclean's (October 6, 2003)*

Chapter 8: A New Roy

Roy Halladay adopts fresh mental approach to the game, by Jack Etkin, *Baseball Digest (March 1, 2003)*

Inside Major League Baseball by Larry Millson, *The Globe and Mail (July 2, 2001)*

Halladay brightens the gloom, by Jeff Blair, *The Globe and Mail (July 27, 2001)*

Halladay continues impressive resurrection, by Larry Millson, *The Globe and Mail (Sept. 19, 2001)*

Halladay received direction from Wells on his road to perfection, by
Tom Verducci, *Sports Illustrated (May 30, 2010)*

Jays, this Buck's all new, by Richard Griffin, *Toronto Star (Feb. 15,
2002)*

Halladay can celebrate, by Ben Bolch, *The Los Angeles Times (Nov.
12, 2003)*

2003 Pitcher of the Year, by Jack Etkin, *Baseball Digest (Jan. 1, 2004)*

Mozart of the Mound, by Marty York, *Maclean's (October 6, 2003)*

Chapter 9: Harvey

Stay in the Moment (with Dr. Baseball), by Karl Taro Greenfeld,
Men's Journal (Feb. 2009)

To baseball greats, a coach of the mind, by T. Rees Shapiro, *The
Washington Post (March 4, 2011)*

The Work of Harvey Dorfman, by Andrew D. Knapp and Alan S.
Kornspan, *The Baseball Research Journal (March 22, 2015)*

Each Branch, Each Needle, by H.A. Dorfman, Hamilton Books
(2010)

The Thing; Nobody Wants to Talk About It, Everybody's Terrified of
It. Can Rick Ankiel Beat It?, by Jeff Bradley, *Chicago Sun-Times
(Dec. 3, 2000)*

More Athletes Turning to Sports Psychologists to Help Cope, by Ron
Kroichick, *The San Francisco Chronicle (July 1, 2001)*

Roy Halladay: 2003 Pitcher of the Year, by Jack Etkin, *Baseball
Digest (Jan. 1, 2004)*

Roy Halladay interview in Lutz, Florida, by Danny Field, MLB
Productions *(2014)*

Halladay back on the ball, by Skip Wood, *USA Today (June 30,
2005)*

Mozart of the Mound, by Marty York, *Maclean's (October 6, 2003)*

Chapter 10: Cy Young

Halladay notches first win of season, by Jeff Blair, *The Globe & Mail* *(May 2, 2003)*

Chicago bats no match for hot Halladay, Canadian Press *(May 28, 2003)*

Halladay's run ends at 15 straight wins, Associated Press *(Aug. 2, 2003)*

Halladay has fling with no-hitter, Canadian Press *(Sept. 7, 2003)*

The Doctor is in ... through 2007, by Jeremy Sandler, *National Post* *(Jan. 23, 2004)*

Chapter 11: The Arsenal

Roy Halladay interview in Lutz, Florida, by Danny Field, MLB Productions *(2014)*

Chapter 12: The Machine

Halladay may face end of season, by Jeff Blair, *Globe & Mail (July 18, 2004)*

Halladay has something new in store for batters: Works on changeup, by John Lott, *National Post (May 31, 2005)*

Halladay primed to carry big load, by David Shoalts, *Globe and Mail (March 31, 2005)*

Doc, by A.J. Burnett, *The Players' Tribune (May 29, 2018)*

Bombers' Bats Forced to Take a Halladay, by Filip Bondy, *New York Daily News (April 29, 2006)*

Roy, oh Roy!, by Kat O'Brien, *New York Newsday (July 12, 2008)*

Chapter 13: Time to Move On

It's getting harder to keep the faith, Halladay says, by Shi Davidi, The Canadian Press *(July 26, 2008)*

Jays will make most of what they have, Canwest News Service *(Feb. 14, 2009)*

Any offer for Halladay would have to be a whopper, by Robert
   MacLeod, *Globe and Mail (July 8, 2009)*
GM open to offers for Halladay, by Jeremy Sandler, *National Post
   (July 8, 2009)*
All eyes on Halladay, by Jeff Blair, *Globe and Mail (July 14, 2009)*
Halladay pitches a gem, by Jeff Blair, *Globe and Mail (July 19, 2009)*
Ricciardi reacts to rift rumours, by Robert MacLeod and Jeff Blair,
   Globe and Mail (July 23, 2009)
Doc's pitching does the talking, by Jeff Blair, *Globe and Mail (July 24,
   2009)*
J.P. keeping his options open, by Cathal Kelly, *Toronto Star (Oct. 24,
   2008)*
Halladay plans a day locked in hotel room, by Jim Salisbury,
   Philadelphia Inquirer (July 30, 2009)
The Rotation, by Jim Salisbury and Todd Zolecki, Running Press
   (2012)
Doc fails stress test, by Richard Griffin, *Toronto Star (July 30, 2009)*
Don't blame Ricciardi: Halladay, by John Lott, *Canwest News Service
   (Oct. 5, 2009)*
Roy Halladay interview in Lutz, Florida, by Danny Field, MLB
   Productions *(2014)*

Chapter 14: Philly

Halladay's regimen inspiring Kendrick, by Matt Gelb, *Philadelphia
   Inquirer (Feb. 20, 2010)*
"I have a window of opportunity that's getting smaller," by Steve
   Greenberg, *Sporting News (Feb. 15, 2010)*
Hooray for Halladay, by Matt Gelb, *Philadelphia Inquirer (April 6,
   2010)*
Halladay, Phillies stymie Braves, by Bob Brookover, *Philadelphia
   Inquirer (April 22, 2010)*

Halladay stoic after first loss, by Matt Gelb, *Philadelphia Inquirer*
(*April 28, 2010*)

Ace displaced: Halladay roughed up by Red Sox, by Matt Gelb,
Philadelphia Inquirer (May 24, 2010)

Tales of Roy Halladay's perfect game, by Matt Gelb, *Philadelphia
Inquirer (May 31, 2010)*

Roy Halladay interview in Lutz, Florida, by Danny Field, MLB
Productions *(2014)*

Chapter 16: Perfection

"We did it together," by Roy Halladay, *The Sporting News (Dec. 20,
2010)*

Tales of Roy Halladay's perfect game, by Matt Gelb, *Philadelphia
Inquirer (May 31, 2010)*

Phillies' Roy Halladay throws perfect game against Florida Marlins, by
Clark Spencer, *Miami Herald (May 30, 2010)*

Perfect Halladay, by Juan C. Rodriguez, *South Florida Sun-Sentinel
(May 30, 2010)*

Roy Halladay interview in Lutz, Florida, by Danny Field, MLB
Productions *(2014)*

Chapter 17: It's Only Going to Get Funner

A Dominant Force, by Matt Gelb, *Philadelphia Inquirer (June 26,
2010)*

Understanding the Doc's bedside manner, by Jeff Blair, *Globe and Mail
(June 26, 2010)*

Phillies defeat Nationals, 8-0, to clinch NL East, by Matt Gelb,
Philadelphia Inquirer (Sept. 28, 2010)

"We did it together," by Roy Halladay, *The Sporting News (Dec. 20,
2010)*

Opposites Collide, by Matt Gelb, *Philadelphia Inquirer (Oct. 16,
2010)*

Halladay proves hittable, especially to Ross, by Phil Sheridan,
Philadelphia Inquirer (Oct. 17, 2010)
Halladay: Early finish to Phillies' season 'bittersweet', by Ed Barkowitz,
Philadelphia Daily News (Oct. 26, 2010)

Chapter 18: The Rotation
What Harvey Dorfman did for the Phillies, by Phil Sheridan,
Philadelphia Inquirer (March 2, 2011)
Happy Return for Halladay Against the Blue Jays, by Matt Gelb,
Philadelphia Inquirer (July 3, 2011)

Chapter 19: He's Human
Skeet Reese & Roy Halladay rescue snake bite victim, Bassmaster.com
(Jan. 6, 2012)
A Jungle Out There, by Skeet Reese, SkeetReese.com *(Dec. 13, 2011)*
Phillies' Halladay expresses affection for Philadelphia, by Matt Gelb,
Philadelphia Inquirer (Feb. 22, 2012)
Halladay leaves with sore shoulder as Phillies lose, by Bob Brookover,
Philadelphia Inquirer (May 28, 2012)
Roy Halladay struggles as Phillies lose to Braves, by Matt Gelb,
Philadelphia Inquirer (Sept. 22, 2012)
Blue Jays minor leaguers rough up Roy Halladay, by Matt Gelb,
Philadelphia Inquirer (May 24, 2013)
Mets light up Halladay and Phillies, 7-2, by Matt Gelb, *Philadelphia
Inquirer (April 8, 2013)*
Roy Halladay offers apology to upset fans, by Matt Gelb, *Philadelphia
Inquirer (May 11, 2013)*
Ailing Halladay exits in first as Phillies lose to Marlins, by Matt Gelb,
Philadelphia Inquirer (Sept. 24, 2013)

Chapter 20: How You Fit In
What Made Roy Fly, by Stephanie Apstein, *Sports Illustrated (July 17, 2019)*

Chapter 21: Second Callings
Roy Halladay spent his final months teaching future Phillies, by Matt Breen, *Philadelphia Inquirer (Nov. 20, 2017)*
What Made Roy Fly, by Stephanie Apstein, *Sports Illustrated (July 17, 2019)*
Calvary Christian High, winners of 44 straight games, carry the memory of their assistant coach, Roy Halladay, by Matt Gelb, *The Athletic (March 27, 2018)*

Chapter 22: I Love You Too
What Made Roy Fly, by Stephanie Apstein, *Sports Illustrated (July 17, 2019)*

Chapter 23: The Legacy
Roy Halladay wants to wear Blue Jays cap if inducted into Hall of Fame, by Mark Zwolinski, *Toronto Star (Aug. 14, 2016)*

Index

A

Aaron, Hank, 312
Abreu, Bobby, 272
Alderson, Sandy, 99, 273
Alexander, Grover Cleveland, 87
All-Star Game (2005), 142
All-Star Game (2008), 129, 153
All-Star Game (2009), 156-157
All-Star Game (2011), 238
Alomar, Roberto, 89
Amaro, Rubén, Jr.
    Doc's death and, 300
    Doc's perfect game and, 203, 207, 210,
      213
    Doc's retirement and, 268
    Doc's trade and, 155, 159-160, 164-170
    Lee and, 232
    Phillies and, 238-240
Amazon River, 247-250
American League All-Star team, 93
American League Wild Card, 50
Anthopoulos, Alex, 163-166, 170, 268, 298
Appel, Mark, 279
Argentina, 256
Arizona Diamondbacks, 67, 91
Arizona Fall League, 55
Armstrong, Lance, 281
Arnsberg, Brad, 127, 135, 144
Arvada, Colorado, 15-18
Arvada West High School, 31-33, 36-37
Asche, Cody, 264

Ash, Gord, 35, 56, 68-70, 74-76, 88, 268
Atlanta Braves, 182, 217-218, 223, 255
Aumont, Phillippe, 169-170
Aurora, Colorado, 15, 18, 23
Aybar, Erick, 161

B

Baines, Harold, 309, 312
Bako, Paul, 52
Baldelli, Rocco, 126
Baltimore Orioles, 57, 241
Barajas, Rod, 135, 145-148, 162, 319
Bard, Josh, 28-29, 36
Barrett, Michael, 36, 154-155
baseball, 17-22, 73-78, 93-95, 104-108
Baseball America, 34, 42, 44, 55, 159
Baseball Hall of Fame, 32, 79, 307-317
Baseball Reference, 241, 270
Baseball Writers' Association of America,
    123, 307-311, 314
Baume & Mercier, 214
Beeston, Paul, 163, 298
Bell, George, 42-43
Bellinger, Clay, 299
Bellinger, Cody, 299
Beltran, Carlos, 39
Bench, Johnny, 312
Bergman, Sean, 64
Berkman, Lance, 242-244
Berry, Jeff, 165-169, 287
Biddle, Jesse, 271-272, 298

Biden, Joe, 211
Biggio, Craig, 159
Billmeyer, Mick, 190
Blanton, Joe, 166-167, 233-234, 242
Blass, Steve, 64
Blue, Vida, 52
Boggs, Wade, 99
Boras, Scott, 94, 101-102
Boras Corporation, The, 94, 101
Boston Red Sox, 60, 85-86, 118, 182-183, 186
Bourjos, Chris, 35
Bourjos, Peter, 35, 161
Bowie, Micah, 64
Boyer, Clete, 99-100
Braunecker, Darek, 166, 169
Brazil, 247-250
Breeden, Scott, 70
Brockport State Teachers College, 98
Brooks Baseball, 240
Brown, Domonic, 159-160, 164-166, 251
Brown, Kevin, 52-54, 57-58, 80-81
Bruce, Jay, 6-10
Bunner, Jonny, 284
Burks, Ellis, 89
Burnett, A.J., 151-152, 154, 164
Burr and Burton Academy, 98
Burrell, Pat, 224-227
Burrs Lane Junior High School, 98
Busby, Steve, 24, 83
Bush, George W., 174
Bush, Homer, 56
Butterfield, Brian, 92-93

C

Cabrera, Orlando, 6, 8
Cairo, Miguel, 10-11
Calvary Christian High School, 282-284
Camiscioli, Kevin, 186-187, 194-195, 213
Campbell, Randy, 27
Campbell, Robert "Bus," 23-29, 33-34, 38, 72-73
Canseco, José, 102
Cantú, Jorge, 202, 205
Capra, Jim, 31-34, 36, 39-40, 50
Carlton, Steve, 64, 120, 312
Carolina Mudcats, 79

Carpenter, Chris
    2000 season and, 62-65
    2005 All-Star Game and, 142
    2011 NLDS game and, 243-246
    Blue Jays and, 35, 41-46, 51, 57-60, 90-91
    curveballs and, 132-133
    Doc and, 13, 84, 105, 195, 247-250, 256, 281, 313
    Doc's death and, 297, 301
    Dorfman and, 94
Carpenter Complex, 257, 284-287
Carrasco, Carlos, 159-160
Carter, Gary, 310
Carter, Joe, 56
Cash, Kevin, 121-122, 140-141, 148
Casterioto, Greg, 232-233, 240
Castillo, Alberto, 58, 61
Castro, Juan, 203-209, 298
Catalanotto, Frank, 54
Chacón, Shawn, 24
changeups, 135-136, 171-173
Cherry Creek High School, 25-26, 36-37
Chicago Cubs, 238-240
Chicago White Sox, 56, 165-168
Cincinnati Reds, 1, 4-10, 221-223
Citizens Bank Park, 1, 168-170, 182, 196, 216-218, 240, 279
Clark, Jane Forbes, 313
Class A Dunedin, 69-72
Clearwater, Florida, 282
Clearwater for Youth, 318
Clemens, Roger, 45, 50, 55, 87, 120, 172, 188, 270
Clement, Matt, 154
Clemente, Roberto, 314-315
Clemente, Vera, 314-315
Cleveland Indians, 89, 122, 159-160
coaching, 23-29, 74-81, 100-101, 171-174, 263, 268-272, 282-284
Coghlan, Chris, 202-204
Colón, Bartolo, 144, 155
Colorado Rockies, 91, 217
Colorado Sports Hall of Fame, 24, 275
Cone, David, 214
Connor, Mark, 67-70, 80-81, 84-86, 90-91, 263

Contreras, José, 172, 227
Cooperstown, New York, 32, 309, 312, 317
Coppenbarger, Frank, 161, 193, 213-214, 218
Cosart, Jarred, 240
Costas, Bob, 156
Cousins, Derryl, 224
Creative Artists Agency (CAA), 165, 168-169, 231-232
Crespo, Felipe, 51-52
Cruz, José, Jr., 38
Cueller, Mike, 232, 241
curveballs, 132-135
cutters, 127-132
Cy Young Award
    Clemens and Hentgen and, 45
    Doc and, 95, 123, 150, 162, 223, 228, 269-270
    Hall of Fame and, 314
    Kershaw and, 241
    Moyer and, 25
    O'Connell and, 309
    Phillies and, 231

D

d'Arnaud, Travis, 159, 166-167
Davis, Ben, 38
Davis, Wade, 166
Dawson, Andre, 310
Delgado, Carlos, 52, 58, 170
Denver Broncos, 24
Denver Nuggets, 24
Denver South High School, 24
Detroit Tigers, 51-54, 68, 121, 140, 150
DeWitt, Matt, 58
DiMuro, Mike, 204
Dobbs, Greg, 183, 205
Dobson, Pat, 232, 241
Donald, Jason, 159-160
Dorfman, Anita, 98
Dorfman, Harvey
    Brandy and, 72
    Doc and, 3-5, 14, 94-95, 104-109, 149-152, 216, 224-225, 242, 258
    Doc's perfect game and, 208
    Doc's routine and, 112-113
    illness and death and, 229-231

    as inspiration to Doc, 271-273, 276, 279-281, 285-287
    The Mental ABC's of Pitching and, 319-320
    psychology and, 97-103
Double-A Reading, 174, 271
Double-A Tennessee, 74-80
Drabek, Doug, 159
Drabek, Kyle, 159-160, 164-167
Drew, Tim, 155
Drumright, Mike, 38
Dubee, Rich
    Doc and, 5-6, 180, 202, 239-240
    Doc's back problems and, 254
    Doc's death and, 300
    Doc's final game and, 264-265
    Doc's legacy and, 319
    Doc's perfect game and, 211
    Doc's training routine and, 189-191
    Dorfman and, 100-101, 216
    NLDS against the Giants and, 225-227
    pitching technique and, 171-177
    Reds and, 9
Dunedin, Florida, 40, 67-68
Dunedin Blue Jays, 41, 118, 174
Dunedin Panthers, 268
Durbin, Chad, 181-182, 198-199, 203

E

Each Branch, Each Needle (Dorfman), 94
Eflin, Zach, 287
Eickhoff, Jerad, 287
Elarton, Scott, 24-26
ElAttrache, Dr. Neal, 261
Eldred, Cal, 24
Elias Sports Bureau, 120
Embry-Riddle Aeronautical University, 275-276
Engle, Bob, 34
Enya, 3
Erstad, Darin, 38
Escobar, Kelvim, 41-42, 57-59, 62
Espinosa, Danny, 219
ESPN The Magazine, 55
Evans, Tom, 52

F

FanGraphs, 241
Fasano, Sal, 128
fastballs, 171-173
Fcasni, Shawn, 264
Fernandez, Tony, 52
Fielding Independent Pitching, 241
Fisher, Brian, 23-24
Fletcher, Darrin, 52-53, 59
Florida Burn, 282-284
Florida Marlins, 6-7, 182
Florida State League, 72
flying, 291-295, 302-303
Fontenot, Joe, 38
FoxSports.com, 253
Francisco, Ben, 160
Francisco, Juan, 9
Francona, Terry, 142
Franklin, Ben, 179
Freeman, Freddie, 196-197
Fregosi, Jim, 56-63
Fryman, Travis, 89
Furcal, Rafael, 243-244

G

Gabler, Frank, 64
Garciaparra, Nomar, 92
Gaston, Cito, 43, 59
Gibson, Bob, 60, 120
Gillick, Pat, 32-33, 73, 157, 159
Gillies, Tyson, 169-170
Glavine, Tom, 130
Gomes, Jonny, 7-10
González, Juan, 89
Gonzalez, Luis, 52
Gose, Anthony, 159-160, 166
Gossage, Goose, 24-25
Grabowski, Reggie, 64
Gradishar, Randy, 24
Granderson, Curtis, 136
Grapefruit League, 68
Green, Shawn, 58
Greene, Todd, 84-85
Gregg, Kevin, 205
Greinke, Zach, 162
Griffey, Ken, Jr., 312

Grove, Lefty, 64, 120
Guillen, Ozzie, 23
Gulf Coast League Blue Jays, 40, 41

H

Halladay, Braden
    birth of, 63
    Brandy and, 317
    Doc and, 257
    Doc's coaching and, 282-283
    Doc's death and, 297, 301-302
    Doc's perfect game and, 211
    Doc's retirement and, 268-270
    Hall of Fame and, 309-311
    NLDS against the Reds and, 10
Halladay, Brandy Gates
    birth of Ryan and, 141
    Blue Jays and, 61-63
    Campbell and, 27-28
    Cy Young Award and, 123
    Doc and, 46-51, 105
    Doc as mental skills coach and, 288-289
    Doc's back problems and, 252, 256
    Doc's coaching and, 282-284
    Doc's death and, 298-305
    Doc's depression and, 70-75, 274-277
    Doc's final game and, 265
    Doc's flying and, 291-295
    Doc's leg injury and, 142-144
    Doc's painkiller addiction and, 259-261
    Doc's perfect game and, 201, 206,
        209-211
    Doc's plane crash and, 296-297
    Doc's retirement and, 268-271
    Doc's trade and, 167-168
    Doc's training routine and, 112, 139
    Hall of Fame and, 307-316
    life after Doc and, 317-321
    NLDS against the Giants and, 10
    Toronto and, 158, 161-162
Halladay, Harry Leroy, II "Big Roy," 15-22,
    23, 26, 34, 50-51, 298, 301, 303-304
Halladay, Heather, 17-20, 273, 298, 311
Halladay, Linda, 16, 20
Halladay, Merinda, 19, 47-48
Halladay, Roy "Doc"
    2000 season and, 55-65

2003 season and, 118-122
2004 season and, 140-141
2009 season and, 153-163
2011 season and, 235-245
2013 season and, 257-258
back problems and, 251-255, 273-274
Blue Jays and, 50-54
Brandy and, 47-49
Bus Campbell and, 23-29
Carpenter and, 41-46, 247-250, 256
catchers and, 145-149
childhood and, 15-22
Class A Dunedin and, 70-73
coaching and, 282-284
Cy Young Award and, 123
death of, 298-301
depression and, 275
Dorfman and, 94-95, 102-108, 229-231
final game and, 264-265
flying and, 291-294
generosity and, 213-215
Hall of Fame and, 307-317
high school career and, 31-37
leg injury and, 142-144
legacy of, 318-321
as mental skills coach, 284-288
MLB First-Year Player Draft (1995) and,
    38-40
National League Championship Series
    and, 223-228
National League East title and, 218-221
NLDS against the Reds and, 1-14
painkiller addiction and, 259-261
perfect game and, 201-212
Phillies and, 171-175, 179-183
pitching technique and, 125-136
plane crash and, 295-297, 302-305
post-2000 season and, 67-69
psychology and, 216-217
public speaking and, 279-281
Queen and, 74-81
rehab and, 276-277
retirement and, 267-272
return to Blue Jays and, 83-93
The Rotation and, 232-235
shoulder surgery and, 262-263
sports memorabilia and, 222-223

trade to Phillies and, 164-170
training routine and, 111-117, 137-139,
    150-152, 176-178, 185-199
Halladay, Ryan, 141, 268-270, 283, 294-297,
    301-302, 309-311, 317
Halladay Family Foundation, The, 318
Hall-of-Fame tracker, 307
Hamels, Cole, 160, 167, 203, 226, 231-235,
    238, 241-242, 301, 319
Hamilton, Joey, 57
Happ, J.A., 159-160, 166
Harper, Tommy, 74
Hawkins, Kirk, 293
Hayes, Brett, 203, 206
Helms, Wes, 207
Helton, Todd, 38
Hendricks, Kyle, 122
Hentgen, Pat, 45-46, 56, 57-58, 87, 298
Heritage High School, 27
Hermansen, Chad, 38
Hernandez, Felix, 162
Hernández, Ramón, 9-10
Hewes, Tim, 69-70
Higginson, Bobby, 53-54
Hinske, Eric, 131-132
Hirschbeck, John, 8
Holtz, Lou, 179
Hooton, Burt, 24
Houston Astros, 181, 240
Howard, Ryan, 12, 193, 204, 208-210, 226,
    244-245, 251, 272, 299-300
Howell, Jay, 24
Hubbell, Carl, 87
Huckaby, Ken, 91-92, 149, 299
Hudson, Orlando, 92-93
Hudson, Tim, 141, 234
Hurst, Bruce, 99

I
Ibañez, Raúl
    Doc and, 145, 218
    Doc's legacy and, 319
    Doc's perfect game and, 204, 209
    Dorfman and, 98, 102, 108-109, 230
    NLDS against the Giants and, 6-7
    Phillies and, 251
ICON A5, 293-296, 302

Inouye, Jay, 111
Iooss, Walter, 234
Iron Mike, 76
Issel, Dan, 24

J

Jackson, Danny, 23-24
Jackson, Reggie, 310
Jay, Jon, 244
Jenkins, Geoff, 38
Jennings, Desmond, 166
Jeter, Derek, 83, 130, 150
Johnson, Davey, 241
Johnson, Jonathan, 38
Johnson, Josh, 204
Johnson, Marc, 25-26, 36-37
Johnson, Moose, 34
Johnson, Randy, 67, 91, 270
Johnson, Tim, 50, 56, 58
Johnson, Tyler, 26, 36-37
Jones, Jamie, 38

K

K: A History of Baseball in Ten Pitches
  (Kepner), 130
Kansas City Royals, 23, 59, 145
Kapler, Gabe, 52
Karsay, Steve, 35
Kendrick, Kyle, 171-175, 185, 218,
  230-231, 242, 300
Kenny, Brian, 312
Kepner, Tyler, 77, 127, 172, 252
Kershaw, Clayton, 241, 319
Key, Jimmy, 83
Kligman, Marc, 298
Knapp, Andrew, 279
Knapp, Jason, 160
Knudson, Mark, 24
Koch, Billy, 111-112
Koufax, Sandy, 312
Kuehl, Karl, 98-100

L

La Russa, Tony, 309
Lamb, Mike, 206
Landry, Greg, 165, 168
Langford, Rick, 59-60, 62

Langston, Mark, 24
Larkin, Andy, 64
Larsen, Don, 9
Lee, Cliff
  Cy Young Award and, 241-242
  Doc and, 2-3, 179, 202
  Phillies and, 163, 166-169, 231-235, 238
  Sheridan and, 185
  trade to Phillies and, 160
Leftwich, Luke, 286
Leiter, Al, 102
Leonard, Dennis, 83
Leyva, Nick, 56
Lidge, Brad, 24-26, 36-37, 218, 227, 230
Lien, Dong, 3, 175-177, 186-188, 191-194,
  202, 263-264, 300, 320
Lincecum, Tim, 156, 223-226
Litsch, Jesse, 154-155
Littleton High School, 24
Lloyd, Graeme, 56
Loaiza, Esteban, 84, 123
Lockwood, Mike, 283-284
Lofton, Kenny, 89
Los Angeles Angels, 56-57, 120, 165
Los Angeles Dodgers, 80-81, 91, 255
Lowe, Derek, 95
Lucas, Ed, 264

M

Madden, Brad, 36, 39
Maddon, Joe, 156
Maddux, Greg, 87, 102, 130, 309
Madson, Ryan, 218, 227-228, 251
Manfred, Rob, 314
Manuel, Charlie, 156, 159, 180-183, 205,
  216-218, 226, 241, 261, 301
Marcum, Shaun, 154
Marichal, Juan, 87
Maroth, Mike, 154
Marson, Lou, 160
Martinez, Buck, 68-70, 83-85, 90-91
Martinez, Edgar, 309-311
Martinez, Pedro, 91, 95, 123, 130, 269
Matsui, Hideki, 119
Matthews, Gary, 210, 219-220
Maybin, Cameron, 203-204, 207
McCann, Brian, 196-198

McDonald, Darnell, 36
McGowan, Dustin, 154
McGwire, Mark, 102
McKean, Jim, 53-54
McMaster, Eric, 37, 38
McNally, Dave, 120, 232, 241
Meche, Gil, 164
Mench, Kevin, 142
Mental ABC's of Pitching, The (Dorfman),
  3, 72-73, 94, 103, 149-152, 272, 287
Mental Game of Baseball, The (Dorfman),
  100
Mesa Junior College, 34
Miami Marlins, 100, 201-211, 258, 264
Michalak, Chris, 68
Middleton, John, 301, 311
Millar, Kevin, 154-155
Miller, Geoff, 285, 288
Minnesota Twins, 223
MLB First-Year Player Draft (1995), 2, 33-38
Montgomery, David, 159, 167, 213
Montreal Expos, 84, 120
Morris, Jack, 46, 121-122, 223
Morris, Matt, 38
Moyer, Jamie, 24-25, 102, 109, 189, 203,
  218
Mulder, Mark, 122, 234
Murphy, Daniel, 199
Mussina, Mike, 130, 134, 309-313

N

National League Championship Series,
  223-228
National League Division Series (NLDS),
  1-14, 221, 242-246, 248
National League East title, 4, 56, 173-174,
  219, 241
National Transportation Safety Board, 302
Nelson, Jeff, 225
New York Mets, 84, 182, 257, 273
New York Times, 234
New York Yankees, 2, 23, 84, 92, 119,
  128-129, 150, 165, 215
Nike, 123, 137, 222
Nolan Ryan's Pitcher's Bible (Ryan), 19-21
Núñez, Leo, 207

O

Oakland Athletics, 99-100, 121, 161, 234
O'Connell, Jack, 308-309
Olney, Buster, 165
O'Neil, Ed, 64
Oswalt, Roy, 231-235, 238, 241-242, 251,
  270

P

Painter, Lance, 58
Palmer, Jim, 232, 241
Papelbon, Jonathan, 251
Parrish, Larry, 53
Patterson, Gil, 68, 90, 93, 113, 133, 148
Paulino, Ronny, 207-208, 211
Pence, Hunter, 240, 244
Penn State University, 317
perfect game, 28, 201-212, 213-215
Perry, Gaylord, 120, 269
Pevey, Marty, 72
Phelps, Josh, 79, 89-90
Philadelphia Phillies
  '95 draft and, 38
  2011 season and, 235-241
  2012 season and, 251-255
  2013 season and, 257-259
  2014 season and, 271
  Cardinals and, 242-246
  Doc and, 1-14, 155, 171-183, 273, 279
  Doc as mental skills coach and, 284-289
  Doc's death and, 301
  Doc's perfect game and, 28, 201-211
  Doc's retirement and, 268-269
  Doc's training routine and, 185-199
  Dorfman and, 230-231
  Fregosi and, 56-57
  Giants and, 223-228
  Hall of Fame and, 309-311, 314-315
  National League East title and, 219-221
  The Rotation and, 232-235
  trade with Blue Jays and, 158-160,
    164-170
  Yankees and, 215
Phillips, Brandon, 6, 8-12, 155
Pinellas-Pasco Medical Examiner's Office,
  302

Pinson, Vada, 74
pitching technique
    changeups and, 135-136, 171-173
    curveballs and, 132-135
    cutters and, 127-132, 263
    Doc and, 86
    Doc's back problems and, 257-258
    Doc's training routine and, 189-191,
        194-199
    Dorfman and, 106-107
    fastballs and, 171-173
    perfect game and, 202-204, 207-208
    psychology and, 149-151
    Queen and, 76-80
    sinkers and, 125-127
Pittsburgh Pirates, 38, 119, 182, 240, 254
Players' Tribune, 151
Plesac, Dan, 41-42, 51-53
Polanco, Plácido, 205, 218, 238
Pomona High School, 31
Positive Coaching Alliance, 282, 318
Poulis, George
    2009 All-Star Game and, 157
    Doc and, 235-237, 251
    Doc's 200th win and, 122
    Doc's death and, 297, 301
    Doc's leg injury and, 141-144
    Doc's legacy and, 320
    Doc's training routine and, 117-118, 138
Prieto, Ariel, 36, 38
Proefrock, Scott, 160, 164-169
psychology
    baseball and, 104-109, 271-272
    Doc and, 73-78, 93-95, 216, 224-225,
        276
    Dorfman and, 97-103
    pitching and, 149-151
Pujols, Albert, 245
Punto, Nick, 244-245
Purcey, David, 155

Q

Quantrill, Paul, 51-53
Queen, Mel, 41, 59, 73-81, 83, 118

R

Ramírez, Hanley, 202-204
Ramírez, J.C., 169-170
Ramírez, Manny, 83, 86
Ramos, Edubray, 279
Redman, Mark, 38
Reese, Skeet, 247, 250
Ricciardi, J.P., 94, 118, 123, 154-160, 163,
    268, 273, 300-301
Richmond, Scott, 155
Ripken, Cal, Jr., 312
Rivera, Mariano, 128-131, 134, 150, 257,
    309-313, 319-320
Roberts, Robin, 87
Robinson, Frank, 74
Rodriguez, Alex, 102
Rogers Communications, 154
Rolen, Scott, 6-10
Rollins, Jimmy, 6-11, 137-138, 218-220, 259,
    264, 299
Rollins, Johari, 299
Romero, J.C., 227
Romero, Ricky, 155
Rose, Pete, 235
Rosenthal, Ken, 155, 252-253
Ross, Cody, 203, 206, 223-227
The Rotation, 232-235, 241-242, 245
Ruf, Darin, 264
Ruiz, Carlos
    Biddle and, 272
    Doc and, 179-181, 218-219, 240
    Doc's death and, 298, 301
    Doc's final game and, 264
    Doc's perfect game and, 202, 205-210
    NLDS against the Reds and, 5-7, 11-13
Rutland Herald, 98
Ryan, B.J., 247
Ryan, Nolan, 19, 310

S

Sabathia, CC, 162
San Francisco Giants, 223-228
Sanchez, Freddy, 225
Sánchez, Gaby, 202-204
Sandberg, Ryne, 261, 264
Sanford, Jack, 120

Santana, Domingo, 240
Santana, Johan, 144, 179
Santas, Donovan, 111-117, 122, 138-144, 187, 193, 235-237, 299, 320
Saunders, Joe, 161
Scherzer, Max, 270
Schilling, Curt, 67, 91, 141, 146, 319
Schneider, Brian, 146-147, 218-220, 300
scouting, 32-36
Seattle Mariners, 2, 145, 160, 179
Seaver, Tom, 112-113
Sheridan, Phil, 205, 215, 221-223
Sheridan, Scott, 177-178, 185-188, 192, 240, 253, 265
Shumaker, Skip, 243-244
Sigg, Chad, 27, 38-39
Sigismondo, Marc, 213
Simon, Alfredo, 64
Singleton, Jonathan, 240
sinkers, 126-127
Sizemore, Grady, 155
Smalley, Roy, 98
Smith, Gary, 234
Smith, Lee, 309
Smoltz, John, 223
Solano, Donovan, 264
Spahn, Warren, 60
Spoljaric, Paul, 58, 298
Sports Illustrated, 55, 234
sports memorabilia, 221
St. Louis Cardinals, 242-246, 248, 254
Stanton, Giancarlo, 146, 281
Stecher, William, 63-64
Stevens, Lee, 155
Stewart, Dave, 61-62
Stewart, Shannon, 52
Stieb, Dave, 53-54, 83
Stubbs, Drew, 10
Sutton, Don, 235
Sweeney, Mike, 220
Syracuse Chiefs, 43-44, 46

T

Tampa Bay Rays, 2, 147-148, 166, 233
Taschner, Jack, 207
Taylor, Michael, 159, 166-167
Taylor, Reggie, 38

Texas Rangers, 68, 118-119, 174, 248
Thibodaux, Ryan, 307
Thomas, Frank, 313
Thome, Jim, 89, 251, 312-313
Three-Rooker Bar, 293
Toronto, Ontario, 113-114
Toronto Blue Jays
    '95 draft and, 32-35
    2000 season and, 55-65
    2002 season and, 111-112
    2003 season and, 118-122
    2009 season and, 153-157
    Detroit Tigers and, 50-54
    Doc and, 2, 41-44, 46-47, 140-141, 273
    Doc's death and, 298-302
    Doc's retirement and, 268-269
    Doc's return to, 83-93
    Doc's struggles and, 67-70
    Hall of Fame and, 309-310, 313-315
    Mel Queen and, 74-76
    MLB First-Year Player Draft (1995) and, 38-40
    Phillies and, 216, 235-238
    trade with Phillies and, 158-160, 163-170
Torres, Andrés, 225-226
Tosca, Carlos, 90, 94, 118
Triple-A, 43, 46, 63, 80
Twitter, 282, 307

U

Uggla, Dan, 202, 206
University of Arizona, 33
University of Colorado, 24
University of Iowa, 24
University of Manitoba, 176
University of Northern Colorado, 24
University of South Florida, 272-273, 276
Upton, B.J., 147, 166
Uribe, Juan, 224, 228
Utley, Chase
    Biddle and, 272
    Cardinals and, 244-245
    Doc and, 238-239
    Doc's 20th win and, 218
    Doc's 200th win and, 259
    Doc's death and, 300-301
    Doc's final game and, 264

Doc's legacy and, 320
Doc's perfect game and, 203-204
Doc's training routine and, 173, 194-195
NLDS against the Reds and, 6-7, 10
Utley, Jen, 300

V

Valdez, Wilson, 7, 11, 203, 206
Van Wagenen, Brodie, 168-169
Vander Meer, Johnny, 223
Verlander, Justin, 162
Victorino, Shane, 1-3, 6-7, 187, 206-210, 218, 221, 238, 243
Votto, Joey, 6, 8-10

W

Waguespack, Jacob, 286
Walker, Larry, 91
Washburn, Jarrod, 95
Washington Nationals, 179, 217-219, 238, 254
Weaver, Jered, 161
Welch, Bob, 24, 102
Wells, David, 56, 57-59, 87-88
Werth, Jayson
    2010 season and, 160
    Braves and, 217
    Doc and, 195, 201-202, 220-221
    Doc's death and, 300-301
    Doc's perfect game and, 205
    Nationals and, 238
    NLDS against the Reds and, 7-9, 13

Wheeler, Rocket, 78-80
Wheeler Avenue School, 98
Wilken, Tim, 34-36, 39
Williams, Mitch, 56-57
Williams, Nick, 279
Wilson, Tom, 95, 119, 148
Winn, Randy, 50
Witt, Kevin, 52, 121
Wood, Kerry, 38
Wood, Travis, 7
Woolf, Jay, 36
World Series (1956), 9
World Series (1991), 122, 223
World Series (2008), 214, 233
World Series (2011), 248
Worley, Vance, 242

Y

Yelich, Christian, 264
Yount, Andy, 38

Z

Zaun, Gregg, 134, 145-146, 149-150, 301
Zeid, Josh, 240
Zito, Barry, 95, 234

DATE DUE

OCT	6 2021		
			PRINTED IN U.S.A.